Convictions

REVISED EDITION

Convictions

DEFUSING
RELIGIOUS
RELATIVISM

James Wm. McClendon, Jr.

James M. Smith

TRINITY PRESS INTERNATIONAL
Valley Forge, Pennsylvania

Original edition published as *Understanding Religious Convictions* copyright © 1975
University of Notre Dame Press, Notre Dame, IN 46556

A section of chapter 2 was previously published as "Ian Ramsey's Model of Religious Language," *Journal of the American Academy of Religion* 41, no. 3 (September
1973). Reprinted with permission. Parts of chapter 2 appeared in "Saturday's Child:
A New Approach to the Philosophy of Religion," *Theology Today* (October 1970). A
section of chapter 3 is based on the authors' article "Religious Language after J. L.
Austin," *Religious Studies* 8 (March 1972).

Trinity Press International, P.O. Box 851, Valley Forge, PA 19482–0851

Library of Congress Cataloging-in-Publication Data

McClendon, James William.
  Convictions : defusing religious relativism / James Wm. McClendon,
 Jr., and James M. Smith. — [New ed., rev. and enl.]
  Rev. and enl. ed. of: Understanding religious convictions. 1975.
  Includes bibliographical references.
  ISBN 1–56338–106–0
 1. Religion—Philosophy. 2. Language and languages—Religious
 aspects. I. Smith, James M. (James Marvin), 1933– .
 II. McClendon, James William. Understanding religious convictions.
 III. Title.
 BL51.M17 1994
 200'.1—dc20   94–30851
               CIP

Printed in the United States of America

94 95 96 97 98 99   10 9 8 7 6 5 4 3 2 1

To
J. L. Austin

Contents

Preface to the Revised Edition

As we note in our first chapter, the world of 1994 is a dramatically different one from the world of 1974, when the predecessor to *Convictions* was sent off to the publisher. Nevertheless, the publication of *Convictions* has more to do with two changes in our more immediately relevant neighborhood of philosophy and theology. With a few luminous exceptions, the philosophy of religion in 1974 was practiced by philosophers who were religious skeptics and theologians who were religious apologists. The philosophers tended to be analytically trained and oriented; the theologians, sensing danger to the faith, disdained analysis. As a result, there was little fruitful interchange between the two groups. In the intervening years, the number of analytically trained philosophers who are also members of religious communities has grown considerably, while the conception of analysis among philosophers generally has broadened and (in our view) deepened. Philosophers can no longer be dismissed as threats to the faith or religious believers as soft-headed dogmatists.

During the same period, there has been a growing dissatisfaction with the general approach to the theory of knowledge called "foundationalism." Technical definitions apart, there is a much greater tendency today to examine the credentials of claims in terms of the disciplines or communities within which the claims are made.

We welcome both of these changes in the philosophical scene. Perhaps, in 1974, we were too sanguine in thinking that our example of theological-philosophical dialogue and our pluralistic approach to justification could change the direction of discussion in philosophy of religion. Now we are happy to make a contribution to that discussion and, we hope, speed its development.

Accordingly, we have made the following changes: chapter 1 is rewritten for clarity, and chapter 2 is almost entirely new, taking account of recent developments in linguistic and literary theory. The last part of chapter 5 reflects new developments in the philosophy of science, and the last part of chapter 6 relates Alasdair MacIntyre's philosophical work to our own. Several paragraphs about theology in chapter 7 are new (our minds having changed), and throughout the book gender usage reflects current rather than earlier customs. As a whole, though, our book says what it said in 1974; our terms are changed but our thesis is not. We believe, not that we are catching up with the times, but that the times have at long last caught up with us.

In addition to the help listed in our old preface, for which we remain grateful, we note here our gratitude to colleague Jim Slinger, who read the whole book afresh, and to editor/typesetter John Eagleson, editors Hal Rast and Laura Barrett, and all the good people at Trinity Press International. Others are thanked where their names appear in these pages. Last and first, we are grateful to our shared mentor John L. Austin, long departed but never forgotten. To him we dedicate this new edition of this book.

JAMES WM. MCCLENDON, JR.
JAMES M. SMITH

Los Angeles County, California
September 6, 1994

Preface to the Original Edition

There is a dark
Inscrutable workmanship that reconciles
Discordant elements, makes them cling together
In one society...
                                    Wordsworth, The Prelude

Our goal in this book is to discuss the discordant elements that divide our own society into fragments and to discover what Wordsworth calls the "dark inscrutable workmanship" that can make even discordant elements one. Since this is our goal, it may be helpful to point out that we two authors are representative of the discord we examine, one of us being a social philosopher who long ago gave up the foolishness of Christian faith and would appear on census as a secular atheist, while the other is a theologian who believes and (unevenly) practices that very Christian foolishness. So we are, in apparent disregard of the Apostle's warning, "unequally yoked together" (2 Cor. 6:14) as writing partners and hence are in better position than some to know the conflicts and paradoxes of a pluralistic world.

Nevertheless, the book that has grown from our discussion and trial drafting is not a debate or a dialog; we have composed it together and are alike responsible for every paragraph, every word. No unequality in *this* sense. That we could do this (and that the course of our friendship has resulted in no small shiftings in our respective conviction sets) is itself a reason for hope regarding wider convictional conflicts. For we believe that here we are indeed engaged with that inscrutable workmanship that the worlds of religion, of race, of politics need even more desperately than does the academic world in which we both live.

Our success here, such as it is, has not come without others' prior work or others' correction and encouragement. Knowledgeable readers will see that the notes within are a very inadequate guide to the help we have received from the literature. The list that follows may likewise (but in this case unintentionally) omit some who have read parts of the successive versions of our typescript and written comments and criticism: Peter Winch, Robert Cunningham, Michael Novak, Hugh Fleetwood, Claude Welch, Daniel O'Hanlon, Paul van Buren, Durwood Foster, John Cobb, Van Harvey, Terrence Tilley, Ismail al Faruqi, John Hutchison, Stanley Hauerwas, David Burrell, David Armstrong, Axel Steuer, John Boler, LeRoy Moore, Nelson Pike. We are indebted to each one for help generously given. We also thank the American Philosophical Association and the American Academy of Religion, where portions of the work were tried before lively audiences, and especially the members of the Pacific Coast Theological Society, who heard most of our ideas in their earliest form and gave us generous critical encouragement.

Portions of our work, noted within, have been published in *Religious Studies, Theology Today,* and *Journal of the American Academy of Religion,* and we thank their editors, H. D. Lewis, Diogenes Allen, Ray Hart, again here.

Many have helped with typing, correcting, and editing: we think especially of Thomas Caruso, Sonja Ridenour, Esther Davis, Charlotte Utting, Yvonne Burke, Aurora Avakian, Joan Creighton, Ralph Frey, and the excellent staff of the University of Notre Dame Press, especially our editor, Ann Rice.

For encouragement and for practical aid with money, facilities, typists, and materials we are grateful to institutions where we have worked: for McClendon these include the Universities of San Francisco, Stanford, and Temple, Goucher College, St. Mary's in Baltimore, and the Church Divinity School of the Pacific in Berkeley; for Smith they include the University of Washington and California State University, Fresno. Our students will see, too, how much or how little they have changed our minds by their good questions and comments on our work.

Our dedication page cannot adequately represent our debt to our two families, whose members have helped in many ways as we did the work. We think especially of their willingness to adjust vacation times and work schedules over eight years (and on two continents) to the demands of this work, while those who were old enough have taken share in reading and correcting as well.

And not least, we thank each other, here in print, for sharing a happy task happily ended for us though only begun for our readers — whom we now cordially greet.

McCLENDON
& SMITH

Convictions

O N E

The statement "There is someone who feeds the cattle upon a thousand hills, who can match the powers of evil and lift up the everlasting doors" is not one to which what is still hidden from us in Space and Time is all irrelevant. But it seems to me it is not only this that makes the question, "Is that statement true?" a hard one. It is also the fact that this question calls upon us to consider all that is already before us, in case it should happen that having eyes we see not, and having ears we hear not.

John Wisdom[1]

The philosophers have interpreted the world in various ways; the point, however, is to change it.

Karl Marx[2]

Convictions and Religion

Twenty years ago, when the manuscript that became the first edition of this book left our hands, the world was very different. A Cold War of twenty-five years duration had frozen the Soviet Union and the United States into permanent confrontation; Apartheid had an ever tighter grip on South Africa, while affirmative action and the civil rights movement moved the United States deliberately closer to full racial equality; sexual liberation and medical technology seemed to have taken all guilt and danger out of sex; a Shah was the secure ruler of Iran while, in the United States, a Republican president had resigned in disgrace, leaving his party permanently weakened. No one had heard of Michael Jordan, Michael Jackson, Madonna, or Oprah Winfrey.

Nevertheless, the issues that moved us to write then remain with us today. There is, first, still great diversity in the world. The simple (if dangerous) division of the world into two camps with an ill-defined third on the fringe has been transformed into a myriad of fragile alliances and occasional enmities, all apparently local and transitory. This political diversity is only one dimension; the variety of ethnicities, cultures, and worldviews is impressive — or, perhaps, depressing.

The facts of these diversities are, however, just that: facts. By themselves, they are no more (if no less) urgent or interesting than the diversity of species or of subatomic particles. Yet the diversities of politics, of culture, and of religion are (for most of us) not only interesting but unavoidable. We are, for one thing, helplessly aware of these differences. If we are residents of Belfast or Bombay, Bosnia or Beirut, Moscow or Miami, Johannesburg or Jerusalem, that awareness is intense; it is fearsome and frustrating. Even in calmer places, however, the technologies of communication and transportation regularly remind us that, whatever our political, ethnic, or religious identity is, most of the world does not share it. This widespread awareness of diversity and the necessity of responding to it is what we shall call *pluralism.*

Of course, some kinds of diversity are so trivial that we respond to them with indifference or even with enjoyment: it is rare indeed that difference in eye color or flower preferences gives rise to violence or even arguments. But differences in those beliefs that guide our lives, that make us what we are — these are another matter. They are indeed the stuff of arguments, manifestos, estrangements, revolutions, and wars. Why is this so?

In a way, the rest of this book is our answer to this question. We can, however, begin by noting features of these latter differences — we shall call them *convictional differences* — that can show the way toward this broader answer.[3]

I. Convictions

Beliefs guide our lives, and beliefs — unlike genetic features or mere preferences — give rise to and are embodied in claims, counterclaims, and denials of claims. The Buddhist and Christian, the revolutionary and the reformist, the materialist and idealist are not mere opponents in a power struggle. Rather, each claims to have a fundamental truth the others lack. All, therefore, would if they could persuade their rivals of the correctness of their view and the rightness of their cause and (at least indirectly) of the incorrectness of their opponent's view and the wrongness of the opponent's cause. Indeed, it is one indication that we hold our views seriously and strongly that we seek the assent of others to them. As Jonathan Edwards put it, "It is the necessary consequence of true esteem and love [of an object] that we should approve and value others' esteem of the same object, and disapprove and dislike the contrary."[4]

Significantly, problems in the outer world of creeds and party cries often correspond to conflicts within thoughtful persons who seek to make sense of their own deep prehensions and tenacious practices, religious or other. It may be that the strongest tension with which we must struggle here is between recognition of the full range of our human wants, fears, hopes, faith, doubts, and commitments on the one hand, and our drive to purely rational understanding of these very phenomena on the other. And we must confront this inner tension in a world convictionally divided, so that there is no easy division between our own inner conflicts and our conflicts with outsiders.

We think Edwards's observation holds not only for our evaluations, which we ordinarily associate with "esteem and love," but for our beliefs generally. When we find an argument valid, a conclusion well supported, or a theory confirmed, we expect others (given the same arguments and evidence) to share our views. Frequently, we are prepared to exert ourselves in support of our views (hence, debates and manifestos), and we are, in varying degrees, frustrated and discontent when our arguments do not persuade except in the cases where we ourselves are persuaded to give up our own views. Such persuasion does occur. We see it in scientific argument, in scholarly disputes, and sometimes even in political and religious forums.

Yet when it comes to convictions that not only guide us but identify us and make us what we are, conflict is more pervasive and serious, and argument is seldom successful. Convictional conflict frequently becomes passionate and violent: Arab against Israeli, communist against capitalist, fundamentalist against secularist, Catholic against Protestant. One might expect that, with an increase in scientific knowledge and the spread of educational advantages and advancing communications technology, the variety of views and perhaps the passion with which they are held would diminish. Should not a view founded on ignorance yield to knowledge, one based on misunderstanding give way to explanation, one based on bad arguments be corrected by sound counterarguments? No such expectations can survive an examination of the history of the twentieth century (or any other century, for that matter!). The end of the great conflict called the Cold War has only served to generate or highlight dozens of other conflicts, many of them of a convictional nature.

We have thus posed again the questions that we first asked twenty years ago: Why are differences in convictions so intractable, so impervious to appeals to evidence or rational argument? And is there a method by which this intractability can be overcome, a method by which convictions can be justified not only to those who already hold them but to those who presently hold other, rival convictions? Our broad answer to these questions will occupy the remainder of this book. We can begin this difficult journey with a modest but crucial step, viz., by defining "conviction," our word for fundamental beliefs. *A conviction* (as we use the term) means *a persistent belief such that if X (a person or community) has a conviction, it will not easily be relinquished and it cannot be relinquished without making X a significantly different person (or community) than before.* Later we shall be saying a good deal more about convictions. For now, we are content to make a few remarks to warn the unwary and soothe the suspicious. We note, first, that we have not defined "conviction" topically. So far as our definition is concerned, a person or community may have convictions about ice cream flavors or hair styles and have no convictions about God, the nature of truth, or the good life. If that situation is unlikely (as we think it is), it is not impossible by definition. What a person cares most about — what makes him or her the person he or she is — is something that must be found out from the person, not settled beforehand.

Of course, what one cares about is not just a matter of argument and evidence. But (we shall argue) these are part of the story. Thus we hold that convictions are a species of belief, intending by "belief" to indicate that they are cognitive as well as conative and affective — convictions are about what we think as well as what we hope or feel. In this sense of the term, 'beliefs'* include not only what one thinks or suspects is true, but also what one regards as highly probable, certain, or even knows to be the case.[5] It follows that while convictions are often the subject of controversy, they need not be, and perhaps some never are.

We have appropriated the word "pluralism" to refer simply to the self-conscious awareness of the diversity of convictional communities. Of course, the word has been used in several other senses; that presents no problems so long as the senses are clearly distinguished and put in their appropriate contexts. There is one alternative use, however, that requires comment, both because of the reputation of its user and the interest of his work. In his book *An Interpretation of Religion,* John Hick states, elaborates, and defends what he calls "the pluralistic hypothesis" about religion.[6] He considers and rejects both the "skeptical" view that religious experience is *in toto* delusive, and the "dogmatic" view that it is all delusive except for one's own tradition. Instead, he defends the view "that the great post-axial faiths constitute different ways of experiencing, conceiving, and living in relation to an ultimate divine Reality which transcends all our varied visions of it."[7]

Hick recognizes, as we do here, the enormous variety of religious beliefs as well as the variety of beliefs *about* religion. He skillfully elaborates both sorts of variety, categorizing numerous approaches to and within the world religions. "Realistic" options hold that existing religions approach a real object of worship; "naturalistic" options deny this. The evidence in favor of either option is ambiguous.[8] This very ambiguity pro-

---

*In the following pages double quotation marks ("...") are used for all direct quotations and for the mention (as opposed to the use) of words or terms, except in the special case of quotations within quotations ("'...'"). Single quotation marks ('...') are used (with that exception) only as 'scare quotes,' that is, to indicate an unusual use of a term.

vides the clue to interpreting each of the religions. In this task, one must distinguish the phenomenal (things as they appear) from the noumenal (things as they are in reality). Only the former is accessible; consequently the "pluralistic hypothesis" is reasonable. What appears religiously (God, gods, or no god), whether ultimacy is personal or impersonal, what the future holds, what the "Real" behind all appearances really is — diverse religious views — are best explained as plural accounts of one "Real," one noumenal ultimacy interpreted by many conflicting myths. Despite appearances, then, by the "pluralistic hypothesis" the religions actually agree.[9]

Is the problem with which we began solved already? Is the proper response to pluralism (*à la* McClendon and Smith) that the diversity we struggle with is only our (limited) perspective on (an unlimited) Reality? Our answer must be twofold. First, Hick may be right: there may indeed be one Reality upon which all convictional systems have a limited perspective. But, we must add, Hick does not — and using his method, cannot — establish that truth in a way that adequately deals with pluralism *à la* McClendon and Smith. What Hick proposes is a useful, perhaps even profound, way of categorizing and thinking about religions, much as Linnaeus proposed a useful (but probably *not* profound) way of thinking about biological species. But there is a decisive absence of analogy in these two efforts at classification. Species do not have a distinctive way of thinking of themselves; religious believers do. And, in our view, it is the testimony of Buddhists or Taoists or atheists that establishes what Buddhists or Taoists or atheists really believe. We may think, after reading Hick, that they ought to believe the pluralistic hypothesis, and we might try to persuade them of that. To do so, however, requires first that we understand what they think now and, further, that we have available arguments and concepts that they will understand and must accept. Nothing in Hick's argument shows that we have that.

Convictions are the beliefs that make people what they are. They must therefore be taken very seriously by those who have them. This means that to take any person seriously we must take that person's convictions seriously, even if we do not ourselves share them. If we regard integrity and a certain degree of consistency as important elements in being a person, we should neither expect nor want others' convictions to be easily changed or lightly given up. On the other hand, if we have a true esteem for our own convictions, we will want them to be shared in appropriate ways by anyone whom we regard. A certain tension appears here. If persons who hold opposed convictions are to come to share common ones,

then some sort of exchange must take place in which the disparate partners communicate with, persuade, change one another in significant ways,
so that one or both become significantly different persons than they were.

Whether, and in what circumstances, such a change or exchange is possible is itself a matter of (convictional?) dispute among three theories or
families of theories about the nature of convictions. According to one
of these theories, conflicts in beliefs among persons or communities are
wholly contingent and, since they are also trivial or illusory, given time
and effort they are completely eradicable. The intractability of these differences is said to be due to ignorance or perversity rather than to serious
differences about what it means to be rational or humane or reverent or
scientific. So if a Marxist and a Christian democrat (or a Buddhist mystic
and a scientific humanist) do not now understand one another or if they
now disagree on any fundamental question, such as the meaning of reasonableness, it is only because one or the other is (or both are) ignorant
of some facts or incapable of thinking straight. We shall call this view
imperialism, with a nod to its older usage in international politics. Of
course we do not intend to accuse convictional imperialists of the racism
or chauvinism that was so large a part of the political imperialism of the
colonial powers. But convictional imperialists do share with their political
counterparts a complacency about their current possession of a truth or a
method of finding it that enables them to correct 'popular errors.' Thus,
instead of "the White Man's Burden" and "the Superiority of European
Civilization" we might have "the Christian's Burden" or "the Superiority
of the Scientific Method."

Second, just as cultural relativists found the colonial imperialist complacency and assumptions of superiority unsupportable in the light of
growing knowledge about other cultures, so the convictional *relativist*
finds imperialist assumptions about ignorance and perversity unjustified
and inadequate to explain convictional differences. The relativist regards
convictional differences as an inevitable, ineradicable, and ultimate fact
of human existence and denies the existence of any common element
relevant to mutual understanding. According to relativism, human communities and their convictions are so constituted that interconvictional
persuasion is impossible; indeed, even communication at any significant level along these lines is impossible. For the relativist, those
with convictional differences see, think about, and speak about different
worlds.

To sharpen our focus on these two: while the imperialist holds that
convictional differences can be eliminated by the application of the cor-

rect method and the correction of (others') character defects, the relativist holds that conflict among convictions cannot be resolved by any means that presuppose serious communication among the opponents. If there should be a conversion from one way of conviction to another, it must for the relativist be the result of some non- or extrarational cause or process, and the shift would put the convert as completely outside his or her former view as he or she had been completely inside it before.

Finally, there is a third view of convictional conflict, which we call *perspectivism*. It regards convictional conflict as expected, but not inevitable, fundamental but not ultimate, enduring but not inherently ineradicable. There are, in this view, common elements among differing sets of convictions, but to discover and use them in resolving conflict requires measures that cannot be limited along convictional lines. Persons or communities with different convictions will experience, think, and speak about their worlds differently, and these differences will not necessarily be the result of mistakes or character flaws. But neither are they walls or electronic scramblers, making communication, understanding, or even persuasion among worlds impossible. Or, at least, so claims perspectivism.

In what follows, it is this third view, perspectivism, that we adopt and defend. But we cannot beg the question by assuming its truth. We must, instead, adopt a method of investigating convictions that does not prejudge the issue. The investigator cannot, for example, simply make up questionnaires asking people about their convictions, or observe their behavior and infer their convictions from that. Both of these methods have the look of being scientific. They start from observations that any investigator can make (public availability of data), and they yield quantifiable results. The problem is that for such methods to be meaningful, relativism must be false, and imperialism or something very like it must be true. For such 'objective' methods to be successful in revealing convictions, it must be possible for the investigator's questions to be understood properly and for the investigator genuinely to understand the answers or the other behavior of the 'subjects.' No doubt the investigator could *attach* some significance to whatever answers were gathered; no doubt the investigator could *assign* significance to whatever behavior was observed. But a proper understanding of such evidence is possible only if communication among those with differing convictions is straightforward and unproblematic. By what right, though, could the investigator make that assumption? On the other hand, neither is there warrant for giving up the investigative task at the outset, as relativism would seem to dictate.

Imperialism, relativism, and perspectivism are not usually asserted as free-standing views. Typically, they are derived from other philosophical views or theological standpoints. Both Christianity and Islam, in some of their forms, have given rise to convictional imperialism: if only all those others knew the truths of Christianity (truths of Islam) and were not blinded by sin, they would be Christians (Muslims). The successes of science since the seventeenth century have given rise to a secular version of the same imperialism, only the truths to be known are about scientific method (or Scientific Method) and the blindness is the product not of sin, but of ideology or ignorance.

Philosophers probing more deeply into that method developed an epistemology that has been called, in retrospect, *foundationalism.* In this view, the way to find truth and avoid error is to believe only those claims that are either (*a*) certain or self-evident, not requiring argument or evidence, or (*b*) derived from beliefs of class (*a*) by rigorous proof or argument. Within foundationalism, there developed arguments about what were certain or self-evident (properly basic) beliefs, and, less frequently, about what were good arguments. Some thought that only beliefs about immediate sense experience could qualify for class (*a*), while others defended abstract truths of reason. Either way, the claims of orthodox Christianity and Judaism and Hinduism or Buddhism faced great difficulty. No rigorous argument applied to any of the historically preferred "properly basic beliefs" seemed to provide any support for the significant claims of any of these religions. (The *loci classici* here are the works of David Hume and Immanuel Kant, especially Hume's "Of Miracles" and his *Dialogues Concerning Natural Religion,* and Kant's *Religion within the Limits of Reason Alone.*[10]) Theologians who accepted foundationalism, as many did, were left either to accept an ever dwindling set of significant claims or to cut religious claims off from the realm of knowledge by concentrating on their emotional or cultural significance alone.

Of course, foundationalism was not without its critics. Among them was William James, about whose views we will have more to say. James's starting point for criticism was a more serious and hence less dogmatic empiricism than his foundationalist opponents espoused. A more recent — indeed, contemporary — group of critics begins at a very different point, viz., Calvinist theology. One theological response to foundationalism was an increased emphasis on natural theology, the attempt to prove claims about the nature and existence of God on the basis of our knowledge of the natural world (cf. "properly basic beliefs"). *Reformed epistemology*[11] rejects the necessity of natural theology. Instead, it suggests that the believer, or at least some believers, are on solid ground in regarding their experience of God as "properly basic." Foundationalists find such claims breathtaking if not nonsensical — as is often the case with claims that conflict with somebody's convictions. Nevertheless, the Reformed epistemologists have both a critical and a constructive basis for their views.

Critically, the Reformed epistemologists point out not only the lack of agreement about properly basic beliefs but also a more serious difficulty: no proposed basic belief has been shown to provide support for such common and commonsense beliefs as the existence of a past, or the existence of other minds like our own, or the existence of material objects. Epistemological systems that do not already include these commonsense beliefs as "properly basic" find it impossible to provide good support for them. Foundationalism is thus rejected for two reasons: First, as the continuing dispute about "proper basicality" suggests, the selection of any one category of beliefs as basic is arbitrary. Second, no proposed basic belief provides support for our common beliefs about material objects, other minds, or history. "Properly basic beliefs" either include such common beliefs or they cannot support them. If we are not content with skepticism, then, we must allow a much richer menu of beliefs as starting points for knowledge. Why not include in that menu a belief about God?[12]

The Reformed epistemologists do not, after all, want to include just any belief about any conception of God. But their constructive proposals do indicate conditions under which such a belief is properly basic, i.e., deserves inclusion in that set of beliefs from which we may properly reason to further conclusions but which require no argument themselves. There is no unanimity among Reformed epistemologists about what these conditions are. For some (e.g., Alvin Plantinga, Nicholas Wolterstorff) what is required for a belief to be properly basic is that it be formed in a "reliable" way, where reliability is determined by the example of an appropriate community.[13] According to Plantinga, since there is no sound basis for restricting beliefs to a well-defined set, members of appropriate communities are entitled to beliefs reliably formed by the standards of that community. (Plantinga's term for such reliably formed beliefs is "warranted beliefs.")[14]

For other Reformed epistemologists (for example, William Alston if he should be counted in their number), a properly basic belief must be one that is the result of a reliable *doxastic practice,* i.e., a regular way of forming beliefs that are neither random nor shown to be false. If a belief is based on an immediate experience of the believer (e.g., "God is speaking to me now") and is formed in accordance with a reliable doxastic practice, it is properly basic for the believer: she or he is entitled to the belief even in the absence of further evidence.[15]

It is worth pointing out here, as Wolterstorff notes, the "polemical" nature of these views.[16] They are not, nor are they intended to be, general theories or accounts of convictions or even religious convictions. They are not, nor are they intended to be, justifications of any particular religious claims or justifications of religious belief to the nonbeliever. They are designed solely to negate or blunt the attack of foundationalist epistemological theories on religious belief. Religious beliefs, and specifically beliefs about God, are *defended* (here is the polemic) by arguing that no foundationalist argument can provide good grounds for holding all religious belief suspect. In the absence of such grounds, the defense goes on, religious believers are entitled to believe (are warranted in believing) some theistic claims.

Conceived in this way, we find considerable merit in the program of Reformed epistemology. Since, as we shall later argue, convictional imperialism is not in general justified, we share the Reformed epistemologists' rejection of foundationalism as a specific form of such imperialism. We also share the emphasis on the (or a) community as the most important unit in assessing belief and establishing knowledge claims. Finally, we are drawn to Alston's idea of a doxastic practice: that recognizing and gathering evidence for our beliefs is not only a learned (and taught) activity, but one intimately related to other learned activities and to our whole pattern of life, whoever we may be.

Nevertheless, we cannot yet say that Reformed epistemology, as we understand it, answers the questions that led us to our present task. Other commentators have argued that Reformed epistemology does not yet provide a clear and defensible criterion for an *appropriate* community or for a *reliable* doxastic practice.[17] Even if these problems were to be solved, however, another issue would arise, one that we ourselves must deal with if we are to be successful. It is one thing to be able to establish that a belief is supported by the practices and convictions of one's community. As a member of that community, one may well be entitled to that belief or find it warranted — we will make our own argument to that effect in chapters 3 and 4. But in a pluralistic world, that is not enough. For there are, in such a world, many convictional communities whose members are entitled on these very grounds to believe contrary or contradictory things. How can we ever claim to *know* (that Jesus is God, that Allah watches over all, that God does not even exist) unless we can justify our belief in the face of these conflicts? This is not a problem merely of persuasion, for in this pluralistic world, each of us is aware of these various convictional communities, and the first person each of us must convince of our beliefs is ourselves. The Scotch verdict — not proven — has its honorable place, but in coming to convictions that define us and guide our lives, we look for something more.

II. Religion

Will it really do, though, to talk about religious convictions in the way that we talk about other convictions? We hope to show that it will. We wish at this stage only to forestall a dogmatic or a priori claim that religious convictions *must* be different and *could not* be studied and analyzed like other convictions. Such a claim might come from two very different sources. On the one hand, there is the person who holds that religious convictions are not to be considered along with political or scientific or aesthetic convictions, but must instead be exposed, along with like superstitious hangovers from the past or prescientific era. Such a person contends that there is nothing to understand *in* religious convictions, and the only thing to understand *about* them is that they are irrational, nonsensical hocus pocus. On the other hand is the person who denies that true religion is open to investigation as a *human* phenomenon. Religion, properly regarded, is a response to the transcendent, the ineffable, to that which is precisely not human or earthly. From this point of view, it is irreverent even to attempt a merely human understanding of true religion.

Now either of these claims might turn out to be right. One might decide, after full investigation, that religious convictions are all irrational nonsense, or instead that they (or some of them) have a grasp of some ultimate and transcendent reality that disqualifies our human attempts to talk about it. Our method does not commit us either to the defense or to the denial of religious or irreligious claims, but only to the understanding of them. Moreover, we are bound as far as we are able to understand them as the members of religious communities understand them, not as we (for whatever reason) would like them to be. We don't quarrel *directly* with either of the claims made against our proviso that religious convictions can be studied and examined for their meaning and justification just as other sorts of convictions can be. We only want to ask how either objector can be so sure in advance that he or she is right? There seems to be only one way to be so sure so soon, and that is by having some grasp of the 'essence of religion,' thereby knowing what religion and religious convictions *must* be. We do not believe that anyone has such a grasp because we do not believe there is such an 'essence.'

When I mention religion, said Parson Thwackum to Mr. Square, "I mean the Christian religion; and not only the Christian religion, but the Protestant religion; and not only the Protestant religion, but the Church of England."[18] The parson's announcement may serve to remind us that this word has a thousand meanings, that we are obliged to specify our own intended sense, and also that even after such specification is made, the other 999 senses remain. Historians of ideas have familiarized us with the fact that many of the concepts we apply to the world, present and past, are relatively new-coined ones. Such is the case with "religion" in its use in the expression "the religions of the world," and in its use to represent the sum or the essence of those 'religions.' As Wilfred Cantwell Smith has shown quite clearly, these current uses arose in the nineteenth century. Before that time, though the noun "religion" and the adjective "religious" were used (as were the corresponding words in other European languages), their meaning was different in a variety of ways.[19] For example, these terms once referred to conscientiousness and scrupulosity (a sense still present in sentences such as "He practices the piano religiously every day"); then to conscientious ritual observance or devotion to gods or to human persons. Later, the 'religious' were those in monastic orders (as opposed to 'secular' clergy who remained 'in the world'). Still later, during the Enlightenment, the *philosophes* used "religion" or its cognates to refer to systems of doctrine or ideas (and sometimes called their own system of thought "the religion of reason"), and it was in reaction to these that Schleiermacher used the term to refer to a feeling or grasp of reality available across many such systems. It remained, then, for the later nineteenth century, with its interest in the many peoples and varied cultures of the world, to designate as religion "not only in the Enlightenment sense the various systems of what people believed, and not only in the Catholic sense what they ritually practiced, and not only in Schleiermacher's sense what they inwardly felt, but increasingly the historical development of all this over the long sweep of the centuries."[20] Thus came the distinctively modern senses of the term "religion," as referring to what we nowadays call "the religions of the world" or, in the singular, "world religion," meaning the sum of these, or (again with a difference) "religion," meaning the supposed "essence" of the latter.

Now we shall have no quarrel with those who want to use the words "religion" and "religious" in any or almost all of these ways evolved in the history of these terms, particularly if they do so with the knowledge that there are also other uses. We shall, however, be somewhat chary of those who speak as if "religion" denoted, or "religious" ascribed, some *one* quality or character or essence. What is that quality supposed to be? Scrupulous conscientiousness? But other human concerns have that quality — for example, the playing of delicate musical instruments. Adherence to a god or gods? But some of the religions turn out to be atheistic. Concern with the sacred or holy? Again the same objection — not all that is called "religion" turns out to have this concern. Our point is only that whatever single property is proposed — ritual, myth, ethical concern, social adhesion, sacrifice, numinous awareness — some 'religion' turns out not to have it. Some writers, notably Frederick Ferré, have proposed that it is exactly their *importance to the holders* that makes certain beliefs and practices religious.[21] The difficulty here is that not everyone does treat his or her religious beliefs as being very important, or act as if they were. This may tempt someone else to say, "Well, then, those are not *really* religious beliefs." That seems, however, to define religion by stipulation, and in that event we are back to Parson Thwackum.

If the lack of an acceptable single defining quality makes the essentialist's position arbitrary, it admittedly makes our own investigation more difficult as well. What language shall fairly be designated religious? What shall we investigate? Perhaps this is the place to take our cue from Ferré's definition of religion:

> The conscious desiring of whatever (if anything) is considered to be both inclusive in its bearing on one's life and primary in importance. *Or...Religion is one's way of valuing most comprehensively and intensively.*"[22]

Now while it may be true, as we have argued, that not all participants in religion regard religion as important, it is *necessarily* the case that all convinced persons and convinced communities treat their own convictions as important. Thus what Ferré has actually done, we believe, is not to offer an all-round definition of religion, but to point to the (necessary) centrality of convictions in human life. So our own approach will be to attend to the analysis and understanding of convictions, leaving the qualifier "religious" to be determined by each according to individual usage and need. As far as we can in this book, we will choose as examples for analysis language used in ways most readers will take to be (in some sense) religious. In this loose sense we will attend to religious convictions, however conceptually elusive religion itself may be. In doing so, we intend to provide ways of understanding we hope will be useful to those of the most diverse schools of thought about 'religion,' without adopting the view of any one school.

We are sensitive, even now, to the charge that there is a certain incongruity between the task we have set ourselves and the problem we described at the beginning of this chapter. There we described a situation, the plurality of convictions in conflict, that has had and continues to have tragic consequences. (We are not forgetting the happier aspects of human plurality, but they do not make the tragic aspects less urgent.) Indeed, given humankind's technological sophistication, we cannot ignore the potential for ultimate catastrophe in the conflict of convictions. Yet what we propose is *another* investigation? More study — and that a study of words! Marx's criticism of philosophers fairly rings in our ears.

And yet... if the world is to be changed, where should we begin? In what direction should we go? What is the most effective means of change? Any attempt to change the world that slights or ignores the answers to these questions is unworthy of the support of reasonable men and women, however passionate and impatient they are. Even to try to answer such questions requires precisely the understanding of the pluralistic human condition (and therefore of human convictions in their plurality) that is our aim. We are sensitive, therefore, but not apologetic. For we recognize that understanding of convictions is a necessary part of changing them and even of knowing which ones need to be changed.

In fact, we make an even more ambitious claim than that. In the present book we shall not only point the way to the understanding of convictions, but also to their justification or rejection. Indeed, we will show that in paradigm cases *the former is the latter;* that fully to understand what a conviction means or is, is the only way, and a sufficient way, to know whether that conviction deserves to be believed; to put it compactly, that the full analysis of some convictions is tantamount to their justification. There are catches in that claim as it stands, but none, we hope, that will be fatal to our work. As, however, we show how, if at all, convictions can be justified, we admit that we do not here try to show *which* convictions pass the test. To admit that is to recognize that our work is more like a *code duello* (the rules) than it is like the actual fighting of a duel. Our only excuse for making it so is that without rules, no one can win a duel (though one might, of course, injure one's 'opponent' in some way); our hope is that we will set down the 'rules' by which the best convictions must prevail. That does not mean, however, that we conceive atheism triumphing over Christianity, or Buddhism over Western secularism (or vice versa, in either case) as the appropriate consequence of our work; it might mean that the triumph of the best convictions would involve a plurality in practice, *or the emergence of new convictional forms.*

The end of understanding, then, is justification. Problems about truth in religion will certainly engage us in the pages to follow. But it may turn out, and should not a priori be excluded, that truth is not separable from other measures of value — from consistency, righteousness, justice, happiness, satisfaction. In that case, we will be obliged to reckon with the interdependence of 'ethical' or 'aesthetic' with 'epistemological' questions. (The scare quotes here mean that already we question the arbitrary nature of these philosophical divisions of human thinking.) The prospect that a concern for truth would not be isolable from a whole complex of other human goals and ideals should surprise no one, except perhaps certain philosophers who have thought to give only the true-false test to human convictions and certain theologians who, rejecting this view, have concluded that the true-false test need not be given at all.

We began this chapter by noting the confused variety of human beliefs including the variety in religion itself. We have so far tried to show that this variety, not proper to religion alone but characterizing human convictions in many departments, presents us with problems to be solved as well as opportunities to be grasped. The problems that most interest us are the discovery and description of common elements among convictional communities and the development of a theory to provide a basis for the justification of convictions, especially religious convictions. Religious convictions, like others, are fully expressed only in the full range of actions of the person or community that is convinced by them. It is, however, the linguistic actions — the speech-acts — that are especially revealing of convictions and of whatever common elements are present to form the basis of interconvictional justification. Our method of investigation requires that we attend to the way the religiously convinced express their convictions in the full context of their utterance. So we must turn again to the variety of religious convictions, and thus to some particular religious speech-acts, to understand and to justify religious convictions. Before this work is done, we hope to show that it points directly toward a structure within which the many-sided task of understanding religion, justifiable or not, may be carried on.

TWO

If an atheist says: "There won't be a Judgment Day," and another person says "There will," do they mean the same? — Not clear what criterion of meaning the same is.

Ludwig Wittgenstein[1]

The answer, implicit in everything I have already said, is that communication occurs within situations and that to be in a situation is already to be in possession of (or to be possessed by) a structure of assumptions, of practices understood to be relevant in relation to purposes and goals that are already in place; and it is within the assumption of these purposes and goals that any utterance is immediately *heard.*

Stanley Fish[2]

But I here fear that I may begin to 'jar upon the nerves' of some of the members of this academic audience. Such contemporary vagaries, you may think, should hardly take so large a place in dignified Gifford lectures. I can only beseech you to have patience. The whole outcome of these lectures will, I imagine, be the emphasizing to your mind of the enormous diversities which the spiritual lives of different men exhibit.

William James[3]

Recent Approaches to Religious Language

> Sticks and stones may break my bones,
> But words can never hurt me.

This singsong children's verse conveys the contrary of what it says. The truth is, words can hurt — or help — and the verse is meant to ward off their power by working a kind of spell: if I say these words, I deflect another's taunts. So words can be both bullets and bulletproof vests. What else can they do? The broader question of the role of language has interested philosophers from Plato to the present. Our plan, we recall, is to investigate religious convictions (defined in the previous chapter) as a way of understanding religion and its conflicts; our task now is to find an approach to the language of religious convictions that will enable us to understand them — or understand them better. It would be quite convenient if a general way of understanding religious talk, *a theory of religious language,* existed to pave the way for our work, provided only that we kept before us, in searching for such a theory, our declared intent to find how religious language expresses *convictions.* For (as the previous chapter concluded) it is convictions that will be the clue to understanding religion and in the long run discovering when, if at all, religion is justified or rational. In fact there are not a few promising theories of language afloat, and in this chapter we will test three sorts of theories, those of the Wittgensteinians, the Saussureans, and the Jamesians, as steps toward finding our own way.

I. Following Wittgenstein

Early in the century now ending, European and American philosophy was in a state of crisis. Neither the advocates of the older idealism nor its standard opponents seemed able to bear the weight that the new times laid upon them, and philosophers turned to radical new ways of thought that had little in common with the old. Principal among the new thinkers was Austrian philosopher Ludwig Wittgenstein (1889–1951), who not only rebelled against previous ways of thinking, but came in time to overturn his own earlier thought, thus producing in his lifetime two upheavals in philosophy. While both were influential, it is the second stage of Wittgenstein's thought that most affects philosophy today, and we will draw upon it here. It is helpful, though, to mention the first stage, since much of what the later Wittgenstein had to say can best be understood as an attempt to overcome or correct his own earlier work. Significantly, this earlier stage was welcomed by the *Logical Positivists,* whose own views about religious language and religion were (to many Christians at least) deeply disquieting, whereas the later Wittgenstein's views have been adopted wholesale by some Christian philosophers.

Logical Positivism was a consequence of that deep disquiet about philosophy, religion, and inherited European culture that became evident in the years between the two World Wars. There was a sense that too much of what had gone before was phony, illusory. Philosophy should instead confine itself to 'logic' in the sense of strictly entailed reasoning free from illusion or compromise, and should be 'positive' in the sense of limiting itself to assured phenomena and facts, without speculation. The great tool of the Logical Positivists was the verifiability criterion of meaning. According to this criterion, there were two sorts of meaningful (or 'cognitively meaningful') statements: those that made no empirical claim at all but were true simply because of the meanings of the words used in them, and those whose method of verification could be specified in terms of certain empirical procedures. Statements of the first kind were called analytic, and those of the second, synthetic or empirical. Sentences that fell into neither category might have a *kind* of meaning: they might be orders or commands ("Shut the door" or "take up your cross and follow me"), they might be expressions of feelings ("Yay, team!" "Good grief!" or "Hallelujah!"), or they might be mixed cases: "The senator is a demagogue" (which the Positivists might analyze as a combination of "The senator persuades people to follow him" and "The senator? Ugh!"). But the philosophically and scientifically interesting meaning, in the Positivists' view, was cognitive meaning: only to the extent that statements had cognitive meaning could they be true or false; only to the extent that they were true or false could they make claims or predictions, state theories or laws, or describe or report facts; only to the extent that they could do these things could they be fit objects of belief. The Positivists drew an explicit conclusion from this: the characteristic and most important utterances of religion, as well as of metaphysics and ethics, were either disguised definitions, elaborate expressions of feeling, or completely meaningless.[4]

The threat of Positivism to many sorts of religious belief was genuine and serious. If its conclusions were correct, most religious language was purely 'emotive' — the Positivist term for language that merely expressed attitudes — and the beliefs expressed in religion were no more capable of being true or justifiable than "Yay, team!" or "Hail to thee, blithe spirit" or "Yum, yum." Even sophisticated twentieth-century theologians, long accustomed to the charge that their assertions were false, were shaken by the implied charge that they weren't asserting anything at all, not even falsehoods. And worst of all, there seemed to be something right about what the Positivists claimed. If religious claims were compared even to very theoretical scientific claims, they did seem peculiarly inaccessible to verification, while no one could deny that an important function of much religious language was to express feelings and evoke similar feelings in others.[5] While logical difficulties arose about the verifiability criterion, leading even its advocates to abandon it as a theory of knowledge, the point it had made — that religious talk lacked scientific or even everyday meaningfulness — still served to express the view of many serious and thoughtful twentieth-century people. Was there any way to assure or even to assert the truth of religious utterances?

It was at this juncture that the second stage of Ludwig Wittgenstein's work assumed such great importance. While his earlier writing, the *Tractatus Logico-philosophicus,* had appeared to support the Logical Positivists,[6] his later writing could not be understood in that way. Language was no longer a construct of logic, supported by universally available 'facts' that it was supposed to depict. Now language was understood as an irregular set of human practices, varying in performance from one field of discourse to another and drawing its viability from the "forms of life" in which it participated and which it shaped. These varieties of language were denoted separate "language-games" whose rules or 'grammar' could not be determined in advance of actual human practices. Thus the possibility of ruling out any entire sphere of language, such as the language of religion, seemed to vanish. Religious language was its own 'language-game.' The primary expression of Wittgenstein's later views appeared in his *Philosophical Investigations,* published after his death.[7] (This was followed by the gradual and still incomplete publication of the rest of his writings.) Two generations of Wittgenstein pupils and inter-preters have unfolded and expanded his philosophy, including his account of religion. Rather than compete with these varied interpretations of the master, we will simply report the work of two of them, Norman Malcolm and Dewi Z. Phillips, asking what light they shed on our present task.

Norman Malcolm, an American philosopher, was personally close to him during Wittgenstein's years in Cambridge, England, and wrote a definitive article on Wittgenstein in the *Encyclopedia of Philosophy.*[8] Mal-colm was particularly adept at showing the changed viewpoint that the later Wittgenstein demanded of philosophers. For example, it was typical of philosophers in Wittgenstein's day to search for the *grounds* of reli-gious belief. Upon what was religion based? What was it, though, that made such a search appropriate in the first place?[9] Was it that in general we have grounds for whatever we think and say? Certainly that is not true of little children: children learn to speak their native language without de-manding to know by what right they must learn *this* language; they learn arithmetic, and the difference between left and right, and (more gener-ally) what counts as human behavior without being given grounds for any of these things. We may imagine, then, that such grounds are provided later. Yet adults, too, accept groundless assumptions — for example, the assumption that material objects don't (ever) simply vanish into thin air without leaving a trace behind. If we thought otherwise, if we imagined that sometimes things do vanish in this way, we would behave somewhat differently than we do. Thus we might give up more quickly when we couldn't find our car keys or billfold, and we would be less inclined than we now are to suspect thieves. Yet, Malcolm points out, there is no infal-lible ground for our ordinary way of thinking: things do disappear and are never seen again, so why should we unwaveringly assume they are still somewhere? To notice this assumption that we all share, along with many other such assumptions, is to understand part of the general truth about ourselves. We inhabit forms of life that are not based on evidence, forms that constitute the *framework* of our thinking.

To reach this point is to be prepared for a further thought: our (ground-less) forms of life are not one, but multiple. Each form is supplied with its own language — not a language such as French or English, but a way of talk embodying assumptions and ways of reasoning that distinguish the various forms. Religion is such a form of life; "it is language embedded in action — what Wittgenstein calls a 'language-game.' "[10] Science is yet another form of life. These are not mutually exclusive forms. There is the language of science, embodying scientific assumptions (e.g., that the causal laws are in effect elsewhere as they are here); there is also, for another case, the language of religion, embodying its 'laws' and assumptions. One might participate in both, as well as in still other forms of life. Sometimes we play one game; sometimes, another. The framework of forms of life escapes our notice if we ourselves are involved in them. Certainly we do not need to have them 'grounded' or proved to us; we follow them without additional reflection, without noticing that we are doing so. A traveler (Malcolm's illustration) sees the name of a place posted on a sign, accompanied by a pointing arrow. A question arises — to reach that place is the traveler to go in the direction of the arrow's head, or in the direction from which the arrow appears to have come? In general, which way does a sign board arrow point? No sign informs the traveler of *that*. At first we may think the question silly, but this is only because we are totally accustomed to the conventional reading. The form of life, the language-game, tells the traveler how to read the arrow. In sum, the language of a way of life, its language-game, has its conventions, never explained because they are beneath the level of explanation, yet quietly determinative of how the language is understood, how the language-game in question is played.

Yet here, says Malcolm, a great difficulty arises. Many, including many academic or university philosophers of religion, are no longer inside the religious way of life, no longer directly engaged in the religious language-game. An illustration of this is the preoccupation of such philosophers with theistic proofs. They teach courses each year designed to test whether the proofs 'work'; the usual conclusion is that these proofs fail to prove the 'existence of God.' Malcolm argues, though, that 'the existence of God' is an alien topic to religious believers — to those actually engaged in the language-game of religion. They believe in *God,* not merely in that empty place-holder, God's 'existence.' For such existence, he points out, might be entertained by someone who nevertheless did not engage in the religious life, someone for whom 'God' didn't matter.

This does not by any means entail that players of the religious language-game (nothing trivial is intended here by terms such as "player" and "game") are themselves thoughtless, do not have exact beliefs and positive differences with one another. They do, but these are doctrinal differences within the language-game. To address and argue such internal differences is altogether different from the external (and for religious folk irrelevant) question of the 'grounds' of religious belief.

So far, it appears that a representative Wittgensteinian such as Norman

Malcolm might be sympathetic to some of the concerns of the previous chapter. While aware of the difference that religion makes (and the differences among various religious standpoints) he is on guard against the convictional imperialism that claims rights over all who disagree with it. He is no imperialist. Does Malcolm swing, though, to the other extreme: is his account of religious language a relativism not only free from invasion by other viewpoints but also inaccessible to them? Are religious convictions simply immune to external criticism? Or, for that matter, is science likewise immune? Can no standpoint be significantly open to other standpoints? Malcolm's answer is not clear.

These questions also confront *Dewi Z. Phillips,* a Welsh philosopher of religion who has written more about religion and its language than any other Wittgensteinian. Phillips's view of religion is expressed throughout his career, but we will concentrate here on a few passages from his writing bearing on the matter at hand. Recognizing that other philosophers have criticized the Wittgensteinian view just related on the ground that it cuts religious language-games off from all others, he has sought to do justice to misgivings about this approach. If religious beliefs are too sharply isolated from other human beliefs, it will appear that there is no compelling reason why people should hold them. They will seem to be a hobby, a private enterprise. Moreover, if anyone should be interested, religious beliefs may seem in the Wittgensteinian view simply inaccessible to nonbelievers' thought and criticism — the view that in the previous chapter we called relativism.[11] So Phillips proposes both to grant the force of these objections and yet to maintain the new standpoint represented by Wittgenstein and his followers.

This standpoint had appeared already in his earlier book, *The Concept of Prayer.*[12] While Wittgenstein's concept of language as constituted by various language-games, and of religious language as itself a language-game (or language-games) is correct, Phillips held, this must not be understood as if each language-game were cut off from all the rest, or in particular as if religion made no difference to the rest of life for its adherents — for almost the opposite is the case. What Wittgenstein's account of language does imply is that the language-games of religion are not founded upon other language-games. Thus religious belief is (in the sense the Wittgensteinians intend) *groundless.* It follows that the following understanding of religion is simply mistaken: We all live, in this 'evidentialist' view, in the same world, have access to the same facts, believe the same truths. Some people, the religious believers, look out over the accessible facts and find among them evidences for religious belief — so they become or remain believers. In consequence, their religion is either true (the religious have assessed the evidence correctly) or false (they have misread the evidence, made a mistake), and philosophers should help us decide which is right.

If the "evidentialist" account of the matter is badly mistaken, as Phillips (we suspect rightly) believes, where does it go wrong? Religious beliefs, he says, are being treated as mere hypotheses, proposals about matters of fact with a greater or lesser degree of correctness. Such a Christian belief as the last judgment, in this case, would be logically similar to the belief that there will be prosperity by the end of the century — one more hypothesis liable to be mistaken, one more in which one ought to place at most only limited trust. Instead, the last judgment functions for believers as an overarching *picture,* not based upon empirical data, not more or less likely, but a picture that (with others like it) controls the believer's present existence. Beliefs such as these are absolute beliefs, not contingent hypotheses. Quoting Wittgenstein, Phillips writes:

> Suppose we said that a certain picture might play the role of constantly admonishing me, or I always think of it. Here an enormous difference would be between those people for whom the picture is constantly in the foreground, and the others who just didn't use it at all.[13]

So such beliefs are not cut off from the rest of life, and yet those who share the rest of life, but are not religious, apparently do not have access to them. In the phraseology of the Wittgensteinians, "The different language-games do not make up one big game."[14]

Phillips recognizes that his own way of thinking about religion is subject to misunderstanding. On the one hand, religious language is for him a separate language, one that is (in the sense indicated) groundless, so that it can be understood only from within. On the other, "religious beliefs cannot be understood at all unless their relation to other forms of life is taken into account." So far, there is no contradiction: religion is about all of life; it is about life's crises and high points in particular. Yet religious believers who "talk of death as if it were a sleep of long duration," or who do not seem to understand that there are senseless evils in the world, have lost their grip on reality. They act as if they no longer know "what we already know." While religion cannot change the facts, which are simply there for all to know, it does nevertheless talk about these things — about "birth, death, joy, misery, despair, hope, fortune and misfortune" — only it understands them in a different way, a way that no earthly event can defeat or falsify.[15]

Certainly this is a lofty, and sometimes moving, way of viewing human existence. Our problem is to know to what extent it is an authentic interpretation of all religion and to what extent it is rather the recommendation of a way of being religious that is so insulated from any matter-of-fact criticism that one can never make in religion's name any claim that risks being wrong. For example, what of those Christians who believe in light of Jesus' teaching that violence is not an option permitted them? Is theirs not a genuine religious conviction? It seems to have been one for Francis of Assisi, for Leo Tolstoy, for Mohandas Gandhi, and for Stanley Hauerwas (a present-day Christian thinker). Yet would Phillips, on the basis of what we have heard, say that the facts are simply against these folk? Would he say that "we already know" that the world lives by violence, that violence is the basis of justice, of law, of peace itself? Must Phillips not conclude, then, that pacifist convictions *cannot* be religious ones? Cannot, since (by his rule) whatever commonsense speakers generally say ("what we all know") must control what is and is not the content of any truly religious language-game.

We suspect the mismove here is that the theory of language-games as displayed by Phillips grants a neutral standpoint, beyond criticism, to some very widely shared convictions (our proffered example is the conviction about the inevitability of violence in this world) while singling out as distinctive language-games what seem to him by comparison only specialized viewpoints — religion and science being his chief instances. Yet if the theory of convictions we are testing in this book proves correct, the way of violence and the way of nonviolence, or for another example the way of belief in resurrection and the way of nonbelief in it, or for a third example acceptance of scientific method or its rejection, are alike and equally convictional standpoints. If we are right, their common status as convinced viewpoints displays itself in the way people actually act and talk. This talk, we think, includes in particular the language of religion as it actually exists. In that case, not only will it be true (as Phillips holds) that those outside religious language-games may lack access to religion and misunderstand it, but also it will be true that outsiders will have no automatic veto, based on their own language-games, over the language-games of those who believe in God. Nor, of course, vice versa.

Exactly where does Phillips stand, then, on the question of relativism — the question to which we found no clear answer in the case of Norman Malcolm? Certainly Phillips has maintained a strong philosophical interest in the relation of religious (and mainly Christian) belief to unbelief, belief in God to the denial of such belief. So how do matters stand between those who believe and those who do not? In *Faith after Foundationalism* Phillips frequently returns to this topic. Negatively, the issue between belief and unbelief cannot be resolved by resort to evidence. The language of religion is not justified or condemned by appeal to common grounds, by facts agreed upon by both sides, or by some foundational beliefs on which all other beliefs depend.[16] Positively, there can be such a thing as conversion — apparently, conversion either to or from religious belief. For instance, Phillips shows how faith may "come alive" in response to persuasive instruction, elucidation from within of faith's contents, so that a hearer will say, "Now I see the kind of thing it is," though previously she or he did not. And again, Phillips envisions a situation in which the primary language of faith is placed in jeopardy and gradually loses its significance for those who still speak it.[17] Yet in neither case is it clear how these possible changes can be or become justifiable ones, different from brainwashing a convert (in the first case) or from sinful neglect of faith (in the second).

To sum up, the Wittgensteinian approach to religious language as envisioned by its strongest advocates recognizes with us the deep divisions that separate people and communities. It even acknowledges, occasionally, that these divisions inhere in certain elemental beliefs, formative for the communities that share them. We have defined these beliefs as "convictions" and are looking for fair ways to understand and assess them. The Wittgensteinians sometimes recognize convictions, though usually under a variety of other labels — "framework principles" (Malcolm) or "basic propositions" (Phillips) or "language-games" or "pictures" (Wittgenstein) — but they seem content not to address the more general question, whether convictions can be expressed in ways that permit someone's assessment and possibly revision or rejection or new adoption of these deep beliefs. They offer no philosophical account of how a community of speakers (players of a language-game) are to know that such profound changes are or are not in order, are or are not justifiable. While the Wittgensteinians are not explicit relativists, they appear to share the dilemma of all relativism: it implies a world in which we are hopelessly divided by high linguistic or conceptual walls from one another. Realistically, this seems all too likely to be the way the world actually is. The question we still face is whether philosophy can see any means to lower these high walls.

II. From Saussure to Deconstruction

The first theory of language treated in this chapter was relatively compact and coherent compared to what we must now examine. This next stream of thought, named by no single name and dominated by no one figure such as Wittgenstein, nonetheless claims our attention. The stream we have in mind runs over a longer period of time, from the scientific linguistic theories of the nineteenth century via Structuralism to Deconstruction and Reader Response theorists, so that whatever broad unity it displays is broken into many diverse currents. Nevertheless, we believe this is a significant stream, and we hope to show here why these theorists of language say what they do. Perhaps in the process we will find resources for our own account in the next chapter — or at the very least note mistakes we ourselves must not make.

While these modern theories of language do not have one name or one dominant figure, they do have a common origin — the work of the Swiss linguist Ferdinand de Saussure (1857–1913). Perhaps the linguistic division of the Swiss population (into speakers of French, German, Italian, and Romansch languages) stimulated Saussure to ask what all languages have in common, or more exactly what task any language performs. The received theory, as old as antiquity, held that words corresponded to things (or happenings): when a speaker of English says "ball," this simply refers to (some) actual ball; no further account is required. Yet long before Saussure, philosophers had noted that in fact the workings of language were not so simple: what about the *idea* of a ball? Without it, the mere sound or written marks have no way of meaning the thing or happening that the sound is supposed to indicate. So philosophers posited something intermediate between words and things, namely, the *concept* or idea. This explained, they felt, how it was possible for speakers of Italian to say *ballo* and speakers of German to say *Tanzfest* where speakers of English might say "ball." In each case, they thought, the *concept* was the same. What Saussure noticed, though, is that this explanation is inaccurate: Italians would call a social event a *ballo* where speakers of English would *not* call it a "ball"; though their meanings overlap they are not simply identical — a difficulty every translator faces every day. It followed, Saussure reasoned, that word and concept could not be separated: each word (or "sign") in a particular language consists in both a sound (the "signifier") tied to its own distinct concept (or "signified"); at any given time, signified and signifier constitute one sign; all the signs of a system comprise a natural language such as French or Hungarian.

Now since there are no single thoughts or things that are merely differently named in different languages (for whether there is even such an event as a 'ball,' for example, depends upon which language-group you are in, depends, we might say, upon where you are in Switzerland), it follows that words do not get their meanings merely by referring to things in the world. Instead, they get them from their relation to and especially their *difference from* all other words in that same language. In English a ball is not a tea-dance and not a café party, and it need not be a cotillion or a prom or a german, either, while in another sense of the word, a ball is not a strike — matters well enough known to writers of party invitations in the one case and equally well to sports fans in the other. Thinking on such facts of language led Saussure to conclude that *word meanings belong to and emanate from the entire system that constitutes one natural language.* Neither the wordless world that language confronts, nor the wordless intentions that some speaker or writer may harbor, but *its own system* confers sense upon the words of any language.[18]

Two further points follow. One is that the contrasts or differences between words acquire great importance in Saussure's teaching. When it comes to temperatures, "hot" and "warm," "cool" and "cold" explain each other: "hot" means not cold; "cold" means not hot; "warm" and "cool" are in between. So it is with all the terms of any language — bright and dull, light and heavy, quick and slow. Moreover, what counts as "hot water" in an English-speaking cultural-linguistic setting differs significantly, as measured by the Fahrenheit scale, from what counts as *heisses Wasser* in a German-speaking setting. (It has to be hotter water to count as *heiss* in German than it does to count as hot in English.)[19] This is not true of every term in every language — sometimes they match very well — but it is true often enough to make Saussure's point. This idea of each language as a system comprising balanced pairs or opposites was of great importance to the Structuralists, the group to be considered next. The other point is that Saussure never meant to say that people couldn't talk about non-linguistic reality. Language-users are not, on his account, isolated from things by their language. On the contrary, we can and do really talk about things and events, even though doing so is not as simple an activity as the ancients or the early moderns supposed: there is not a simple, one-to-one correspondence between the words of any language and whatever is there to be talked about, nor even between any language and a universal system of concepts that in turn match up with the world. A system of language indeed makes it possible to refer, but does so in the systemic ways just offered as examples, and not by simple word-thing correspondences.

We can correctly talk about hot water only because "hot" in English is not the same as "warm" or "cool" or "cold." Yet this point about reference was grasped by some of Saussure's successors only hazily, or not at all.

Saussure's points about system and difference and especially about opposed pairs (hot-cold, left-right) mightily impressed not only linguists but workers in allied fields, issuing in the movement called "Structuralism." A Structuralist anthropologist might attempt to interpret an entire society, as Saussure had interpreted languages, as a structure of interrelated parts, kinship and marriage, male and female, hierarchy and membership being interpreted by their complex, paired roles in a given social structure. Structuralism seemed a powerful tool offering insights that had eluded previous theorists. A bit closer to our interests is the Anglo-American counterpart of Structuralism called New Criticism. The New Critics attempted to interpret works of literature not in terms of the unspoken *intentions* of their authors, or in terms of the external real or imagined *world* to which a book was supposed to refer, but strictly in terms of the *internal structure* of a text. In reading such a poem as William Blake's "Tyger," the New Critic would not ask what Blake had meant by the poem (that was called the "intentional fallacy") or ask who or what Blake's "tyger burning bright, in the forests of the night" referred to, but only how the related parts of the poem revealed the meaning of the whole — a meaning available only in terms of its language. Such 'structuralist' rules came to be followed by many twentieth-century teachers of English literature and (not incidentally for us) by teachers of "the Bible as literature" and other academic interpreters of religion.

In several ways the theory of the New Critics, in particular those interested in religion, was rather awkward. They insisted that their subject, literature, was important for human life, yet their theory seemed to cut literature off (as misreaders of Saussure had supposed his theory cut language off) from the real world. So how could it be important? In addition, their rule against asking for an author's intentions, while perhaps logically coherent, isolated texts even from their own authors. They found a way around these difficulties: while works of literature did not directly refer to the real world, they did in some way reflect it. One favored term was "mimesis." Literature and perhaps other human utterances mimed or imitated the world. Many of the New Critics were at least vaguely religious; the structural pairing (remember Saussure) they now discovered in all great literature somehow conveyed the metaphysical world of divine truth: the words of a poem (any poem) reflected the reality of "all things, seen and unseen," the creation and the Creator.[20] So Structuralism in this instance seemed on the side of inherited religious verities.

This brings us to Deconstruction.[21] The Deconstructionists shared with the Structuralists the heritage of Saussure, his belief that the entire system of language (and not simple reference to things or events) yielded meaning, his emphasis upon structured pairs of words, and his focus upon the conventional or formal element in language as essential to meaning. They did not deny but continued to assume these features of language. They called attention, however, to something else that this understanding of language brought with it: every word-meaning, since it is paired with an opposed word-meaning, inevitably calls attention to that opposition. For example, speech calls attention to and thus implies writing; faith implies doubt; order implies chaos — and of course the contrary in each case. A second feature of Deconstruction was one instilled into Western thought by such "masters of suspicion" as Nietzsche and Freud: we cannot take people to mean what they say or say what they mean; in general others' writing and speech must be subjected to an analysis that finds in it subterfuge and hypocrisy not directly expressed (or even directly intended) by its authors. When speakers say "hot," perhaps they suggest cold, and so forth. Thus the world that shows itself, the apparent world, is only a deceptive world of appearances. This hermeneutics of suspicion provided a further motive for deconstructing (i.e., reinterpreting in this suspicious way) classic literary texts, finding senses contrary to traditional readings. It also became a stock way of deconstructing rival critics' views. Finally, the Deconstructionists' political and religious views often called for a radical rejection, not simply of this or that political view or religious commitment, but of the entire "oppressive" system of things as usual. This oppression was implemented, they believed, by the institutions of language with its conventions. The features that Saussure had identified in the nature of language, its conventional qualities, the arbitrary nature of a language-system, were now seen as true but oppressively true: "logocentrism," the oppressive rule of words, was an enemy to be destroyed, but (quite paradoxically) the verbal techniques of Deconstruction would provide the means of its destruction.[22]

How does Deconstruction bear upon our own present task? Apparently it makes it an unworthy one. We have set out to find the convictions by which people live and to understand the communities of conviction that either unite or divide people from one another. If that could be accomplished simply by taking what people say or write and inferring the contrary as their true convictions, our task would be complicated, but not immeasurably so. In that case, those who say, "We believe in one God" (the words of the Nicene creed) might be understood to mean that there are many gods, and those who find no place for God in their life and thought might be taken to confess God's being and presence. These are not ridiculous thoughts; they may in certain cases be substantially correct. Yet surely they need some substantiation other than the post-Saussurean thesis that each concept suggests its contrary. And surely suspicion itself is appropriate in a given case only if there are some cases where suspicion is unfounded. For if suspicion is always appropriate and people always mean the contrary of what they say, *if,* to condense the point, *everyone always lies,* then lying itself is utterly ineffective; it has itself become an ineffective convention, and the truth can be reliably discovered merely by standing what each of us says on its head and 'hearing' its contrary. That may produce considerable confusion (we may not know, for example, whether those who say the Nicene creed imply that actually there are many gods or actually there is no god at all — at least we know there is not for them one God as they confess), but the Deconstructive rule then fails the apparent purpose of the Deconstructionists to expose the oppressive system of the world and liberate themselves and us from it. The world is simply its own mirror image, and we are not oppressed. How can words oppress when everyone helplessly tells the truth by lying? Or for that matter, when everyone helplessly blurts the truth? Isn't the real world (with its oppressions and deceptions) more complicated than either of these — a world of mixed truth and lies? Or are we to take the Deconstructionists to be telling us just this, since (applying their own rule to themselves) they, too, must forever be lying? It seems that at best Deconstructionism must remain only a technique, not *the* technique, of interpretation. Indeed, from time to time Deconstructionists grant as much. In chapter 6 of this book we will consider the case of the *rebel* who seeks to change an unsatisfactory world without being in position to offer a better one. We will show that to be a difficult but not impossible convictional stance. With other stances, it may contribute to the ultimate justification of some better set of convictions. We note here in advance that 'Deconstructionist' techniques may be part of the arsenal of such a rebel. Here we must leave Deconstruction.

Yet it may be that Saussure, the Structuralists, and the Deconstructionists have among them hit upon still other points of considerable importance for our overall task of getting straight about how the language of religious convictions works. We found this to be true of the

Wittgensteinians; may it be true of the Saussureans as well? Pursuing that question leads to a school of interpretation closely linked with Deconstruction but differently labeled, namely, *Reader Response criticism.* The themes and advocates of the two are similar, but the Reader Response movement more plainly makes two or three positive points that we find instructive. Whether these are points it shares with Deconstruction others can decide. In any case we believe that the preceding pages make it easier to understand the goals and tools of Reader Response. A collection of essays titled *Is There a Text in This Class?* by Stanley Fish, an American literary critic, furnishes a useful guide to Reader Response.[23]

Fish began his work as a member of the Structuralist (or formalist, or New Critical) school of interpretation. Here one is to look at an entire text, considered as a whole, with the meaning determined by all the (paired or opposing) elements that compose it. We will not get the meaning of *Hamlet* or the meaning of the book of Genesis until we have read the entire play, the entire book; only then are we in position to see what it is saying line by line. This was the standard Structuralist approach. Then a new insight appeared for Fish: while he or she is actually reading, the first-time reader of those texts has not seen the end, does not know how everything will come out at the end, and much of the reader's interest lies in that fact. (Even readers who *do* know how the story ends may on a fresh reading participate in the suspense to a considerable degree; otherwise children would not enjoy having a story told the second time.) This led Fish to concentrate his interpretations upon the *response* of the typical reader at particular points in the progress of the story — say in Genesis the point in chapter 37 where young brother Joseph has been favored with a special coat, to the irritation of his brothers. A reader sees trouble brewing, but the immediate response will be not to the undisclosed fact that the annoying Joseph will be the means of his brothers' survival in Egypt, but only to the youthful troublemaker and his wicked brothers in Canaan land.[24]

In Fish's words, he had now "displaced attention from the text [spread out on its pages] to the reader and his temporal experience." That created a problem, though, for there are many readers and they have many responses. Fish therefore had to claim that there was a "level of experience that all readers share, independently of differences in education and culture."[25] This solution was not surprising: he was now assigning to the typical reader what other New Critics had assigned to language itself and what Noam Chomsky had assigned to "linguistic competence" — the ability of any speaker of any language to share in an internalized set of rules that explained how everyone used language. Fish's special contribution at this point was to insist upon the *emotional* component of the reader's response to the text. So readers' responses to what was written might after all vary (as people vary); still, there was a standard response, happily the one embodied by Professor Fish himself.

In retrospect, Fish saw that at this point there was a severe tension in his theory of reading: on the one hand, reading was necessarily and as a matter of course controlled by the formal conventions of the text itself (the old Structuralism); on the other hand he was insisting that a text's meaning was identical with the responses it created in the (so-called typical) reader. Increasingly, it seemed to him that both could not be true, and his next step was to abandon the role of stylistic convention altogether: now there was no meaning embodied in the text, but only the meaning that arose as a reader *read* the text. (At this stage of his work, we might say in the language of our next chapter that everything hinged upon "uptake.") Fish notes that he had one very powerful argument on his side against critical opponents who insisted upon the *objective* meaningfulness of the text: they always disagreed with one another about the content of that objective meaning. And he was able to furnish plenty of instances of such basic disagreement to substantiate his view. Here, then, he had achieved a characteristic postmodern insight: all facts, including the facts about any text one seeks to interpret, are already interpreted facts — there is no such thing as an uninterpreted fact. "Indeed," he says in retrospect, "the *text* as an entity independent of interpretation and (ideally) responsible for its career *drops out* and is replaced by *texts* that emerge as a consequence of our interpretive activities."[26]

The text drops out! It sounds as if the Deconstructionists' goal has been attained. Something had to account, though, for the element of continuity and agreement that kept various readers' readings and interpretations from dissolving into a myriad of unrelated fragments. How could people even *argue* about what Milton's poems meant if there were no (objective, uninterpreted) texts of *L'Allegro* and *Il Penseroso?* (To keep our own parallel goals in mind, how are we ever to discover what religious speakers mean by what they say if there *is* no "what they say" to address?) Fish's solution was to recognize that there were *communities of interpretation* that shared "interpretive strategies" not for reading but for writing texts, for constituting their properties. Such strategies "exist prior to the act of reading and therefore determine the shape of what is read rather than, as is usually assumed, the other way around." He had but one step left to take: There is more than one interpretive community, so that "what was normative for the members of one community would be seen as strange (if it could be seen at all) by the members of another."[27]

And who is to adjudicate between interpretive communities? It seems that Fish has escaped the iron formalism of his (Structuralist, New Critical) beginnings only to fall into another iron clasp, that of relativism. This would not make his standpoint a unique one: we have already seen in the previous chapter that there is good reason to be attracted by relativism, even if it is an unstable (in fact an incoherent) final resting place for those who seek as we do to understand communities of conviction. Still, it has been worth while to take this brief look at Stanley Fish. For in the course of his own intellectual journey Fish touched on almost all the points we will think important in presenting our own plan for understanding religious convictions.[28] There was the (apparently arbitrary) role of linguistic convention, which Fish inherited from the New Critics. There was the emotive role played by readers (or hearers) of what others write (or say) — part of our notion of 'uptake,' which Fish seized upon in his focus upon reader response. Finally, there was a background of assumptions, understandings, shared beliefs special to an interpretive community, and writers themselves also belong to such communities.

This brings us to the variety of interpretive communities and, as just noted, to the special problem of relativism (which community? whose interpretation? whose truth?) that we will address in the second half of the present book. And it certainly brings us to the question about representation or reference, the sense in which religious convictions (or for that matter, literary texts that express such convictions) can tell us the truth about heaven and earth, or conversely fail to do so. Reader Response critics seem clearer and more helpful about many of these urgent matters than are their close cousins the Deconstructionists, and for that reason we have reached a terminus with the Deconstructionists' work here.

III. From James to Ourselves

Recent approaches to language, including religious language, are surprisingly varied. Where Saussure and his followers started by investigating the *system* of language, started we might say with all the words in the dictionary, the later Wittgenstein and his followers instead started with language-in-practice, that is, with *uttered speech,* with the distinctive shapes of language-games in particular settings. William James, whose life span (1842–1910) overlapped these other pioneers, had still a third approach. James was an investigator in many fields: he was one of the founders of the modern science of psychology; he came relatively late to philosophy but made important contributions there also; he retained as well a lifelong interest in understanding religion — an interest closely connected with his father, an eccentric religious theorist who sponsored the Swedenborgian movement in America. The combination of these interests led James to approach religious language psychologically, by way of a theory about human thought. In an age preoccupied with the machine, with science, and with the relentless impersonal forces of nature, James hoped to recapture the dignity of human personhood, the difference thinking made, the right to believe, and the free will he believed to be a significant part of existence in the world. In the end, he hoped that "science, metaphysics, and religion may then again form a single body of wisdom, and lend each other mutual support."[29]

Jamesian psychology was introspective: we learn about minds by noticing ourselves thinking. The mind (he found) is a stream of feeling, appearing now as sensation, now as particular concepts and the words that express them. The first thing we may notice in consciousness is our concepts, each of which means exactly what it means, discrete and single. Yet concepts are only a convenient dividing up of the stream of feeling, and that ongoing stream is endlessly complex. "It shows duration, intensity, complexity or simplicity, interestingness, excitingness, pleasantness or their opposites." All is flux, all overflows into all else, so that if one succeeds in abstracting one's attention from particularized conceptual thought and attends to this vast, underlying stream itself, one finds "a *big blooming buzzing confusion*."[30]

Of particular present interest is what James believed lay at the margins of the thought-stream, away from the usual center of introspective attention. At least in certain human minds there is not only the central stream of consciousness; there is also a margin of memories, thoughts, and feelings not readily accessible, yet not completely beyond attention, either. This is the realm of the "subconscious," consciousness extending beyond its ordinary field. Nineteenth-century psychology had discovered that this threshold area of the mind made powerful incursions into the more accessible central stream. Most important, the subconscious was the margin of mind whence religious impulses came; there, as it were out of sight of the everyday, the deep prehensions had been formed that came to light in overt religious belief.[31]

It might seem, then, that James was a psychologist-philosopher-religious theorist not particularly interested in the questions about language that preoccupied other theorists such as Saussure and Wittgenstein and their followers. Indeed, James was a hearty optimist concerning the efficacy of language. It successfully conveyed thought and effectively represented thought's objects. In his unfinished textbook of philosophy, James brushed aside the worries of some philosophers about the "misuse of terms"; he took people generally to say what they mean and mean what they say.[32] Yet this bluff optimism did not issue in total neglect of the problems of language. The great strength of *The Varieties of Religious Experience,* James's Edinburgh lectures on the philosophy of religion, lay in the enormous care with which they presented case study after case study based upon the very words of subjects who reported first-hand religious experience of their own. While James sorted and arranged these cases in order to make his own cumulative argument for a pragmatic sort of religiousness, he exercised scientific care to see that he did not distort his reports, and our own judgment (based on familiarity with some of his cases) is that he is remarkably faithful to his human sources.

We cannot in this brief chapter reproduce full samples of this work. Yet a couple of excerpts may begin to give their flavor. Consider first a few sentences from one Henry Alline, whose *Life and Journals* James had perused:

"These discoveries continued until I went into the house and sat down. After I sat down, being all in confusion, like a drowning man that was just giving up to sink, and almost in an agony, I turned very suddenly round in my chair, and seeing part of an old Bible lying in one of the chairs, I caught hold of it in great haste; and opening it without any premeditation, cast my eyes on the 38th Psalm, which was the first time I ever saw the word of God: it took hold of me with such power that it seemed to go through my whole soul, so that it seemed as if God was praying in, with, and for me. About this time my father called the family to attend prayers; I attended, but paid no regard to what he said in his prayer, but continued praying in those words of the Psalm. Oh, help me, help me! cried I, thou Redeemer of souls, and save me, or I am gone forever; thou canst this night, if thou pleasest, with one drop of thy blood atone for my sins, and appease the wrath of an angry God. At that instant of time when I gave all up to him to do with me as he pleased, and was willing that God should rule over me at his pleasure, redeeming love broke into my soul with repeated scriptures, with such power that my whole soul seemed to be melted down with love; the burden of guilt and condemnation was gone, darkness was expelled, my heart humbled and filled with gratitude, and my whole soul, that was a few minutes ago groaning under mountains of death, and crying to an unknown God for help, was now filled with immortal love."[33]

A rather different flavor appears in the testimony of one of Starbuck's case studies quoted by James, that of a woman who has abandoned her religious beliefs:

> "Away down in the bottom of my heart, I believe I was always more or less skeptical about 'God'; skepticism grew as an undercurrent, all through my early youth, but it was controlled and covered by the emotional elements in my religious growth. When I was sixteen I joined the church and was asked if I loved God. I replied 'Yes,' as was customary and expected. But instantly with a flash something spoke within me, 'No, you do not.' I was haunted for a long time with shame and remorse for my falsehood and for my wickedness in not loving God, mingled with fear that there might be an avenging God who would punish me in some terrible way.... At nineteen, I had an attack of tonsilitis. Before I had quite recovered, I heard told a story of a brute who had kicked his wife downstairs, and then continued the operation until she became insensible. I felt the horror of the thing keenly. Instantly this thought flashed through my mind: 'I have no use for a God who permits such things.' This experience was followed by months of stoical indifference to the God of my previous life, mingled with feelings of positive dislike and a somewhat proud defiance of him. I still thought there might be a God. If so he would probably damn me, but I should have to stand it. I felt very little fear and no desire to propitiate him. I have never had any personal relations with him since this painful experience."[34]

These poignant accounts, a tiny fraction of the scores of reports sprinkled through the *Varieties,* may just begin to convey the flavor of James's work. Certainly he has been criticized — for paying too much attention to extraordinary cases, for concentrating upon the striking individual (the "saint") at the expense of both religious institutions and religious thought, for narrowing "religious experience" to certain concentrated moments in life at the expense of the entire lives of those he studies, for attending mainly to Western, Christian experients at the expense of others. While these criticisms have force, they should not diminish the credit due James for taking real-life religion seriously. This success encompasses two prominent features: attention to the actual (spoken or written) utterances of individuals, coupled with the outcome in their lives of what they say — in James's biblical phrase, the fruit of their lives. What they do gives its value to what his speakers say.

James provided his own theoretical analysis of this material. He thought his cases revealed the contents of the human subconscious, evidence that pointed to a "More" in the cosmos that he identified as God.[35] Our present interest, however, is in his linguistic method rather than in the speculation he next pursued. Has anyone adequately followed up the

Jamesian investigation of what religious people actually say and do (and the close connection of these two) as a clue to interpreting religion itself?

Process philosophy, a largely American philosophical movement, displayed two broad tendencies. One branch, characterized by Chicago philosophical theologian Charles Hartshorne, concentrated on the speculative and rational dimensions of the Process heritage. The other, characterized by other Chicagoans, was drawn to the empirical and experiential aspect of Process thought. This side claimed a special relation to the thought of William James. Prominent among these empirical philosopher-theologians was Bernard E. Meland, for decades a member of the faculty of the Divinity School of the University of Chicago and editor of a 1969 volume that set out to sum up the achievements of this approach.[36] The name of William James recurs throughout that volume. Yet the emphasis is upon "radical empiricism," another side of James than that we have called attention to here.

Toward the end of his days, James had referred more and more to a philosophical doctrine which he named radical empiricism. In a brief summary, he said that it consisted in a postulate, a statement of fact, and a generalized conclusion. The postulate or unproved claim is that philosophers shall debate only things definable in terms of experience. The "fact," (so James tells us) is that the relations between things are matters of "direct particular experience" just as much as the things themselves are. "Causing," as in the observation that eating grass *causes* cattle to grow, would presumably be such a relation, such a matter of direct experience. We experience the causing just as we do the cattle, the grass, and the increase in beef. Cattle and grass and 'being caused' are all equally observable, the causal connection as much as the things caused or causing. While 'radical empiricism' so defined might seem simply a statement of common sense against fancy academicians, James meant it as a sophisticated rampart of his pragmatic philosophy.[37] Things are what they seem; there is no further need for transcendental deductions and the Absolute Idea.

Now the mid-century Chicago philosophers who followed James in this approach were interested in religion even more than he had been — it was their main business. Yet they hoped to display a perfectly 'natural' religion, one not propped up (as they would view it) by popes or Bibles, far less by philosophical proofs and arguments. Religion for them had to be a matter of experience, preferably everybody's experience equally. They recalled James's doctrine of the "More" that he said was found in the subconscious margins of (some) human experience.[38] For James, that subliminal awareness had been only a set of data that might lead a philosopher to form a hypothesis about God. But truly radical empiricism, the "radical empiricism" of James's last writings, could not be satisfied with inferred hypotheses that led from the subconscious margins of the consciousness-stream to an "over-belief" about God as their cause. That would not be in the Chicagoans' eyes radically experiential. They needed a "More" that (or Who) was immediately given in human experience itself. How, then, did the language of religion appear to these latter-day admirers of William James? Meland's title, *Fallible Forms and Symbols,* answers the question in brief. Not only language, but conceptual thought itself, is fallible, errant, inherently insufficient to describe or express the deep prehension of "More" believed to lie in the borderlands of human awareness. Yet those borderlands were by Meland's account the source, the only possible source (since their theory closed these theorists off from other sources) of religious truth.[39]

Such a conclusion may seem about right. Surely religion deals with the ineffable; the mystic approaches things not lawful to be uttered; religion and God or the gods are shrouded, properly shrouded, in deep mystery. Yet that would not be a conclusion that adequately grasped the move that empirical Process thinkers such as Meland made. Nancy Frankenberry, herself in the radical empiricist camp, has provided a close analysis of Bernard Meland's version of radical empiricism. She quotes in cryptic summary his definition of experience, which is:

> simultaneously a patterned occurrence exemplifying and bodying forth the stream of ever recurring concretions as a communal event and an intensified channeling of that stream into individuated life-spans, each with its own legacy of inherited possibilities as given in the structure of experience and with its unique fund of possibilities as an emerging event.[40]

Frankenberry nicely dissects this rather dense definition: "The realities of faith transpire," she says, "within (1) lived experience as perceptual events, are known consciously in (2) 'appreciative awareness,' are lived intermittently in (3) common social events, and are mediated, sustained, and altered by virtue of (4) particular 'structures of experiences.' "[41] While her version still contains technical terms we cannot unravel here, we can surely see in it the connection with William James, for (1) refers to James's undivided stream of experience, still "perceptual" and not yet "conceptual"; (2) brings elements of this flow to consciousness and language; (3) correlates what is thus dredged up with such common elements of religious life as church and Bible; and finally (4) relates all the above to human culture and history.

Now, however, comes trouble: what Frankenberry calls "the linguistic gap." On the one hand, she finds that Meland has (admirably) insisted that religious experience, to be intelligible, must be brought to clear expression "with all the critical facilities at our command." On the other hand, the validation, the root, the heart of religious experience always lies in the prelinguistic or extralinguistic "depths of lived experience" — this is (1) in the preceding summary — depths that *by definition cannot be spoken or written. Here is a gap, a fatal gap, in Meland's project.* How can anyone in any language speak the unspeakable? Perhaps, Frankenberry suggests, the real need is to reexamine the thesis of "a primal disparity between language and reality."[42] Frankenberry has her own way of facing that severe problem, but it is not one that returns, as we hope to do, to an earlier clue from William James's thought, one that takes what religious speakers *say and do* as itself the primary material for understanding what religion is about.

Before investigating that clue, we need to acknowledge another portion of the Jamesian heritage, one that looms still larger than Chicago and Process philosophy on the current scene. This is Pragmatism. When William James moved into philosophy, he found it dominated by what he called Absolutism — a view of philosophy that not only believed in an Absolute, but also believed itself absolutely competent to settle every important human question for everybody. James found this pretentious: why should philosophy or the philosophers think they could decide so much about other people's morals, taste, politics, and religion? His own version of philosophy he called Pragmatism, and by it he meant that people have rough and ready ways of finding for themselves what is good enough, true enough, or beautiful enough, a way that James might have summarized under the motto "it works for them." Of course, now that he was a philosopher, he had to express this in somewhat more elegant fashion, and he did so in a number of writings late in life — *Pragmatism* (1907), *A Pluralistic Universe* (1909), *The Meaning of Truth* (1909), and others.[43] In his day James's work was paralleled, with important differences, by C. S. Pierce (from whom James 'stole' the name "Pragmatism"), and it was continued, again with differences, by John Dewey and others. More recently, a new school of Pragmatists, whose leading light is Richard Rorty, has appeared. The high-level, abstract philosophy of language of these new Pragmatists is not one we can usefully (or pragmatically?) report here,[44] but the broad philosophical thrust of the newcomers faithfully returns to James's own: to free human thinking from domination by philosophy and philosophers. As Rorty ironically writes, "The traditional image of philosophy is of a discipline that will (any day now) produce noncontroversial results concerning matters of ultimate concern." Rorty effectively attacked this traditional 'foundation-alism' in *Philosophy and the Mirror of Nature* (1979)[45] as well as in his later writings. The first edition of the present book (first published, 1975) was a still earlier instance of a nonfoundationalist approach to its subject matter. Thus there are broad sympathies (as well as differences) between ourselves and the new Pragmatists, though we cannot pursue all of them here.

For now we must indicate our own relation to William James, which focuses upon his link between saying and doing — between attending to what (religious or antireligious) speakers actually say as interpreted by what they actually do. We shall find that the saying-doing distinction is not a sharp one: saying is in fact a kind of doing, and so the question becomes one of interpreting religion by attending to one kind of doing (namely, saying) as an important clue to all the rest. In this regard if no other we are here Jamesians.

What we propose is examining in its context the language in which people express, appeal to, and reveal their convictions, particularly their religious convictions. The precise details of this method will be set out in the next chapter, but we can state here the basic principles from which we will work.

(1) The starting point of our inquiry, the data or givens, will be what the members of the religious communities say (including what they write) especially to each other. Here at the outset is an important correction of James, aided by such as Stanley Fish: it is in interpretive *communities,* not simply in solitary individuals, that we find characteristic religious speakers.

(2) In determining what is meant by what these speakers say, the cru-cial evidence will be the testimony of the community as it is embodied in its linguistic and other *practices.* "Linguistic practices" is a more contem-porary (and we believe more precise) way of describing our topic than the vaguer if more colorful Wittgensteinian term "language-games."

(3) The categories of assessment (true or false, appropriate or inap-propriate) to be employed for the utterances of the community will be, insofar as possible, those dictated by the sorts of utterances they are within that community. This guideline marks an important distinction be-tween the tasks of the first part of this book (chapters 2 through 4) and the second (chapters 5 through 7). For in the later chapters, we will address a question that we will only be able to address properly after first attending

to assessment within particular communities: namely, what happens when diverse or rival communities disagree?

(4) It is *not* assumed (though it may be true) that the standards of adequacy appropriate in one community are appropriate in others, or in general — which gets at the point just made about rival communities of conviction.

No method, ours or any other, can guarantee a complete, precise, and undistorted account of religious (or any other) activity. What these procedures will amount to in the present work can become clear only as we do the work itself. But it is already evident that our method presupposes that the language of convinced communities does reveal their convictions — an instance of the more general principle that our beliefs are shown in our actions. Lipchitz's *telling* us that he believes it will rain is as much his act as putting on his raincoat or opening his umbrella. Which act gives us a better idea of Lipchitz's belief will depend on the surrounding circumstances, including his other beliefs, intentions, and desires, which we come to know in the same ways. (He may be putting on his raincoat by force of habit, or he may be saying "I believe it will rain" insincerely.) In either case, we need to know more. Still, there is an especially close connection between our speech and our beliefs. In fact, there is a set of actions, "speech-acts," whose point in human communities is just to make beliefs (desires, aversions, etc.) known, and while our utterances may be hypocritical or phony, so (psychology points out) may our beliefs and even our feelings be false to ourselves and of course false to the way things are. Moreover, these often go together. People with phony beliefs often reveal them in phony speech. What of the case, then, where somebody thinks one thing yet says another? Of course this happens (one instance being lying), but as all parents and many children know, we often catch liars at their game, and we do this by the very method proposed here — attending carefully to what they say.

Such attention will require lively consideration of the variety of ways in which religious and other speakers (and writers) make language work for their purposes. The schools of theories about this that we have just surveyed (the Wittgensteinians, the Saussureans, and the Jamesians) do not fully encompass the variety, and there is no way we can do it here. However, recent workers in the field of religion have made one of the features of language not so far mentioned here — its employment of *models and metaphors* — so prominent in their work that we must say something about it before moving on, even though what they say has organized itself around no single figure and has been dominated by no single organizing theory. Sallie McFague, a Protestant feminist theologian, published *Metaphorical Theology: Models of God in Religious Language* (1982).[46] Its main point was to insist that inappropriately dominant masculine-gender models and metaphors represented God in a way that sponsored sexism and male domination in the Christian church. This could be remedied, however, by discovering other, feminine or gender-free models and metaphors in Christian Scripture and tradition and employing these instead of or as well as the masculine ones. God as "Friend" might supplement and correct God as Father; Jesus as God's Sophia (wisdom — a Greek term of feminine gender) might supplement and correct Jesus as God's Son.

Although her application of these literary devices was distinctive, the emphasis upon models and metaphors was not new. A generation earlier, Ian T. Ramsey, an Oxford philosopher of religion (and later, Anglican bishop) had made much of models and metaphors in his work.[47] Rather like William James, Ramsey believed that religious language sprang from "religious situations" in which human beings had enjoyed certain sorts of discernment and from which religious commitment typically grew. These "situations" could be distinguished from the situations of everyday life by the unique discernment or awareness that took place in them; Ramsey was endlessly resourceful in providing new and illuminating examples of ordinary, or nonreligious, disclosure situations: a gestalt pattern, seen first as a mere set of dots, is then seen to form a portrait or a landscape. Or (in a different sort of everyday example) all the lights go out while a party is in progress, and the party-goers, relative strangers to one another, are 'made human' for one another, disclosed, by the awkward situation. In like ways, Ramsey thought, some situations are religious: in them, something or other causes the situation to take on a different coloring, and religious discernment occurs. Examples might be a situation in which a mother stoops to care for her infant — and for one who sees, the mother's stoop 'discloses' the parental care and love of God; or a massive granite peak rising in the mountains 'discloses' the awesome grandeur of the divine.

Finally, Ramsey believed that characteristic religious language *models* such disclosures — repeats them, as it were, in words, so that both speaker and hearers (or writer and readers) may find such a disclosure evoked afresh by the words. In such circumstances, it is appropriate to say (metaphorically) that God is a Mother, not merely to this infant, but to all the earth, appropriate to speak (metaphorically) of the Mount of God, where it is not the granite peak but an infinitely greater moral and mystical height that is intended. Ramsey understood the religious sentences that were formed in this way to constitute instructions to the imagination to think progressively along certain lines — this mother, a still better mother, the best mother who ever lived... — until, in cases where the language works, God's Motherhood becomes a 'disclosure' for the listener, evoking an appropriate commitment to God.

While it would be possible here to offer a full critique of McFague's views of model and metaphor, or of Ramsey's rather more fully elaborated theory,[48] it seems unproductive to do so, because no one theory of this sort has commanded the widepread allegiance of other workers in the area. There are still other theories of religious models and metaphors,[49] but this gives the flavor of one of the best of them. Paul Ricoeur in France (and America) and Anthony Thistleton in Great Britain have surveyed the field of religious language rather thoroughly (except that each has omitted all reference to our own work). Their surveys cover many topics drawn from linguistics, literary studies, biblical hermeneutics, and still more, and they, too, refer to models and metaphors in religion.[50] Yet these surveys leave the language of convictions as such unaddressed, and until we have seen for ourselves how to understand such language including all its tropes we cannot be much helped by these loosely related studies. Of course, we too may fail to provide an adequate theory — that will be for others to judge. Yet how can anyone make that judgment before what we have to say here is read and debated?

That is enough, though, about what we are going to do before we do it. Not every case of words that work differently than they may seem to is a case of lying. Think of the children's ditty, "Sticks and stones...," with which this chapter began. The verse seems to say one thing, but it works only because it assumes another — words can indeed hurt me. Our goal in the chapter has been to find theoretical help about how words work. Wittgensteinians might have told us that "sticks and stones" is part of a language-game; Saussureans might have said that it need not be taken at wooden face value. Beyond that, we need a regular way of discovering what religious language is and does: we need, that is, a speech-act theory of language.

THREE

So far, however, we have scarcely begun in earnest: we have merely felt that initial trepidation, experienced when the firm ground of prejudice begins to slip away beneath the feet.

John L. Austin[1]

If you feel that finding out what something is must entail investigation of the world rather than of language, perhaps you are imagining a situation like finding out what somebody's name and address are, or what the contents of a will or a bottle are, or whether frogs eat butterflies. But now imagine that you are in your armchair reading a book of reminiscences and come across the word "umiak." You reach for your dictionary and look it up. Now what did you do? Find out what "umiak" means, or find out what an umiak is? But how could we have discovered something about the world by hunting in the dictionary? If this seems surprising, perhaps it is because we forget that we learn language and learn the world together, that they become elaborated and distorted together, and in the same places. We may also be forgetting how elaborate a process the learning is. . . .

Stanley Cavell[2]

A Speech-Act Theory of
Religious Language

The hope of finding the seeds of a theory of religious language in the
work of the Oxford linguistic philosopher John L. Austin may strike
some as comical, for Austin never devoted himself to religious language
as such, and his sardonic *obiter dicta* on religion did not tend to in-
spire a surge of confidence in the breasts of the faithful. Moreover, many
have supposed that the doctoral dissertation of Donald D. Evans gleaned
whatever could be harvested in the field of philosophy of religion using Austinian tools. In reality, Evans's work on Austin concentrates upon
the notion of 'performative' language, recognizing only in a brief note
that Austin in his culminating work had abandoned the performative and
had developed instead the theory of speech-acts.[3] So while on the one
hand the account we are about to give of religious language represents
Austin's own views no more than did Evans's account, on the other hand
we do hope to provide a foundation for the analysis of religious language
starting from the latest and most considered views of Austin and his successors.[4] Concretely, this should permit us to give a satisfying account of
the convergence of historical, sociological, and linguistic factors in any
significant utterance, thereby advancing beyond the theories described in
the previous chapter. We propose to set out an account of speech-acts, to
apply this to sample utterances, one nonreligious (nonconvictional) and
one expressing a religious conviction, and then to examine these results
as critically as we have the work of others.

I. Speech-Acts

Austin was a philosophical iconoclast who took a certain pleasure in
overturning what had been considered central doctrines in philosophy

in his day and in disregarding the received dichotomies of philosophical thought. Thus it is not surprising that he should have begun his systematic explorations of language by attending to forms of speech that refused to fit into traditional linguistic categories and in any case were generally regarded as trivial by analysts. Suppose I say, "I bid one heart," when it comes to my turn to bid in a game of bridge. One way to understand my utterance, one that had commended itself to some philosophers, was to take it as a description of myself, a statement about me. Such an interpretation would assimilate "I bid one heart" to "I have one heart," or "I have one kidney." That seemed, though, a wrong-headed view of the matter. If "I bid one heart" is a statement, it is either a true one or a false one — but even to ask which it is seems to miss its point, as it is certainly to mistake its role in the game of bridge. So long as we maintain traditional dichotomies, however, denying that it is a statement seems to imply either that it is meaningless (which it certainly isn't), or that it is some sort of command, or an expression of feeling, which seems equally to miss its point in the game.

What then is that point? Clearly, to bid one heart! Then, suggested Austin, let us call it, not a statement, nor a command, nor an expression of attitude — but a *bid*. Thereby we recognize that when I say, "I bid one heart" (it being my turn to bid in a game of bridge), I have *done* something, namely, bid one heart. Having tried this, it is easy to multiply examples of utterances that exhibit the same intimate relation between saying and doing. Thus if the judge, while performing his function, robed and on the bench, says to the prisoner in the courtroom, "I sentence you to thirty days in jail," he has thereby *sentenced* him, not described sentencing (or expressed a feeling or a wish). And if your physician says, "I advise you to exercise daily," she has *advised* you, certainly not described you or your regimen. And so with many other such utterances in this form: consider "I pronounce you (man and wife)," "I pray that (my soul may be delivered)," "I invite you (to my house for dinner)," or "I resolve (to pay off my debts this year)." Austin first dubbed utterances of this kind "performatives" and set out to find the characteristics that distinguished them from the apparently nonperformative, true-or-false utterances that had received so much attention from philosophers and that for contrast Austin called "constatives," for example, "That barn is red."

Austin found, however, that the performative-constative dichotomy broke down upon examination.[5] What had seemed to be two classes dissolved into only one. For he could find no characteristics that would unfailingly distinguish his new class of performatives from the old class of constatives. At one point he had suggested the "hereby" test for per-formatives: an utterance was performative, according to this test, if it could be put in the form "I hereby (warn, sentence, bid, etc.)..." Thus, "I hereby bid one heart," "I hereby promise to pay you five dollars," and "I hereby sentence you to five years" all make good sense, and the "hereby" does not change that sense but functions to show explicitly what would be true even if the "hereby" were for convenience omitted — that *saying it is doing it.* Therefore, the utterances even without the "hereby" were seen to be performative utterances, and the verbs "sentence," "bid," and "promise" were performative verbs.

So far, the test works. But what about the verb "state"? Take any state-ment, such as "I am a citizen of Washington." If we change the utterance to "I state that I am a citizen of Washington," it remains the same state-ment, and so does "I *hereby* state that I am a citizen of Washington." But if "state" is performative, the same must be true of "assert" also, yet these are the paradigmatic nonperformatives. So the "hereby" test failed to work. The same thing was true of every proposed test: both the pur-ported classes were liable to be unhappy in utterance if the facts did not support them, both were dependent upon the context or circumstances of the speaker as well as the speaker's intentions, both could occur in identi-cal grammatical forms. What had been hoped for from the distinction was not realized. The 'performative' distinction neither separated the class of utterance to which "true/false" applied from all other classes; nor did it separate utterances that could be felicitously or infelicitously uttered from all others; nor did it divide utterances into two mutually exclusive classes of any sort.[6]

The collapse of the performative-constative distinction, while at first glance representing merely the failure of one more hopeful theory, in fact opened the door to a more promising approach. Beginning with the ob-servation that performatives were a saying that was doing, it had been possible to describe the various ways in which this doing could go wrong, or be subject to challenge, or fail. But if performatives were indistinguish-able from the others, all utterances could be usefully treated as kinds of action, having the sorts of linguistic liability and linguistic asset that performative acts had been seen to possess.[7]

To call language a kind of action will not be very helpful unless we can say what we mean by that. The philosophy of action has come in for considerable discussion,[8] and philosophers will see what path we perhaps incautiously take here, among several possible ones. Let us begin with a nonlinguistic story: the body of a heavily padded human, marked in large numerals "43," is somehow attached to an inflated, elliptical object. Man and object are seen to move into a group of similarly padded but differently numbered humans; after a time, the movement slows and stops. Already, we have before us a number of different senses of action. In the broadest of these, we can describe the motion of man plus object as his (or their) action; this sense corresponds to describing any physical motion, say, of pool balls on a table, as 'action.' Again, attending to the fact that '43' is self-propelled, we can speak of *his* (physiological) movement as action, without so far intending to discriminate between this sense of action and the action of his heart in beating, or of his sweat glands in secreting. Next we come to a more interesting sense in which '43' has acted: he has moved across the ground (cf. drawing in a deep breath or raising his head), but this sense interests us here only because it leads to the next.

Suppose now that we say, "43 was slanting off tackle." That is significantly different both from breathing, or digesting lunch, but also from raising his head, drawing a deep breath, or moving about. What we have done is to put 43's movements into the context of a game, with the consequence that there are ways in which his actions can be successful or go wrong. The notions of "off tackle" and of "slanting" cannot be explained without referring to the game of football, so that the assessment of 43's run will require a knowledge of both the rules of the game and the aim of the team playing the game, which is to win and not lose. We can illustrate this by noting circumstances in which we would not say that 43 slanted off tackle. He would not have done it if (*a*) he had been playing a different game, say one in which there are no tackles; or (*b*) if he had not been a player in this game; or (*c*) if he hadn't had the ball or had fumbled; or (*d*) if he had been tackled before he got to the line.

If, however, difficulties like (*a*) to (*d*) do not arise, we may also be able to attribute another action to 43: making a first down. That can be true only if the run comes off. But it requires that other conditions be satisfied as well; certain yardage must be covered, and there must be official recognition of his success, which in turn rests upon certain well-known objections not having arisen or been sustained — penalties incurred, end of the game, or the like.

Again, whether 43's action was successful or not, he will perhaps delight, dismay, encourage, or disappoint various spectators, cause bets to be won or lost, money to change hands, statistical records of team and player standings to change, even coaches to be hired or fired. These results are not provided for in the rules, nor are they the point of the game, but it is significant that it is moves in the game, not mere physical movement, that have these effects. It is also significant that they are effects on people who understand the game, at least in the sense of knowing that there are sides, knowing what counts as succeeding, and so on.

We wish to focus upon the last three senses in which 43 has acted: he has (1) *moved;* (2) thereby, and under the circumstances, he has *made a move* in the game; (3) thereby, and because they knew the game, he has *had an effect* upon players, spectators, and perhaps others.

Now let us shift to a verbal situation and, guided by Austin, note the ways in which saying something is action. Consider the man in the striped shirt with the players. His mouth opens, his chest heaves, sounds come forth. This may seem to be of a piece with heartbeats and breathing until we specify that Striped Shirt moved his jaw, issued the sounds. But this becomes interesting, in turn, if we (1) acknowledge that Striped Shirt has *said something* (cf. 1 above), has, we may say, performed a *sentential act.*[9] If further we ask *what* he said, we are inquiring for some recognizable words appearing in a recognizable sentence (in some recognizable language) that will specify the sentential act he has performed. Suppose he said "Time out." If so, this is so far no different from what the alumna in the stands does in explaining to her son, "Time out," nor from what the son does in echoing his mother's explanation by saying "Time out." But we recognize that the referee has not only said something but also thereby made a move in the game — he has (2) *called time out.* Austin referred to this second kind of action as an illocutionary act;[10] we will simply call it a *speech-act.* Striped Shirt has inserted his words into the situation and made a difference. Time out has been called. Whereas what the alumna did by inserting her words into the situation (her speech-act) was explaining, not calling, and what the son did (his speech-act) was repeating, not explaining. (3) Once again, other persons and other states of affairs are *affected* by the referee's act in the game. (This is even more evident in the case of a penalty assessed by the referee.) And these effects, too, can be attributed to the referee, though in some cases not to him alone. Austin calls the act by which such effects are produced the referee's *perlocutionary act:* he disappoints or delights, decreases or increases the sales at the concession stand, causes bets to be won, the score to be changed, the statistics to be compiled differently than if he had not done what he did. Though, of course, there are cases in which he might not do any or all of these. In general, action in sense 3 is dependent on action in sense 2, and 2 is dependent on 1; whereas there can be sentential acts (1) without speech-acts (2) (we can just say sentences over like pupils in a reading class), and there can be speech-acts (2) without perlocutionary acts (3) (in such cases there would be no effects to be listed).

It may be objected by now that our comparison of the notion of speech-action to acting in games, while it may do for certain ritual or social patterns of conversation ("games people play"), is an inevitably reductionist treatment of utterances that express religious or any other central human convictions. To treat these as moves in a game is already to misunderstand their import. But this objection would reflect a misunderstanding of the point of the preceding paragraphs, which seek to show, if only by a simple example, that as actions rise in grade to the level of meaningful human utterance they necessarily rise also to a setting in complex human structures (languages, linguistic institutions) and occur in connection with complex human practices in such a way that their meaning presupposes these structures and practices. It is not our intention to claim that the significance of all such structures and practices is on a level with those of organized sport, but to show how meaningful action is based upon the social world in which it plays its role. Our main point may be succinctly summed up thus: *saying something, talking, speech in the full sense that saying something is a way of acting meaningfully, is to be understood in terms of the crucial significance of the speech-act* (Austin's "illocutionary act"), rather than in terms of the sentential act or the perlocutionary act.[11] This is to be our guiding principle in the present search for the significance of religious utterances.

Now the speech-act theory can serve us as the foundation for a theory of language only if it can help us account for those aspects of language whose omission we have criticized in earlier theories, while it nevertheless retains their insights. We propose to investigate this possibility by stating the conditions that must be fulfilled for the successful completion of two particular speech-acts. We expect these to be complex enough to reflect the various aspects of meaning we have suggested and yet allow for the evident capacity of large numbers of people to speak a language. Now rules are often best understood by noting what would violate them, so we will ask what a speaker of English (for convenience, but any other natural language would do as well) must do to make a nondefective, faultless, or happy *request* and then, a happy (religious) *confession.*

This choice of samples may strike some readers as revealing a fatal indirection in our work. Should we not rather deal with 'statements' and 'religious statements,' thereby confronting the central difficulty: the 'cognitivity' of religious speech? To raise this objection in this way, however, is to display a basic misunderstanding of Austin's work in breaking down the misplaced barrier between statements and all other forms of speech. In discarding the performative theory, Austin was discarding the 'statemental' (or, as he might have put it, the "constative") theory as well, and the latter was the more significant discard. Nevertheless, the statemental theory dies hard[12] and for legitimate although misplaced concerns. We share the concerns and therefore wish to place them within a more adequate (speech-act) theory of meaning. To make this clear it may be helpful to say more about the sometimes misleading term "statement."

In a rough-and-ready way, the vocabulary of our language, or any other natural language, will employ certain verbs to designate certain speech-activities — blessing, promising, suggesting, advising, objecting, begging, answering, stating. But these categories are not always mutually exclusive, nor equally precise. Thus in *telling* someone something, I may be advising, or ordering, or objecting. "Tell" is a more general class of speech-act, which, according to circumstances, may or may not be specifiable in more exact ways: when you told me to get a new secretary, were you advising me or ordering me? But "state" — like "tell" and "say" and (sometimes) "assert" — can be used in this more general way also. This more general and historically more recent use of "statement" has been employed by traditional grammarians, who distinguish statements from questions and commands, and again by those philosophers who employ it as a synonym for "sentence" or for "utterance," or more narrowly for any sentence or utterance that is true or false. Sometimes, on the other hand, philosophers have used "statement" to mean an abstract entity, the content or 'proposition' that might be expressed by an indefinite range of sentences or utterances. (In this sense, the same statement is said to be expressed by sentences that translate one another in two or more languages.) And there are still other technical philosophical uses, but we can comprehend these only in terms of the ordinary uses.

Returning to ordinary speech, we note that "statement" and "state" are sometimes used in an older and more restricted sense, which is suggested by their etymology (from the Latin *stare, status,* to stand). In this sense, statements are speech-acts issued in relatively formal circumstances by persons who have reason to be informed on the subject of the statement and consist in setting forth (generally in the interests of or even at the request of the hearer) the matters about which the speaker is so informed, generally within certain restrictions as to content and style. Thus prisoners of war may state their name, rank, and serial number, trespassers may be required to state their business or move along, and participants in an argument may state their case. These instances remind us that those making statements are presumed to have special access to the subject matter of the statement — the serviceman is presumed to know his own name, rank, and serial number; the trespasser but not the Pinkerton guard can state the trespasser's business (though the Pinkerton guard may be called upon to state her own suspicions); we state the other person's case in an argument only after we have heard it, and then normally subject to correction. They also remind us that not everything belongs in a statement, though certainly something other than facts may belong there: Thus one may state a claim, state an argument, state conditions, state limitations. "Just state the facts, ma'am," is probably not designed simply to limit the police officer's interogee to *facts;* rather it is designed to limit her to facts of which *she* has direct knowledge — to what she knows to be facts, and can therefore *state,* as opposed to her surmises and hypotheses.

We may test this understanding of the ordinary and strict use of "statement" by noting some natural limitations in the language. We do not say "state" whenever we are dispensing facts, for I can *admit* this fact, and *advert* to that one, and in neither instance will "state" do the required work. Nor can we always use the verb "state" in speech-acts where "say" is called for: the believer *says* her prayers; perhaps she *offers* a prayer; but she does not *state* her prayer. When the reporter is called to take down the suspect's statement, it is understood by the experienced that certain matters are to be set out in the resulting document — matters concerning which the suspect speaks from the 'privileged' position of his firsthand knowledge and which bear upon the subject matter at hand. His 'statement' will be recognizable as such only if it observes, within reason, these limitations. In this sense all of us can, and regularly do, *say* far more than we *state;* our statements are a weightier and a sharper-edged fraction of our talk. Clearly the question of what in the religious realm we are in position to state is closely related to the question of what in that realm we are in position to know to be true. But this is very different from saying that all that is true, or even all that we know to be true, can be stated.[13]

It is in this light, we think, that the following passage in Austin's essay "Performative Utterances" is to be understood:

> Suppose for example you say to me 'I'm feeling pretty mouldy this morning'. Well, I say to you 'You're not'; and you say 'What the devil do you mean, I'm not?' I say 'Oh nothing — I'm just stating you're not, is it true or false?' And you say 'Wait a bit about whether it's true or false, the question is what did you mean by making statements about somebody else's feelings? I told

you I'm feeling pretty mouldy. You're just not in a position to say, to state that I'm not'. This brings out that you can't just make statements about other people's feelings (though you can make guesses if you like); and there are very many things which, having no knowledge of, not being in a position to pronounce about, you just can't state. What we need to do for the case of stating, and by the same token describing and reporting, is to take them a bit off their pedestal, to realize that they are speech-acts no less than all these other speech-acts that we have been mentioning and talking about as performative.[14]

Austin's point here is not that one cannot ever make statements about other people's feelings, for that claims can be made about feelings even by the 'feelers' themselves is evidence that they are not *completely* private, and what is in principle not private may in practice become public. Rather what Austin sees to be possible is that some circumstances may arise in which, although we are there and can speak, yet we are *in no position* to make a statement about another's feelings — and a chance meeting in the hallway seems to be such a circumstance. I can't in the normal run of things state what your feelings are this morning simply because I've walked past you in the hallway.

This notion of being in position may bring into focus the difficulty in treating religious utterances uniformly as statements, even though we may concede that such utterances have cognitive content. Inability to state is a commonplace of everyday life. The difficulty may be physical (drunkenness, or aphasia; or consider the circumstances in which one could state, "I am now gargling vigorously"), but these are generally surmountable. The inability may be due to the privileges or circumstances of the speaker's life. Although I can surmise, I cannot state what the British prime minister wore to bed last night, since I was not there — but someone who was can perhaps state that he wore pink pajamas, and I may then be able to state that on the other's authority. The president's physician cannot state, is not in line to state, current U.S. policy in some Lebanese crisis, while the president and the secretary of state are and can. Or the inability may be one based on the moral certainties of the case: thus in some Oscar Wilde play, a frivolous fop may say, "Madeleine, I love you passionately. Marry me, do, do," when we know that the fop is not passionate about anything, so that his utterance is not a falsehood but a misfire, a giant bark from a Pekingese pup.[15]

We begin to see, then, what difficulties might be involved in a genuine religious statement and to ask what circumstances might justify classifying a given religious utterance as the speech-act of stating. Can there be, within Christianity or Judaism, *statements* about God? We remember the theological caution in the presence of mystery that led Israel to avoid even the nameless name of God. We recall the theological tentativeness of the Greek Christian Fathers, and (to shift to our own time) we remember that Buber said God could properly be only addressed, never expressed. If there is in these traditions nevertheless much talk about God, we must ask whether this is not confession, or praise, or explanation, rather than statement. For in their view of the matter, no human person is ever in position to make statements about the biblical God. Never, because in the tradition that acknowledges this God, nothing counts as getting into position to make statements about God, and obviously outside it nothing does. The gargler cannot, while gargling, make statements about gargling because she is too close to it. I cannot make statements about the prime minister's pajamas because I am not close enough to his bedroom. The president's physician cannot make statements about U.S. policy because the physician is not in the line of responsibility. In the strands of Jewish and Christian tradition that we have just recalled, it might be said that believers cannot make statements about God because God is too remote ("God is in heaven, and you upon earth" — Ecclesiastes 5:2) or because God is too near ("In him we live and move and have our being" — Acts 17:28). If on the other hand there is a strand in these traditions that holds that such statements can be made by some in virtue of a special position of participation or of faith that they occupy, we will shortly single out that position in specifying the conditions for confession. Perhaps in the eyes of some that will come down to the same thing as examining the conditions for a (special, religious) act of stating, and if that is true, we will be content. We think we have said enough to indicate how our starting point differs from that of the 'religious statement' school of language analysts.

II. Requesting and Confessing[16]

A certain diner, Beth, while sitting at table with others says, "Please pass the bread." Now let us ask what has happened, what must have happened, if Beth's utterance is counted a *happy request?* How do we know that Beth has not only made sounds or issued some words but has thereby, in these circumstances, successfully and happily asked that the bread be passed?[17] We will list the conditions for happily requesting in summary form and then offer some explanation of each of them.[18]

1. *Preconditions.* The speaker (in this case, Beth) and some hearer know a common language (in this case, English); both speaker and hearer are conscious and free from relevant physical impediments so that the speaker's sound-production and the hearer's hearing of speaker are normal.

2. *Primary conditions.*

    2.1 The speaker issues a sentence (performs a sentential act) in the common language.

    2.2 There is a convention of the language to the effect that this sentence is a way of (performing the speech-act of) requesting.

3. *Representative or descriptive conditions.* In issuing this sentence the speaker describes or represents a possible future state of affairs with sufficient exactness that it can be identified as the requested state of affairs.

4. *Affective or psychological conditions.*

    4.1 The speaker wants the requested state of affairs to come to pass.

    4.2 The speaker's intention in issuing this sentence is to use the language's convention for requesting (see 2.2) and the speaker intends the hearer to understand (by her use) that she is so using it.

    4.3 The hearer on the basis of the issued sentence takes the speaker to have the requisite wants and intentions just listed (see 4.1 and 4.2).

    4.4 Neither the speaker nor the hearer foresees that the possible future state of affairs (see 3) would come about or has come about in the ordinary course of events, that is, without the speaker's sentential act.

To return to our old analogy, the *preconditions* are related to the speech-act in somewhat the way in which, in football, the requirement that the players and officials shall be on the field and functioning is related to making a move in the game (slanting off tackle). While the preconditions are the most constant of the sets of conditions we have specified, they are not invariant for all classes of speech-acts. Some speech-acts require no hearer (cursing? practicing speaking? cheering?). It might also be claimed that some religious speech-acts (e.g., prayer) require no human hearer and within some contexts no hearer at all. These facts indicate that the preconditions are not necessary conditions for the faultless performance of *every* speech-act and that the precise relationship of the preconditions to successful performance of a particular speech-act must be determined case by case, involving nonlinguistic (for example, theological or scientific) considerations as well as linguistic. Nevertheless, it does seem correct to say that without the existence of hearers and a common language there would be no such things as speech-acts to begin with. Given the common language and its conventions, speech-acts that dispense with one or more of these preconditions become possible.

As we shall see, there is no a priori way to say which conditions can be dispensed with; we must know what other conditions are met and which speech-act is in question. Given the presence of other conditions, any one might be dispensed with; given the absence of others, any one condition might be necessary for a given speech-act. That we must admit 'nonlinguistic' considerations may seem regrettable, but it also seems inevitable. As we indicate later (and as Austin and Quine, in their different ways, showed) the search for the purely linguistic or the irreducibly logical apart from a particular context seems doomed to failure.

The condition we have called *primary* is one that we were once disposed to call the essential condition for the performance of a speech-act.[19] Yet bizarre cases can be imagined in which fulfilling the primary condition is not sufficient, and extreme circumstances in which it is not necessary, for the performance of the act of requesting. The positive point to note is that not just any sound (see 2.1) or just any sentence (see 2.2) can normally be used to make a request: the range of possibilities may be wide, but it is not boundless. "Bread, confound it!" will not normally count as a *request,* nor will "Please *fine* the bread" count. The trouble with the latter is that we don't know what it means; that is, we have no bread-fining convention, though one can imagine a world in which we had that and not a bread-requesting convention. There are many ways of getting the bread: Beth might wire electrodes to a subject's elbows and close the circuit; she might hypnotize someone and instruct him to pass it on a signal, say the ringing of a bell; she might order someone to pass it, threaten him if he did not pass it, or audibly speculate on how it would be if she had the bread. Any of these might result in her getting the bread, and some of them have some things in common with requests, but none of them are requests for bread. What they fail to be and what a request must be is a sentence whose utterance is a conventional linguistic device (a device recognizable by speakers of that language or dialect) for making a request. Only in that case can its utterance be the performance of a speech-act of requesting.

If someone objects that 2.2 is circular, defining a linguistic act in linguistic terms, this should be admitted: the circle could be made less obvious (to the careless) by circumlocution; it can be avoided altogether, however, only at the greater risk of obscuring the conventional character of the illocutionary act.[20]

There may be speech-acts that involve no reference to or representation or description of anything, though we are hard-pressed to think of examples: only in certain circumstances do we greet or thank someone,[21] and clearly requesting does have a *representative* or *descriptive condition,* as do appraising, pardoning, and, as we shall see, (religious) confessing. For requesting, the requirement is that she must make it reasonably clear *what* she is requesting, and the requested state of affairs (the bread being passed) must be a possible one, which means that there must be bread available, someone who can pass it (all the hearers not helpless paralytics), and the bread must not already be in Beth's hands, if her request is to be a happy one.

By this time, the point of the search for the conditions of a happy, or successful, speech-act, as opposed to a merely possible or minimal one, should be coming into focus. For if someone objects that saying "Please pass the bread" while holding the bread, the only bread, in your hands is *some* kind of request, we would grant that this may be true (though the burden seems to be on the objector to say what such a speaker is up to). But we would add that such an act would not work well linguistically; hearers would be puzzled, or suppose that they had misunderstood, or perhaps take it that the speaker did not know what she had just said. Now such responses are indications that all is not well linguistically, while our conditions taken together set out the broad range of cases in which linguistically all *is* well. Under these conditions, though all may not be well dietetically or morally or socially, Beth's utterance is linguistically happy, and that is our present concern.

If this point is kept in mind, the remaining, *affective conditions* can be briefly explained. As in the other conditions, it is important to remember that they will differ for different speech-acts: sincerity, for example, seems appropriate enough an affect for stating and promising but is not a linguistic requirement for requesting. The relevant condition in the latter case is that Beth must want the possible future state of affairs referred to in 3 to come to pass. The strength of her desire, however, is not to be measured by her 'sincerity,' but only by what is necessary for the total success of the act — want it enough to accept and not refuse the bread when it is passed. (To refuse it would be to incur such a linguistic reproach as, "But you *said* please pass it.") Beth may want other things as well — all the bread she can ever get her hands on, the undivided attention of her hearers, perhaps the moon, but those wants do not go to the happiness of her request.

The next condition shows the way in which the speaker's intentions are woven into the fabric of her action. The correct description of these intentions (4.2) shows the necessity of steering between the Scylla of supposing that happening to say words in an appropriate order counts as a happy request (for in fact, if she didn't intend to say those words, she will have to make some excuse to those who heard and acted upon them) and the Charybdis of supposing that intentions count for everything, so that it doesn't really matter which words were spoken or in which order or that it doesn't matter whether Beth intended to be taken as requesting (suppositions so extraordinary that we should have to invent fantastic stories in order to illustrate them).[22] Making what we intended to say the absolute determinant of what we have in fact said would have the general effect of opening too wide a loophole for speakers, in more weighty situations, to wiggle out of what they have said — welsh on bets, break promises, and slander their neighbors with impunity.

The next condition, called "uptake" (4.3), is simply the recognition that utterance involves a receiver as well as a sender and calls attention to the necessity that the hearer grasp Beth's intentions and wants as a result of the employment of the convention. And the final, negative requirement (4.4) points up the hollowness of requesting what is taken already to be the case.

If we have succeeded in our purpose of setting out the conditions for one type of utterance (in this case, a request) and relating them to one another, it will be seen that affective, representative, and primary illocutionary forces are not competing rivals for the bearing of meaning in an utterance, nor are they mere conjuncts, so many assorted apples, oranges, and pears in a bowl. Rather the representative and affective conditions make for the meaningfulness of an utterance whose primary condition (in this and every such case) is that it belongs to the possibilities of the language, as a possible (conventional or rule-governed) move within that language. Representation (description, reference) is certainly not eliminated, but neither is it given a favored hierarchical status. Austin felt that earlier theories were mired in the 'descriptive fallacy' — the view that the proper business of words was to make (verifiable) statements, whose virtue was to be true and vice to be false. Others have spoken of a 'performative fallacy,' presumably an overemphasis on the conventional aspect of language. We hope to avoid both errors. If the utterance of a sentence under a certain convention is primary, it is only because such conventions constitute the language and make *linguistic* meaning possible. That descriptive or representative conditions are often necessary reflects the fact that language is not a self-contained activity but comes to grips with a *world* that language alone cannot replace. And the affective conditions arise from the fact that language is the instrument of *persons,* for whom desires, intentions, beliefs, and so forth, have central significance. On special occasions any of these conditions could be unfulfilled and a request could still be made. But this is only to say that we can understand the exception to a rule well enough — as long as there is a rule. We can understand an enjoyed or sought-after punishment as nevertheless punishment, even though it breaks the (general) rule that punishments must be unwanted, but we so understand it only because it is the exception and we know it. Sometimes, of course, the exception becomes the rule; language does grow and change. But it does not grow without starting from rules, nor without making new rules as it develops new forms.

Some may feel, however, that our linguistic account of Beth's speech-act is defective. What of the changed situation at the dining table, what of the active roles of her hearers, what of the whole sweep of consequences of her speech-act? While these may be trivial in the case of "Please pass the bread," that does not make it an unsuitable example for our inquiry. We note that even "Please pass the bread" may have astounding consequences. The bread may be poisoned or, less dramatically, someone may have resolved to leave the table if Beth asks for bread just one more time. And so on. The trouble with talking of consequences lies in just this indefiniteness: while it is possible, as we have shown, to set out the conditions for a successful (illocutionary) speech-act, there can be no successful formulation of all its possible consequences. One act may cause another, and causal chains go on and on. Our attention centers on the speech-act proper since our interest lies in discovering what can (rightly) be said and what can (happily) be believed. One point, however, should be made with care. We must distinguish the reaction of Beth's hearers that is *essential* to her request from that which is merely *produced* by her request (its perlocutionary effects). The former reaction (see condition 4.3 above) was called by Austin "uptake."[23] Uptake can be distinguished from the perlocutionary effects in the following way: if without the effect in question, it is questionable whether the utterance is entitled to be called a request (or if it is taken as an order or a complaint) then we are talking about uptake. Requests are requests *of* someone; there must be uptake for any request to have been made. On the other hand, felicitous requests do not need to be honored or fulfilled — Beth can request the bread without getting it, as every beggar knows. We note, too, that where the normally central features of the illocutionary act are missing or unknown or distorted, an observer may use what would normally be perlocutionary effects as tests of what sort of speech-act has been performed. For example, if some hearer hands a speaker some object that satisfies the speaker and that elicits gratitude, we may classify the speaker's earlier unheard or indecipherable utterance as a request, plea, demand, or petition. But in singling out, with Austin, the illocution or speech-act proper, we are choosing that way of viewing language which contains the key to justifiable utterance and so the key to justifiable (religious) convictions.

Now we will apply the method we have just demonstrated to a religious utterance. Consider "God led Israel across the Sea of Reeds" (which we will call utterance G), drawn from a tradition with which most of our readers (and we ourselves) are somewhat familiar. It will bring up most of the problems we want to discuss. It is not self-evident that G as it stands is a speech-act nor is it self-evident that it is religious. For one could merely say or write those words (as we have in preparing this page), thus performing a sentential act but so far not a speech-act. Furthermore, a variety of speech-acts might be issued via that sentence: a historian of religions might use these words to relate the traditional belief of the ancient Hebrews, just as we might say, "Ceres blessed the crops of the ancients" to report *that* tradition, without ourselves being believers in Ceres' bounty. Or again these words (or rather their equivalent in an ancient language) might have been used by a Hebrew of the time of Exodus, say Moses. Or in a different way by one of Pharaoh's charioteers. Or, again differently, by a later chronicler or psalmist. As before, we must locate the utterance, find its setting or story, in order to discover its force.

Let us say that G is used by a Christian or Jewish teacher today: call him Aleph. With the utterance of G he is confessing his faith in the past providence of God as he teaches his class. We shall regard such a use of G as one genuinely religious case.

As before, we will ask what has happened if Aleph's utterance is properly to be classed a *happy confession*. We will list the conditions for happily confessing in summary form, with explanations following. The numbers will correspond as nearly as possible to those in the requesting case.

1. *Preconditions.* These are identical with those for the requesting case (see page 57).

2. *Primary conditions*

   2.1 The speaker issues a sentence (performs a sentential act) in the common language.

2.2 There is a convention of the language to the effect that this sentence is a way of (performing the speech-act of) confessing.

We explicate 2.2 as follows:

2.21 In issuing this sentence the speaker takes up or maintains a certain stance, to which the speaker is thereby committed.

2.22 In issuing this sentence, the speaker displays, i.e., witnesses to, this stance.

3. *Representative or descriptive conditions.* In issuing this sentence the speaker describes or represents the relevant state(s) of affairs with sufficient exactness to make it possible for the speaker to take up that stance (2.21) and to display it (2.22).

The relevant state(s) of affairs will vary from confession to confession. In our story, Aleph's G requires:

3.1 In a certain historical context, a certain event (being led across the Sea of Reeds) has occurred to a certain people (Israel).

3.2 This event is attributable to the God acknowledged in this context.

3.3 This God exists.

4. *Affective or psychological conditions.*

4.1 The speaker has a certain affect, namely, awed gratitude, and in issuing this sentence conveys his possession of it to the hearer.

4.2 The speaker's intention in issuing this sentence is to use the language's convention for confessing (see 2.2), and he intends the hearer to understand (by his use) that he is so using it.

4.3 The hearer on the basis of the issued sentence takes the speaker to have the requisite affect (see 4.1) and intentions (see 4.2), and he takes the speaker to have displayed or witnessed to the stance (see 2.22 and 3).

To seek the *primary condition* for confessing is to inquire what is involved in being a confessor, what one must do to confess. In our analysis, the primary elements are stance-taking and witnessing. By "stance," whose synonyms are "outlook," "position," and the like, we mean the entertaining (as true and important) of certain alleged facts, the embracing of certain pervasive theories about what matters in life, the hoping of certain hopes, the adoption of certain roles in certain communities, and the undertaking of certain patterns of behavior with regard to those facts, theories, hopes, and roles. The stance of Aleph is that of one who remembers and is heir to the storied crossing of the Sea of Reeds and who therein is committed to God and to his fellow-heirs.

Thus if, having issued G, it is put to Aleph that he certainly doesn't *act* like a believer, he may, with consistency, either defend his behavior as misunderstood by the objector or plead weakness of will. If however he replies, "So what? Never mind how I live; I'm just telling what I believe," then linguistically something is wrong. Either Aleph does not know what a confession is, what his words (normally) mean, or his intentions were mistaken by his hearers (he was, perhaps, a historian, not a confessor). The point, we emphasize, is a philosophical and not a theological one. It is like the situation in which Beth, told that there *was* no bread, angrily replied "So what; I said *pass* it." Our concern is not with her manners but her intelligibility. What could she mean, or what, in the case at hand, could Aleph?

Aleph's is one possible stance, but there are others that may also be embodied in confessions: an ancient Egyptian might confess, "God" (or "Jah") "led Israel across the Sea of Reeds, but I'll still serve the sun-god Ra," or perhaps "Ra drove Israel away, across the Sea of Reeds," while a modern Promethean might confess, "God led Israel across the Sea of Reeds, yet I defy Him to tamper with my independent life." Our point in these perhaps farfetched examples is that merely and even sincerely to *say* the words of G is not *eo ipso* to take up or even to understand Aleph's stance; we must learn what Aleph's stance is from Aleph and his community. In that community there is something that those words cannot but mean, something they necessarily mean.

The other primary aspect of confessing is witnessing — the term that we believe most nearly does justice to the signaling quality that coheres with stance in the act of confessing. The witness is called, not to lecture or to argue, but to testify. She tells us not so much what she thinks as where she is, where she finds herself. We may catch the difference between the reporter and the witness by remembering the characteristic work of Pascal and of Hegel: Pascal sets out to show us where he finds himself; on the basis of what he shows us we can infer something about the way things are, the way the world is. Hegel on the other hand sets out to tell us how it is with the world and more, overall and in general, and from this we may infer the stance in which Hegel finds himself: Hegel is by intention a philosophical reporter; Pascal, again by intention, a philosophical witness. Again, this point may be illustrated by imagining that when Luther at Worms said "Here I stand," he was misunderstood as reporting his location in the cathedral: "I'm over here, sir, by the north transept. Were you looking for me?" But that would make more than one mistake: not only a mistake about the sense and reference of the speaker's words, but also a mistake about the kind of speech-act he was performing. Luther was not describing or reporting; he was confessing. And confessing entails bearing witness, not only taking a stand but showing it, which is different, as we have said, from stating it.

Have we captured the force of confessing? We may test our understanding by reference to the forefather of Western literary confessions, St. Augustine. The *Confessions* constitute a sketch of the landscape of reality with which that convert to a new set of convictions found himself confronted. He begins with praise to God: "Great art thou, O Lord, and greatly to be praised."[24] He then continues with an account of his own personal history from infancy through the adventures and perplexities of his young manhood to the conversion that set his subsequent life's direction. There is the admission of sins and the expression of intense regret. He reflects upon the possibility of knowing God, upon the nature of time, and upon the ideas of creation, sacred Scripture, and church. In all these ways, Augustine is giving account of the setting in which he takes his stand, his horizon; he is taking up that stance and thereby affirming it, and he is exercising the loyalty (to God, to church) that his setting and stance require of him. If we turn to the *Confessions* of Jean Jacques Rousseau (1712–78), again there is personal history, again there is the self-searching attempt honestly to know the true meaning of the personal past, again the author confronts a certain landscape and takes his stance with respect to it. The common features of these works, in some ways so diverse, focus on their self-involving quality — the writing is not merely *about* the author, as some autobiographies manage to be; rather the confession *shows* us the author in action, attempting to give a faithful account of what shapes him. Thus the act of confessing involves, both in this literary genre and in our own account of confession, the appropriation of a place, a taking up of those commitments or loyal ties that are seen to be appropriate to the place, and a self-involving display of these.

Thus a confession such as Aleph's points inescapably to a context that is taken to be real. We recognize that not every Jew or Christian employs G as does Aleph to celebrate a real crossing of an actual sea under divine guidance. Their confession of G might still be happy, but it will be so under a different set of conditions for happiness. Whether or not it is Jewish or Christian to do so, it is possible for confessors to hold nonhistorical, as well as nontheistic, religious convictions. We have chosen the conservative and traditional faith of Aleph as our illustration both because Aleph represents a large number of actual believers, past and present, and because this illustration shows clearly how the analysis must take account of every dimension, whereas confessions with a suppressed or diminished representative aspect might not.

The central feature to note in this case or any other is that the *representative condition* is just what is required for the fulfillment of the other conditions. In Aleph's case, the Israelites must as confessed have crossed that sea; this event must be placed within a wider stream of biblical narrative, here called the "context" of the event; God, the God to whom the context refers, must be God, must exist. Note in particular that the happiness of Aleph's confession on its representative side depends *on these conditions* and not merely on his belief in them; for example, if Aleph, depending on older Bible versions, confessed that it was the *Red* Sea that Israel crossed, his confession, as Aleph's community now knows, would have been in that regard unhappy, Aleph's sincerity and blamelessness notwithstanding. Sincerity is not a sufficient condition of happy confessing any more than of happy requesting.

As with the Red Sea, so with a God who acted in this case and who therefore acts in Israel's history and in world history; if this is not the way it is, Aleph's confession is unhappy as it stands. But how are we or how is anyone in this pluralistic world justly to say that these conditions are or are not fulfilled? Here we seem to have run directly into contested convictional ground. Here the relativist would have us back away, unable from any perspective other than Aleph's to say what would count as satisfying these conditions, while the imperialist would perhaps say, let science (or philosophy, or common sense: in any case let *my* view) settle the matter, thus proposing, it seems to us, that we sail our inquiry right over the dry land in a miracle of transconvictional justification greater than the parting of the seas at the Exodus.

But what other way can we propose? We admit that the answer is not easy, and we will be occupied for the rest of this book in giving our full reply. Yet some preliminary things can be said here, and others when we discuss the affective conditions for the happiness of Aleph's G.

The sorts of problems that are here intertwined in the evaluation of Aleph's utterance may be roughly labeled historical, hermeneutical, and theological; something must be said about each. At the outset, the historical problems seem most straightforward. Was there a crossing of the Sea of Reeds by a people called Israel? Let us suppose that 'objective' historical inquiry, at least in the decade in which Aleph issues his confession, tends to answer that there were at the relevant time tribal movements of Semitic peoples from the region of the Nile toward the eastern desert and beyond. But G requires much more than this. These "movements" are taken, within the biblical context represented by G, to have been a deliverance, a redemption, the rescue of a people from servitude in order that they might serve a holy and righteous God. Is it appropriate for Aleph's community to take its ancient confession as the interpretation of this 'objective' claim? Can the 'inner' history of the community thus coalesce with the 'outer' history of detached scholarship?

Theologian readers will recognize in the 'inner/outer' distinction the language of H. Richard Niebuhr, who, wrestling with a similar problem, thought that 'inner' history (defined as 'our' history, or as the history of persons) must be sharply distinguished from 'outer' history (defined as 'their' history, or as the history of things or objects). Yet he also thought these two accounts referred in some way to the same realities and might usefully correct one another.[25] While this last claim seems to us correct, for reasons we will later give, it appears that Niebuhr made two mistakes, though these come down finally to one. He spoke as if 'inner' and 'outer' history could be sharply distinguished in the first place, and he spoke as if 'outer' history was not shaped by human goals, drives, and convictions just as is 'inner' history. If we can doubt the God of Israel who is said to preside over Israel's self-confession, asking whether Israel's self-understanding is not fallible, we can equally doubt the god of scientific historiography, asking whether that muse does not slumber or sleep. Yet we draw from these double doubts not hard skepticism but a less dogmatic caution: the testing of a biblical outlook on history is sure to be slow and full of pitfalls for the rash confessor (or the rash professor).

Even the optimism implicit in the last sentence, however, is overstated, and for this reason. The context of biblical thought lying behind G is a world of narrative whose leading actor is God himself — a God who acts in a world of action. But the hermeneutical question is this: does it still make sense, today, to say, as G presupposes, that God acts in history? How can God act in history? Notice that the form of this question (and not merely the answer it seeks) is historically conditioned, being in part a function of our modern cosmology. This is not to say that the "how?" did not arise before modern times. It did arise in antiquity, and again in medieval times, where we find theologians at pains to provide explanations of the acts of God, explanations given in terms of the cosmology that they had inherited from Aristotle. The dawn of the modern era, however, brought with it a new cosmology (Galileo, Kepler, Copernicus, Newton), and it became difficult to say how God, who as Jews and Christians regarded him was neither the universe nor a part of the universe, could be said to 'act' in the universe. The interesting possibilities were in principle four: (1) one could cling to the old cosmology in spite of the changing intellectual climate; (2) one could accept the new cosmology but continue to talk of God's acts in the old ways; (3) one could accept the new cosmology and give up talking about God's acts; (4) or one could find new ways to describe God's acting and (therefore) a new way to describe God himself. The first, or reactionary/rebellious, route was taken by some. Perhaps the real point of the Catholic Church's condemnation of Galileo is to be found in the (understandable if hopeless) attempt to hold on to a *particular* way of being able to talk about what God does. That way, as it turned out, was not a live option. The second, or accommodating, route became what we know today as theistic orthodoxy. God was said to act in the world by providence (ordinarily) and by miracle (extraordinarily). The trouble was that the traditional theistic account (as we find it, for example, in a philosophical theologian such as Samuel Clarke, 1675–1729) left an unclosable logical gap between the theistic God and the world in which he was supposed to act, the Newtonian world. For it was never made clear how an otherworldly God could affect a this-worldly world, a world that ran on Newtonian principles very well by itself.[26]

The third view arose about the same time as the first and second, was apparently more logical, though less interesting in the religious sense, and was dubbed deism. In this view, God did not *act* in history. God started the world and would end it with a final judgment, but in between the world was on its own. Deism removed the problem of God's acts from the current scene, however, only by the expedient of reinstating the same problems at a temporal distance — in connection with history's beginning and end, where once again God must act and where therefore the logical problems inexorably reappear. The fourth alternative belongs especially to the nineteenth and twentieth centuries. In it, the notion of God is reconceived (as by Spinoza, Schleiermacher, or Whitehead) with a view to providing a sense of "God acts" that is compatible with modern cosmology.

The historical conditioning of "How can God 'act'?" then, is not only a function of a changing cosmology, but also a function of a changing theology — that is, a changing conception of God. Logical consistency and grammatical correctness are insufficient conditions for the intelligibility of G. It must make sense in terms of the cosmological and theological understanding available at the time of its utterance.

Perhaps we can make this point clearer with an example. People have long spoken of the "rising" and "setting" of the sun. In the geocentric view of the ancients, the sun, moon, and stars 'really rose' and 'really set.' A changed cosmology, however, produced another account. It is the earth that moves, people said, rotating on its axis; the sun's motion, then,

is 'apparent motion.' Once that fact was fully accepted in a culture, it became possible to speak again (or still?) of the rising and setting of the *sun.*
"Sunset" remains in our vocabulary after all. Now, however, a new analysis is offered on demand: "When we say 'The sun rose' what we mean
is..." The child who has learned the terms "sunrise" and "sunset" has
more to learn about astronomy but not about proper English. But there
may also have been, for some speakers at least, an intervening time, between the passing of the old theory and the widespread acceptance of the
new, in which it was felt that "the sun rose" was simply an unacceptable
way of speaking.

Now, with the appropriate changes, it is the possibility of just such
a difficult time for a certain form of speech (and we do not here judge
whether the time is temporary or permanent) that we contemplate in specifying the present linguistic condition. Does Aleph issue G in such a
historical context, at such a time in history, that an important part of its
representative aspect, requiring that we be able to assign some sense to
"God acted here," is (in this time) impossible? If so, G is unhappy in this
respect.[27]

There may be some who are impatient at this point. "Let's cut all
the chatter about speech-acts and felicities and theories of religious language," they might say: "Get down to brass tacks. Is there any God, or
isn't there? If you think there is or isn't, give your reasons, and I'll look
into them. If you can't say, why bother with all this business? Why bother
with *anything* else until that is settled?"

To such a position we are truly sympathetic. Only, we will all ask,
which *is* the present condition (3.3) — true, or false? Our object has been
to note the way in which *possible* and *happy* speech-acts must mirror
reality; we believe, in other words, that the present inquiry, so far from
being beside the point, is a direct journey in search of the answers that
our brass-tacks critic wants, or rather it is a tour book saying what such
a journey must be like. What we are seeing for a special case here, and
will argue in detail within, is that there is no such journey that ignores
the convictional communities to which Aleph, and we, and Brass Tacks,
each belong — no nonconvictional road to the truths around which our
convictions cluster.

Briefly to illustrate this, consider the objection to our view that goes
as follows: "I've no particular problem with statements about God. I can
state flatly that God doesn't exist. And I can do it because of the modern
scientific worldview." If for "modern scientific worldview" we substitute
"modern philosophy" or "logical incoherence in the concept of God" or

"the course of human history," we will have represented the views of very many convinced atheists. Only now, as the term "convinced" suggests, we will have stepped across a convictional line separating those of Aleph's tradition from certain of those outside it, and will thereby have raised, though in a different way than for Aleph, the question of what makes the atheist's 'confession' (or 'statement' — let him choose the term for the moment) a happy one, that is, how may *it* be justified? And we know no shorter route to the answering of his question than the one we are already pursuing.

That is to say, it appears to the present writers (whose religious beliefs differ radically on the issue) that because of the convictional nature of the particular belief in question (the existence and nature of the God of the Hebraic and Christian traditions), *and* because of the convictional nature of still other beliefs that it involves, it is not possible to answer the question about the fulfillment of certain of the representative conditions of G directly, save by means of utterances that partake of the same logical nature and leave us with the same difficulties as does G itself. To put the point in the terms we have been employing, it seems that for a member of Aleph's community, and certainly for anyone else, happily to make the straightforward assertion that the representative conditions of G are all fulfilled (including the condition that God did in fact lead Israel across the sea and therefore that God does indeed exist) he must issue a speech-act that is itself a confession, or (what comes to the same result) this 'straightforward assertion' can be issued only by one who is in position to make such a confession. And this is not the tautologous point that only those who believe that God exists believe that God exists, but is the rather richer one that such assertions *happily* occur, *can* happily occur, only in connection with the rich involvement in stance, in commitment, and in appropriate affect (yet to be discussed) that make up the happiness of G.

The *affective* or *psychological conditions* for Aleph's G are noticeably more complex than those for a request at the dinner table, and partly because of that complexity, here we are even more willing than elsewhere to be corrected by anyone who can show that we are mistaken. We will however give our reasons for listing those we do, and will particularly note, as before, how the affective conditions interlock with the primary and representative ones (so that changing the others may not be as simple as some religious revisionists might suppose).

Awed gratitude is itself an affect of a rather high order of complexity and sophistication. Everyone has wants (to name the chief affect of requesting), but gratitude, humility, awe, and their convergence in awed gratitude are the outcome of a long development in the world to which Aleph belongs. But why awed gratitude here? For certainly we are not suggesting that this is the only affect appropriate to religion — joy, dread, hope, guilt, detachment, fear, ecstasy come to mind at once, and all of these *may* characterize the confessor of G. But the requirement of awed gratitude may be explained by noting that if Aleph shows, or is taken by all hearers to show, either by his attendant behavior or by the manner of uttering G itself, that his attitude is not in fact awed gratitude, G is thereby exposed as unhappy in utterance. If, for example, when challenged by such a reply to G as: "Then why act so ungrateful to God?" Aleph replies: "I don't believe all that baloney about God; I'm just teaching Religion 101," his consistency is saved, but now our story about him must change; he is not after all in uttering G confessing his faith. Or if the conversation goes, "Then why don't you seem at all grateful to God?" "What's *gratitude* got to do with it? I'm just stating a fact," Aleph would here be showing, given our original story, that he does not understand *what* he has said, does not understand the affective force of his own utterance, does not know what his words (in this case) mean.

A word should be added about Aleph's "conveying" his possession of the affect via his utterance (see 4.1): we do not mean that confessional speakers should tend to histrionics; rather we mean that it is normal, expected, and conventional for these words of confession to imply that the speaker has just such an attitude, and thus abnormal, unexpected, and deviant for the speaker to lack that attitude.

The evidence for awed gratitude as the appropriate affect of G can be found by consulting the tradition in which we have placed Aleph. Among the Psalms we find those that celebrate the mighty past acts of God, such as Psalm 105:

> Then he led forth Israel with silver and gold,
>   and there was none among his tribes who stumbled.
> Egypt was glad when they departed,
>   for dread of them had fallen upon it.
> He spread a cloud for a covering,
>   and fire to give light by night.
> They asked, and he brought quails,
>   and gave them bread from heaven in abundance.
>   (Ps. 105:37–40, RSV)

Now this Psalm begins with an injunction that sets its tone throughout: "O give thanks to the LORD" (Ps. 105:1). In other words, the recital of the mighty deeds of God that follows is viewed as cause for gratitude and, as the use of the tetragrammaton (in our versions represented by capital-letter LORD) shows, gratitude in which God is exalted and the worshiper accordingly stands in awe. Thus the gratitude the worshiper is called to express is humble or awed gratitude.

Of course this might have been an isolated occurrence; however an examination of the whole Psalter shows that whenever the theme is the mighty, saving acts of God in Israel's history, the characteristic feeling-exhortations are to thanks (*hodu*), blessing (*baraku*), and praise (*hallelu*). Of these three, the *hallelu* is a call to sound the note of praise — the exaltation of God and the abasement of all else before God; the *hodu* is a summons to thanksgiving, that is, gratitude itself, and the *baraku* calls for a combination of these two elements of praise and thanks: "the term [*barakah*] is to be understood as an ascription *of praise and gratitude* for blessing received."[28] To be sure, other affects as well are proposed and expressed and evoked in these 'psalms of recital,' but the others vary; ours is constant. What we have called awed gratitude, then, was for the psalmists who shared in the formation of Aleph's tradition the natural affective accompaniment of their confession.

But what can be argued for the tradition's beginning can equally be argued for its later stages. In the early Christian period there arose in the worshiping communities a liturgy that became central, its origin being attributed to Jesus himself. A characteristic feature of this liturgy was a central prayer that *recited the wonderful works of God* both in creating the world and in guiding his people on a journey through history, a journey that included deliverance from Egypt and that finally led to the coming of the Christ, who "on the night when he was betrayed took bread, and when he had given thanks, he broke it" (1 Cor. 11:23f., RSV). as the prayer goes on. The function of the prayer was to recite and celebrate God's saving acts; thus it is like G. But the name of the prayer and of the whole liturgy of which it formed the central part was the eucharist, i.e., the thanksgiving.[29] Again the note of awed gratitude sets the affective tone for the recital of God's deeds.

Finally one might give attention to contemporary Jewish worship. In the Kiddush, the prayer of consecration at meals in pious Jewish homes and now also a part of the Friday evening service of many synagogues, the Exodus from Egypt is recalled:

> in love and favor Thou hast given us the holy Sabbath as a heritage, a reminder of Thy work of creation, first of our sacred days recalling our liberation from Egypt.

And this prayer begins and ends with the Hebrew words "Blessed art Thou, O Lord our God."[30] What we have is again an expression of awed gratitude to God — in the first instance for the Sabbath, but, behind that, for the "liberation from Egypt," which the Sabbath recalls. Alongside this we may mention the Passover Seder service. Here the ritual is introduced with the Four Questions, whose answers point to the meaning of the Passover meal as a memorial of the Exodus. Then there comes a midrash on Deuteronomy 26:5–8, reminding the hearers of the mighty deeds of God in the deliverance. To this midrash is attached the Dayyenu, a hymn or chant that singles out those deeds one by one:

> Had he given us their substance
> > but not torn the Sea apart for us
> > > Dayyenu
> Had he torn the Sea apart for us
> > but not brought us through it dry
> > > Dayyenu
> Had he satisfied our needs in the desert for forty years
> > but not fed us manna
> > > Dayyenu.[31]

What then is "Dayyenu"? It means "for that alone we should have been thankful" or more literally, "it would have been enough for us." Humble or awed gratitude, occurring just where we would by now expect it. Not only here, but also in the great Hallel

> O give thanks to the Lord
> > for He is good
> > for His mercy endureth forever[32]

and indeed throughout the whole Seder, the tone is that of deep and humble gratitude for God's deliverance of his people. Thus, if Aleph remains in the tradition that gives his G both its point and its particular sense, his confession expresses awed gratitude.

The remaining affective conditions are parallel to the requesting case, including the requirements for intention (see 4.2) and uptake (see 4.3), and though they possess intrinsic interest, they need not detain us now.[33]

Now see what follows from this analysis. Aleph cannot *happily* confess that God led Israel across the Reed Sea unless he is in position to do so. To be in position is among other things to possess the affect we have called grateful awe. Without that attitude neither Aleph nor anyone else can in this sense confess what God has done. The outsider cannot happily make that confession (without becoming in the act an insider to Aleph's confessing community), but the outsider cannot happily deny that God has so led Israel, either; not without meeting the affective conditions for *that* utterance, which are not the same, but which would themselves require some particular getting into position for felicitous utterance (and this is true whether it is a rival religion — "there is no God but Ra" — or irreligion — "secular atheism is the only honest outlook" — which undergirds the denial). So far, we seem to be led toward relativism.

On the other hand, there are the representative conditions (see 3.1, 3.2, and 3.3) to remind us that confessing stance and witness (see primary condition 2.2) together with awed gratitude (see affective condition 4.1) are not sufficient to make a confession happy. I can, like Don Quixote, take up my stance against the evil giants that threaten us all. If, however, the giants are in truth windmills, my stance will be comic, however noble it may be as well. No one can say that Don Quixote has not taken a stance, has not confessed. But no informed Sancho Panza can say that Quixote's confession was a 'happy' one if the representative conditions are unfulfilled — that is, if the giants are not giants. Indeed we are now in position to see just the degree to which the representative condition must be fulfilled in order for the confession to be happy — namely, that degree which is required by the assumed stance itself. In other words, the speech-act requires that a certain state of affairs shall prevail if the act is to be happy, but the demand is not a tyrannical one; there is some margin for error in representation in every speech-act where representation is involved. It does not matter, for the happiness of G, whether "Israel" is five thousand or five million strong; nor does it matter how 'transcendent' or 'immanent' the God referred to in G may be, provided only that he can be identified as the God of the Israelite tradition in which G stands. We may with good reason be interested in such matters, but that interest lies beyond our concern here.

What does matter is the intimate interdependence of affective, representative, and primary conditions for happy utterance, the interconnection of language structure and persons and whatever else there is beyond both. As to the issue dividing imperialism, relativism, and perspectivism, we will address that in chapters still to come. That issue will not be settled, however, save by constant reference to the actual structure of language, a structure we have seen revealed in speech-act analysis.

III. A Critical Review

It seems natural to ask whether the understanding of religious language developed in the preceding section can be applied to the analysis of utterances outside Christianity and Judaism. The most satisfying sort of answer would be to repeat the exercise, taking as illustration an utterance drawn from another religious tradition. Now it is no part of our intention to offer such an exhaustive demonstration, but we will summarize the conditions for happiness of another sample utterance, namely, F, "There is nothing." We will suppose this to be spoken by a Buddhist mystic in order to explain the third *Jhāna* of Buddhagosa's mystical path.[34] This permits us to note that religious utterances need not be issued as confessions: we can envisage injunctions, self-committals, disclosures, and still others, while our present example is an *explanation*. Here in compressed form are its conditions:

1. *Preconditions:* same as before.

2. *Primary:* the speaker issues a sentence that counts as a convention — employing an attempt to explain, i.e., to relate that which the hearers do not understand to that which they do.

3. *Representative:* A mystical state occurs with sufficient reliability to call for and to sustain the explanation; this state apprehends a truer 'picture' of the world than that of the previous *Jhāna,* and this 'picture' is blankness — all is washed away. Nonmystical 'pictures' of the world are therefore in an important way false.

4. *Affective:* The speaker wants the hearers to understand the mystical state, its appropriate world-picture, and the true status of the apparent world; the speaker has the corresponding linguistic intentions; the speaker is so understood and so taken by some hearers, for whom the 'picture' of blankness is evocative of the speaker's point.

It is interesting that if as we stipulate here F is *explanation,* then the affect appropriate to the mystical state (detachment?) need not be possessed by the speaker herself in order that her speech-act be happy, whereas if a more strongly self-involving speech-act is issued, say by one of the disciples who after meditation *testifies* attainment of the Third *Jhāna* by issuing F, there would be stronger affective demands. However, even if an explanation is issued by a nonmystic, it carries *representative* freight unless suitably qualified. One such qualification would be for the explainer to say, "This is the explanation a *mystic* would give of the Third *Jhāna.*" These sorts of points are of course fully explicable only in a full account such as we have given for G above. In a less formal way, we will explore other convictional speech-acts in chapter 4; we leave to interested readers the (not inconsiderable) task of working out others for themselves.

Plainly, the speech-act theory we are proposing differs in many significant respects from the approaches of the Wittgensteinians, the Deconstructionists, and even the Jamesians. Nevertheless, it is most useful to see those differences against the background of some important similarities.

To begin with, all the theories (including ours) are developed with an awareness of the diversity of experiences, ways of life, and beliefs, including religious ones. It was, of course, a central aim of James's work to note and describe that variety, and if he reports it as (not quite) sober fact, Deconstructionists and Reader Response theorists celebrate it. This awareness of diversity — our *pluralism* — presents to each of the theories a certain problem. Phillips and Malcolm (like the Reformed epistemologists) see it in defensive terms: how can we preserve the integrity and wholeness of the religious way of life in a hostile intellectual context? Fish and the Deconstructionists have a more global approach. They want to liberate everyone from the hegemony of the 'Structure,' so that each community can develop and value its own text, its own way of 'reading' the world. For James (with whom we have the closest affinity) the variety of religious experience (with its language) and the power it exerts over those who enjoy it present a twofold problem of justification. Is the power of the experience legitimate (i.e., does it give the experiencer a basis for religious belief?), and what conclusions can be drawn about religion by others who do not have the experience? All the theories emphasize attending to the members of the religious (or interpretive) communities and so, implicitly or explicitly, reject what we have called convictional imperialism.

With respect to relativism, matters are less clear. Both Phillips and Fish have (many) moments when they seem to embrace the idea that it is a bad idea, and perhaps an impossible one, for one convictional community to question or criticize another. Neither of their theories provides a clear way to engage in this criticism, and they do not mourn the lack. James, for all his talk of legitimation or justification, is also silent on a method or technique for seriously questioning another's claim to legitimate belief. Here, we think, the speech-act theory shows its superiority. Like the Wittgensteinians, it regards understanding the practices of the community (especially its linguistic practices) as indispensable to understanding its religious beliefs and hence for either agreeing or disagreeing with them. Like the Reader Response theory, speech-act theory insists that an adequate theory of meaning or interpretation must include the affective response both of the speaker (or writer) and the audience. Like James, speech-act theory begins with what the members of the community say (and what they do in saying it). But, unlike these other approaches, speech-act theory includes a representative condition as part of successful or happy speech-acts. For a speech-act to be *happy,* it is not sufficient that it be a possible speech-act in that community and that both speakers and hearers have the appropriate affective states for that speech-act in that community. Language, including religious language, is not only a way of connecting the members of a community with each other — including the connecting of those past others who helped to create the linguistic community and those future others who are its heirs. Language also connects its speakers, the members of the community, to the world, and *that* connection must be appropriate if the conventionally permitted speech-act with its successful affective conditions is to be happy.

In this regard, we too seem to have failed, because we seem to have no *theory* of representation at all, while at the same time we incautiously hold that valuations such as true and false do clearly apply to some religious utterances — God either did lead Israel across the Sea of Reeds or did not. And in this we differ not only from the Positivists (who held such claims not false but meaningless) but also for all the post-Positivists we considered in chapter 2, for they in effect conceded that point to the Positivists.

But should we not be able to say in general what we mean by calling such a claim false or true; or should we not at least be prepared to say which is the case in our sample utterance?

In response, we remind our readers that we disagree with one another on the latter question, and we expect that our readers disagree in similar ways. But we believe that we have come upon an understanding of why that disagreement is (in the short run) inevitable, while not (in the long run) invincible. Such disagreement is lamentable to the extent that we might have hoped for a simple and clear test by which to vote utterances such as G in or out. It will seem to some readers that what we have been saying *must* be mistaken. How can there be an utterance that makes a claim of truth whose truth is hidden by the very conditions of its happy utterance? Isn't it just obscurantism to entangle questions about the truth or falsity of an utterance with questions about the commitment or stance or attitude of the utterer? Surely (the question now becomes rhetorical) questions of *fact* cannot be so confused with questions of stance, of *value,* as we have made it appear?

To such complaints, as we have said, we are quite sympathetic. Indeed, it appears that Austin's term for characterizing the point of view behind this protest, "descriptive fallacy," is not quite the one we need. For "fallacy" suggests that the one gripped by these expectations about getting the facts straight (and thus unreceptive to this part of our account) is making some *logical* mismove that has stultifying consequences. That however is not the way we find the so-called 'descriptive fallacy' arising. Rather the descriptivists (and we in our descriptivist moments) are captivated by a picture, see things in a *certain* way. The picture here is of a world of 'facts,' independent of us and (perhaps) of each other, facts the description of which would tell us the whole truth about the world. In such a world, whatever was a fact, whatever was true of the world, could be described or stated. If we don't have the right statement, the full description, we must simply try harder: attend to new arguments, gather more facts, and so forth. What can't be stated or described is just what can't be the case.

What remedy have the authors for such a state of mind? We certainly do not mean to repudiate the descriptivist's concern with truth and falsity — we are as concerned as he or she to say what is true about the world. But if it turns out that the representative, primary, and affective elements of our utterances are intertwined as it seems to us they are, then saying what is true will sometimes truly be an elusive goal. The history of convictional controversy (political and social as well as religious) seems to offer reasons for believing that just collecting facts or thinking up new arguments (important as such tasks are) is insufficient to resolve such controversies. To that extent, at least, the picture of the world that captivates the descriptivist seems to be an incomplete one. And insofar as our more complex pluralist picture accounts for these difficulties in arguing about convictions, it seems to be a better picture of reality — truer to the facts, if we are still allowed the expression.

There is one further point of view that we are happy to share with the Wittgensteinians and with James. Speaking, uttering speech-acts, *doing* by and in speaking, is a way of participating in a way of life. Language is no mere epiphenomenon, the verbal cherry on the sundae of life. It is the very stuff of which the sundae is made. We differ with Phillips and James on this point only in thinking that speech-act theory offers a clearer and more articulate way of showing how this is so. That point is, in turn, connected to our standing promise (chapter 1) to show that fully to understand the speech of convictional speakers is to learn whether what they say is *justifiable*. Clearly, our analysis so far has not fulfilled that commitment. For we have found Aleph's confession embedded in the language frame of his (convictional) community in such a way that we can neither fully understand it nor find it adequate or inadequate until we attend to that wider frame, the whole set of religious convictions in which it is embedded. We must now turn to exploring that wider set.

FOUR

If the formation of concepts can be explained by facts of nature, should we not be interested, not in grammar, but rather in that in nature which is the basis of grammar? — Our interest certainly includes the correspondence between concepts and very general facts of nature. (Such facts as mostly do not strike us because of their generality.) But our interest does not fall back upon these possible causes of the formation of concepts; we are not doing natural science; nor yet natural history — since we can also invent fictitious natural history for our purposes.

. . .

Grammar tells us what kind of object anything is. (Theology as grammar.)
Ludwig Wittgenstein[1]

It is the erotic sense of reality that discovers the inadequacy of fraternity, or brotherhood. It is not adequate as a form for the reunification of the human race: we must be either far more deeply unified, or not at all. The true form of unification — which can be found either in psychoanalysis or in Christianity, in Freud or Pope John, or Karl Marx — is: "we are all members of one body." The true form of the unification of the human race is not the brothers, Cain and Abel, but Adam the first man, and Christ the second man: for as in Adam all die, even so in Christ shall all be made alive.

Norman O. Brown[2]

How Are Convictions Justifiable?

What anyone can happily say, indeed what one can say with any meaning whatever, is intimately related to one's action and to the way things are ('the facts') and to one's (affective) participation in both of these. To action, because speech itself is a kind of action and because our acts affect one another; to the way things are, because speech-acts typically have some sort of representative force relating them to the existing world; to the speaker's (and hearer's) affects, because they engage both of these. Thus the happy speech-act is not the grammarian's grail that our preceding technical inquiry may have suggested to some; rather 'happiness' in speech-acts *is* closely related to the happiness of the speaker in the world; to inquire about the speech-act is to inquire about the state of the speaker in his or her situation, and thus about the situation too.

I. Convictions

Our speaker, Aleph, was a man of religious belief, and in every case would be someone with some beliefs. It was this very fact that gave rise to our linguistic inquiry when (in chapter 1) we indicated the connection between beliefs and talk. These are not two disparate or disconnected sorts of human phenomena; what we believe and what we say are tightly connected. Now, however, we are in far better position to see how this is so. What one believes is expressed in what one does but most clearly in that special form of doing that constitutes speech. If one says nothing (which is so extraordinary as to require minimal attention here) or lies or is insincere (less extraordinary), we all have ways of detecting, interpreting, and dealing with these modes of verbal behavior, for they are logically dependent upon the normal mode, which is saying what one means, thinks, believes. Even if most of the time, or all the time, a particular speaker speaks ironically or hypocritically or deceitfully, her speech is fully intelligible if and only if we measure her irony, hypocrisy, or deceit, against straightforward speech, so that in those cases, too, belief and speech are inseparable. Aleph's speech-act (his confession) is an expression of Aleph's belief; it is indeed a *confessio fidei*.

Are we enunciating a startling doctrine of linguistic philosophy or rehearsing a truism? Perhaps this is one of those cases, so interesting to philosophy, in which the commonplace seems startling because it has been overlooked or even denied. In any case, one very important consequence follows: *the conditions for the happy utterance of a speech-act are also the conditions under which the belief(s) expressed by that speech-act are justifiable.* Suppose Beth, at a table where there is no bread, believes the Yorkshire pudding to be a loaf of bread. If then, requesting, she says, "Please pass the bread," her request is unhappy because its representative condition cannot (then and there) be satisfied. Note however that her belief, too, is 'unhappy' and for the same reason, — there is no bread; the Yorkshire pudding is not bread; her belief is mistaken. Similarly for Aleph: his belief that Israel crossed the Reed Sea, or that God led Israel, will if mistaken make his speech-act, G, unhappy, and the belief, so far as it is mistaken, is an 'unhappy' belief.

Note that it is no more true of beliefs or similar mental states than it is of speech-acts that their 'representative' failures (such as failures in description or reference) are the only ways they can go wrong. We have treated speech-acts first and at some length because their more public character makes these possibilities more evident in them, but beliefs and the like (attitudes, intentions, hopes, and so forth) are also subject to a wide range of flaws. Let us refer to beliefs alone for the time being, since they are crucial in the work ahead, and recall some ways in which, paralleling speech-acts, beliefs can go wrong. Most important, a 'belief' can simply fail to be a belief at all by being some other mental state or act instead, so that we have misnamed it a "belief"; or it may be a mere jumble or confusion. These failures may be compared with the failure to fulfill the primary condition of a speech-act — the failure to use an appropriate linguistic form. Thus "Bread pass please the" hardly qualifies as a request, or any other speech-act, if the language in use is English; correspondingly the 'thought' designated "Bread pass please the" is not a belief; no one thinks *that*, and it is hard to say what the "that" is; it is not a wish or a desire or a feeling, either. Likewise, some other words or even G in the mouth of a person with a different stance than Aleph's may not express a *confessional* belief but a guess or a supposition instead.

It hardly need be pointed out that a similar parallel exists between the affective conditions for the happiness of a speech-act and the affective conditions for the happiness of a belief which that speech-act expresses or to which the belief corresponds. If the utterer of Aleph's G is not a man of grateful awe in the measure demanded by his speech-act, his act is affectively unhappy. But the same is true of the (confessional) *belief* that God led Israel across the Reed Sea: happily to believe this is to feel one way and not another, just as to say it happily is.

Thus with a few appropriate changes, the apparatus of appraisal that applies to utterances applies to beliefs and thoughts as well.[3] To be able to understand what anyone says is to be able to understand what that person thinks; the unhappiness or the happiness of what he or she says or can say shows the justifiability or the unjustifiability of what he or she believes, also.

It follows that for any belief, there are a certain number of possible challenges that might arise, roughly those that could arise in connection with the issuance of the speech-act expressive of that belief. Of a belief that can meet such challenges, we will say that it is *a justifiable belief;* of one concerning which (some of the) possible challenges have arisen and been met, we will say that it is in these respects or in that degree a *justified* belief; of a belief that has been challenged by and has met every such possible challenge, we may say that it is *fully justified.* The process by which challenges are met or responded to is the process *of justification.* This process (and connately the achievement, also called "justification," which results when the process is carried out) will be of central interest to us in the pages ahead. Here we emphasize that while "justifiable," "justified," and "justification" are important terms for us, they are not technical terms on which we have a copyright. Like most of the terms we use in the present work, they are ordinary words used in their ordinary ways and are thus not employed with special precision. Our goal is to be plain about what constitutes the justification of belief in the ordinary case, not to erect special or arbitrary standards of success.

At this point the most important fact to note is that the challenges to one's belief that can arise are evidently limited in number. We recall the three 'dimensions' or 'forces' in terms of which speech-acts can be assessed — the primary, the representative, and the affective. We have just seen that a similar grouping is possible respecting beliefs.[4] However, the threefold scheme was itself only an arrangement, whose purpose was to order the conceivable challenges to a given speech-act (in Beth's case, "There isn't any bread," "You're not asking, you're ordering!" "It's right in front of you, dear," etc.) conveniently. The responses to these challenges, rather than any particular arrangement, constitute the clearest means of showing the point, the thrust, the *meaning* of an utterance. If these challenges do not appear or if they are met satisfactorily, we have clear evidence that the issuing of the speech-act is happy.

This dependence of meaning and happiness in speech-acts upon a limited number of conditions is paralleled by the dependence upon a like set of conditions for determining the meaning and the happiness — or, as we shall usually say in their case, the justifiability — of beliefs. Indeed, so direct is the parallel that it is needless for us to repeat the exercise of chapter 3, this time attending formally to the belief(s) expressed by Aleph's speech-act rather than to that act itself. Nevertheless, there was a point in attending to utterances first. For in their case, some matters became clear that would remain obscure if we attended to beliefs alone.

Take the notion of justification, just introduced afresh. How well justified do the beliefs of our own community of conviction have to be in order for *us* to be justified in accepting them as our own? At one extreme, we are tempted to answer "Not at all. I have a perfect right to think my own thoughts, to believe as I please." Yet that temptation clashes with another, more precisian, urge, which wants to answer "Infinitely well! There *is* no limit, no requirement is too great, no doubt too small to entertain." Here the parallel with language may be profitably invoked. For similar temptations to latitudinarianism and puritanism may arise in the question "How happy must a speech-act be?" and here too we may be tempted to answer with either the precisian "Infinitely happy" or the latitudinarian "I have a right to say whatever I like." But we have just seen that neither of these is fair to the linguistic facts. We can't say just anything (though we can indeed say anything *sayable*), and what we can happily say is subject to fairly definite and (in principle) satisfiable tests. If someone has done what we all do when requesting bread (or thanking a helper, or advising a neighbor), it does not matter, linguistically, what else the speaker may or may not thereby have done. If the (enumerable) challenges are not applicable, that's all there is to be said.

Now we can compare this account with the parallel case of beliefs. While, to be sure, each is entitled to her own thoughts, this may express no more than the self-evident truth that only she can have *her* thoughts. Or, perhaps, that there is no practical or morally acceptable way that we can stop her from thinking her thoughts. In fact, of course, she cannot believe just anything, for her 'belief' may not be *belief* at all, as we have noted above. Or it may be in various ways unsuitable, in which case, although she (so far) believes it, the possible challenges show the ways in which it is untenable and in need of revision. Suppose Jason reports to us his belief that the dean (known to be an upright man) is actually an arsonist. "Why do you believe that?" "No reason, I just think he is." "Well, have there been any suspicious fires lately?" "No." "Has he behaved strangely?" "No." "Are you possessed of past records, or some psychological data about the dean, or something else the rest of us do not have?" "No, nothing; I just think he is." But even a hunch requires some circumstances that make it appear an appropriate hunch, and if Jason is honest about having no reasons *at all,* then his belief is patently inappropriate, perhaps even unintelligible — a belief to which he has no right.[5] Note that it is not merely the *announcement* of his belief that is unhappy. We say, "You shouldn't say that," to such a person, but we do so, in this case, on the ground that he has no right *to that belief.* Of course we have chosen an easy, if extraordinary, case in which the belief is of a slanderous character, so that challenging it seems important. It does at least illustrate, however, that beliefs are not unchallengeable any more than speech-acts are.

The other parallel also applies: the demand for justification cannot be an unlimited one in the case of beliefs, either. If my belief is a suspicion (that the dean is an arsonist or that the milk is sour), it need have no more reason for happily existing than suspicions normally require (need not be already proved, need not be self-evident, need not be widely accepted). If we know how to recognize ordinary, *bona fide* suspicions, we are also in position to reject the spurious and to identify justifiable or justified ones.[6] As in the case of speech-acts (cf. accusations, promises, requests), the conditions for believing, and for happily believing, are limited in number and can normally be listed, even though in practice no one happens to list them.

If, once a challenge has appeared and been examined, one is not confident that the conditions are satisfied or is persuaded that they are not, he will be able to say that the belief in question is (to that degree) unjustified, even though it had been his own. On the other hand, until such a particular challenge does arise, there is no reason to suppose that the beliefs one holds are fraudulent, defective, or bogus, any more than one would normally suppose that whatever someone *says* is inappropriate, false, or unintelligible. To be unjustifiable is, we repeat, to fail to meet one or more of these conditions for happily believing, and the task of justification is that of responding to *actual* claims that one or more of the conditions is not met, or to *actual* doubts that it is. Justification is a response to challenges, and these challenges are both limited in number and definite in content.

Now an important clarification must be introduced. We have spoken of "challenges," and this term seems to suggest that the difficulties with speech or with belief come from outsiders, with the speaker or believer always playing the role of attorney for the defense, while someone else attacks what he or she thinks and says. In fact this is an inadequate portrayal of the real situation. Sometimes, to be sure, it is someone else who points out my faults in speech and thought. Very often, however, it is I who first doubt whether what I said is what I meant to say or should have said, while unexpressed beliefs can hardly be challenged save in this way. Even external challenges have no effect unless we ourselves see that they have some merit. It is our own experience, our own (shared) standards, then, that often question our beliefs, and the 'challenge' most often takes the form of an internal dialogue.

This internal dialogue, however, is made more intense by two external factors. One is that it is a rare thing for any of us to have totally unshared beliefs. Many of our beliefs are shared by most people; some beliefs are so widely held (that sky is blue, that grass is green, and that water runs downhill) that we may spend a lifetime without meeting anyone who cares to challenge them in any way. We are accustomed to and generally dependent upon the sharing of many cultural beliefs. The other factor to be mentioned is that some of our most important beliefs are nevertheless *not* shared by all, and we know that they are not. Indeed, we know that besides our own community of belief-sharers, there are other belief-sharing communities that may doubt, challenge, or by their very existence even threaten important beliefs we do hold. These two factors — that of community and that of pluralism — are of great importance in justification, and we must say more about them.

First, however, let us narrow the range of beliefs to be discussed. We would speak of beliefs like Aleph's — but like Aleph's in what respect? His utterance expressed a religious belief, yet as we said in chapter ɪ it is difficult or impossible to delimit the class of 'religious beliefs' in any satisfactory way; "religious," like "religion," escapes any straightforward definition. Besides, we shall have to decide what to do about irreligious beliefs, which clash with religious ones and thus are logically similar to the latter. Further, not *all* beliefs on religious topics are either very important or very interesting. The importance of Aleph's G is not merely that it is religious, but that it holds a special place among the utterances and beliefs of those who accept it. G, we may say, is a *convictional* utterance, and the belief(s) that it expresses are Aleph's *convictions.*

Here, then, is the special sort of belief with which we are concerned. Convictions *are* beliefs, and they do bear a special relation to the rest of our beliefs and to ourselves as well. "We are our convictions," said Willem F. Zuurdeeg.[7] We now have a more exact way of speaking about these central elements in our thought (and speech) and can use them to explain the definition of convictions we offered in chapter 1. Convictions, we said there, are persistent beliefs such that, if X (a person or a community) has a conviction, it will not easily be relinquished and cannot be relinquished without making X a significantly different person (or community) than before. Convictions, then, are a class of beliefs, to which the considerations we have made about beliefs in the preceding pages — their intimate relation to speech-acts, their liability to the flaws and capacity for the success or happiness that speech-acts may have, and their corresponding links with the speaker-believer and the world in which he or she lives — all apply. This is the exact sense in which "we are our convictions" can be taken: a sense in which all our beliefs are immediately related not only to our world but also to ourselves.

Further, we see the senses in which convictions are 'important' beliefs and thus more central to the lives of their holders than are their other beliefs. For one thing, they are *persistent.* "Persistent" does not merely mean continuous or long-lived. Being persistent implies the capacity to resist attack, to overcome, to continue in the face of difficulties. I may have held a belief all my life, unchallenged, only to discard it the minute some evidence of its falsehood or any other sort of unsuitability is presented to me. Such a belief is therefore not a conviction. On the other hand, I may have acquired a belief only yesterday, but if it is in fact persistent in character — that is, the sort of belief that I *will* cling to in the face of difficulties, maintain against doubts within and adversaries without — and if it meets the further condition of a conviction, then, new though it is, it is already my conviction, though I may not yet have recognized it as such.

Now there may be persistent beliefs, stubbornly held, that nonetheless have no *significant* role to play in the lives of their holders, but these, failing the second of our criteria, will not qualify as convictions. By "significant" beliefs, we mean those that exercise a dominant or controlling role over a number of other beliefs held by their believers, or those that govern (or correspond to) broad stretches of their thought and conduct. Every belief is related, at least prospectively, to one's conduct: minimally, one will be disposed to identify it as one's belief or to conceal one's possession of it. Some beliefs, however, are much more decisively related to the lives of their owners than this. We have explored in some detail just such a belief in our examination of Aleph's convictional speech-act, G, in the previous chapter. That speech-act, or the belief that it expresses, is happy only if in identifiable ways Aleph's (other) words and Aleph's other, nonspeech deeds correspond to it. Further, these other words and deeds are of great moment in his life. If, for example, he fails to live a life of awed gratitude in face of God's historic act of deliverance of his people, Aleph's belief is unhappy as a conviction. Beginning to live a life of awed gratitude (or ceasing to do so) is a good instance of a significant change in the sense proffered in the paragraph before last.

What would be an instance of a belief that fulfilled the first, but not the second, criterion, that is, one whose change was nonsignificant for the believer? Suppose a woman believes herself to have been born in a certain city and state where she remembers living in early childhood. Suppose that her belief about her birthplace is supported by what she regards as good evidence — a birth certificate, a parent's word, the beliefs of others whom she trusts. Now someone tells her she is mistaken; she was born across the state line. She is distrustful of the new claim, as we all are when persistent beliefs are challenged. She doubts, she argues, she resists. Finally, she is shown overwhelming new evidence of her birth in another state and given a reasonable story to explain her previous misinformation — parents who for such and such good reasons lied to her, forged the birth certificate, etc. Reluctantly, she changes her mind. Her persistent belief is finally abandoned, replaced by a new one. Yet she is in character and action very much the woman she was before. She has only acquired new information (including new information about her parents' veracity), perhaps a new practice for answering place-of-birth queries on questionnaires, but nothing more. Her belief about her birthplace was not, in the required sense, a conviction, for *its change produced no significant change in her.*

Our point is not that beliefs about God's dealings with Israel are necessarily convictions, while beliefs about birthplaces cannot be. We can imagine nonconvictional views about God (though perhaps these require a changed sense of the term "God"); alternatively we can envision circumstances in which a belief about a birthplace is indeed convictional, that is, one that is not only persistent but that also affects the character and attitudes of the holder in such a way that changing the belief would mean a changed person.

Let us concede, however, that it is not always easy to recognize 'significant' changes. For one thing, there may be marginal cases. Some ethical beliefs, though persistently held, play only a peripheral role in the lives of their holders, and these may be beliefs associated with religion as well. Indeed one of the characteristic problems of religious ethics in a changing world is the religious community's difficulty in dealing with beliefs that are of marginal importance for contemporary life and faith but that are maintained as if they were central. A little reflection upon the beliefs of a community, perhaps the reader's own, will show that these lie in a spectrum ranging from most to least important. It may be questionable in a given case whether the change of a tenacious belief somewhere in the spectrum is correlated with significant character change, but this is not a grave difficulty for the notion of convictions we offer. For there are similar borderline cases in many definitions.[8] That we generally, or normally, are able to identify cases of significant change of conviction is shown by the fact that we talk about such a change as a "conversion," or perhaps of the significantly changed community "like a new bunch of people." Such expressions bear witness to the sort of change we have in mind when we say that convictional changes are significant changes in persons and groups.

Now, however, we must acknowledge a more radical difficulty raised by the definition of convictions we have proposed. Not everyone will agree on these cases of 'significant' change. Take the case of Aleph, the hero of chapter 3. If Aleph should painfully but truly relinquish his faith in the God of Israel, give up his conviction about God's leadership of his people in the archetypical exodus, cease to live under the shadow of that numinous event, we can imagine that, nevertheless, *someone* may say, "That's a trivial matter, not a very significant change at all. All this business about gods and miracles and providence in history — quite immaterial to a man's life; a little more superstition here, a little less there, but it's six of one, half a dozen of the other." While on the other hand, our counterpart may regard our story of the woman who gets a new belief about her birthplace as an inescapably convictional occurrence: "Blood and soil — that's what makes us what we are!"

Our point is that to count a change as significant involves a judgment that may itself be convictional. While our example may be a bit forced, still one must recognize that those of vastly different views from one's own might see the world, and what matters in it, so differently that neither Aleph's change, nor the conversion of St. Paul, nor the Protestant Revolt against Rome, nor the enlightenment of Gotama would count in their eyes as convictional. No matter what is changed, something is sure to remain the same, and it is always logically possible that what changes will seem to someone insignificant (although we shall argue later that not every consistent opinion on what matters can be maintained in practice). It follows that while our definition of convictions is conviction-neutral (or nearly so), its *application* can be affected by the convictions of the applicant. This must be recognized; it is one of the complexities with which pluralism confronts us.

We have just noted the topical neutrality of convictions. They can be beliefs about whatever their holders are convinced about: gods, devils, the social security system, or the sanity of their neighbors or themselves. It is clear that convictions may be disputable (and disputed); it should be made clear that they may be undisputed (or even indisputable). Some philosophers in examining beliefs and systems of belief have emphasized the distinction between knowledge and certitude, but convictions are likely to include both beliefs that the holder is said to know (have evidence or authority for, be able to defend) and those of which the holder is (merely) certain (feels sure about). Moreover, convictions will sometimes be the conclusions of reasoned arguments and based upon evidence. But the premises of such arguments may themselves be the convictions of the arguers, even presupposed ones of which the holder is hardly aware. There is no guarantee that a person or a community will be aware of each conviction that is operative; in fact we can be as mistaken about what our convictions are as we can about almost anything else. (It does not follow from this that we *must* be mistaken, or that ordinarily we will be, or that we could be mistaken about everything all the time.)

Convictions, then, are a varied class of beliefs, a fact that should not surprise us. After all, in the way we have shown, we *are* our convictions, and we humans are a varied lot ourselves. Some of us think things through; others act and live intuitively, in the main. Some of us have many convictions; others only a few. Some of us are deeply involved in convictional communities; others are lone wolves, convictionally speaking. Some seem to have acquired settled convictions long ago; others (especially the young) are consciously in process of convictional formation.

With so many things to be considered, any general principles of justification may be hard to come by. Against the difficulties, however, we must weigh the desirability of achieving our goal. While convictions may be obscure, varied in character, and determinable only on grounds that are themselves partly convictional, they are nevertheless central to the lives of their holders and affect even nonconvictional beliefs. Thus the justification of convictions may be difficult, but so much rests upon the results that the difficulties must be somehow confronted.

We have already hinted that the convictions of a community or of an individual are related to one another in a variety of ways. Thus the justification of any one conviction is not likely to be achieved without regarding its relation to other convictions embraced by the same community or the same believer. If the question is whether Aleph justifiably believes that God led Israel across the Sea of Reeds (or whether Jane Jones is justifiably convinced that there is a Star Wars master plot to take over the world or whether anyone should be convinced that the scientific method is a reliable source of truth), one must attend not only to *that* conviction but to others that are a part of the wider set of convictions of the holder. We must at least consider whether the conviction in question is dependent upon others in the set — and therefore its justifiability dependent upon theirs. In any case, it is noteworthy that convictions do not occur in isolation; they are found in their holders along with other beliefs, some of which are, in the usual case, also convictions.

II. Conviction Sets

Let us attend to this clustering phenomenon, for it certainly affects our task. For convenience, we will refer to the set of all convictions held by a person as that person's *conviction set* and to the set of all convictions held in common by members of a community as the community's (shared) conviction set. Of course, it may be that not every member of a convictional community (whether it is the Roman Catholic Church or the Society of Friends) shares *all* the important or central or defining convictions of the community. In such cases, we may still refer to the community's conviction set, meaning the set of beliefs that shape the actual life and practices of the community. Often these are guarded by its teachers, or elders, or authoritative leadership cadres. Thus the community as a community could not relinquish these beliefs without being significantly changed.

Since our own inquiry is aimed specifically at religious convictions, it may be useful to designate that subset of person X's convictions (or community R's convictions) that are religious as X's (or R's) *religious conviction set.* However, our previous strictures concerning definitions of religion and religiousness hold here also: we had better not rely too heavily upon our ability to discriminate, in practice, religious and nonreligious convictions. Fortunately it is not crucial, for present purposes, to be able to do so.

One aspect of cultural pluralism is that persons normally belong to a number of overlapping convictional communities, a fact with important consequences for the justification of convictions. The conviction set of a given person may include subsets shared with several communities — one may be at once a union member, a Baptist, a Democrat, an American, and a white racist; or at once a college professor, a health food faddist, an atheist, and a Slavophile. (That each of these is among other things a *convictional* community would of course require evidence.) What usually happens, Zuurdeeg suggests, is that the sometimes agreeing, sometimes conflicting convictions connected with these several communities are held by the individual hierarchically — that is, where X's nationalist convictions and X's Catholic convictions conflict, one subset will tend to dominate X's life, thereby reducing the force of the other subset.[9] Evidently the interrelation of anyone's convictions may be a complex business, and there is no guarantee that he or she will manage the resultant conflicts easily or well.

To illustrate the complexity of relations among convictions, let us consider a model much simpler than the one just referred to. Let us provide the believer of the previous chapter, Mr. Aleph, with a religious conviction set having five member convictions. One of these will be the now familiar

G "God led Israel across the Sea of Reeds."

Let us further specify Aleph to be a Christian, whose remaining religious convictions are:

D "Jesus said, 'One thing is needful,' "

E "Jesus opened the blind man's eyes,"

J "God was incarnate in Jesus of Nazareth," and

T "(This) God exists."

Consider first D. To see how it may function convictionally let us recall its source in a story found in the Gospel of Luke. Jesus, in the story, visits the household of the sisters Martha and Mary. While Mary sits at Jesus' feet to listen, Martha is, in the winsome archaism of the King James version, "cumbered about much serving" and finally complains that Mary should be directed by the Master to help her. But Jesus instead says, "Martha, Martha, you are anxious and troubled about many things; one thing is needful. Mary has chosen the good portion, which shall not be taken away from her" (Luke 10:38–48, RSV). To investigate the religious employment of this story in Christian history would be a task similar to the investigation of the role of the Reed Sea crossing story. We will not attempt such an investigation, merely noting that the Martha-Mary story has sometimes been taken as an injunction against a busyness in life that causes the busy one to miss the main point, life's true meaning. Let us say that Aleph takes the story this way. Thus when he finds himself distracted by the whirl of events, annoyed, anxious, his perspective distorted, he is disposed to remind himself (and perhaps others as well) that "Jesus said, 'One thing is needful.' " This reminder expresses D, his conviction. Often, of course, it will be shortened in his speech and memory to the simple "One thing is needful." Aleph finds in that reminder a redirection to purposefulness and confidence as he faces his day's affairs. Another might have had another motto: "Take it easy," or "Cool it," or "Observe priorities," or perhaps "Trust God for everything," but it is important not to obscure the differences between any of these and D.

To say that D is his conviction, and thus not *merely* a motto, is to say that Aleph holds it persistently and that its change would be a significant change in him.

Now the same sorts of points that were made about D can be made about E, "Jesus opened the blind man's eyes." Here, too, the origin is a story in Christianity;[10] here, too, let us stipulate that by this saying Aleph is reminded of one of Jesus' mighty works, which he takes as a sign of the role that Jesus may play in his own life and in the lives of others. Jesus is the enlightener, the dispeller of moral and spiritual darkness, the restorer of *vision*. Full explication would show the function of this conviction in Aleph's life by describing the sort of occasion on which he is prone to recall and act in the light of E and the conditions under which he can happily embrace it (compare the discussion of G in chapter 3).

It may be objected that D and E are not themselves Aleph's convictions; they are at best reminders of some conviction or other. They are perhaps like the little signs that some workers put over their desks: "Smile!" or "Think!" These latter cannot be convictions for the reason that they are not full-fledged beliefs, though as mottoes they may remind their owners of real beliefs. In this view, E would remind Aleph of something like "One ought to expect new insight in the course of one's life." Is not something like this, rather than the overparticularized D or E, the real candidate for convictional status for Aleph? This objection seems to us misguided. While "Think!" and "Smile!" may not be beliefs, "Jesus said, 'One thing is needful,' " is.[11] Thus D *can* be Aleph's conviction. What the substitutes like "You ought to observe priorities" lack, and D and E have, is just the peculiar flavor of such a belief. Lacking it, they partly miss the role that D and E can play in the life of a believer. Wilfred Cantwell Smith, a historian of religions, relates an episode on a journey in the Himalayas that is instructive here. He finds "a humble fruit-seller," weighing out his oranges by means of a simple pan scale and (for weights) three rocks said to equal two pounds — for the fruitseller is too poor to own metal weights. "He was far from any possibility of having his dealings checked; and there was no external measure of his honesty, which I found was sustained rather by a verse from the Qur'an which runs 'Lo! He over all things is watching.' " How poor a substitute for the fruitseller would have been a generalized platitude ("One ought to be honest"). No, his conviction was that *Allah watches* — or more exactly it was these words of the Qur'an themselves.[12]

Still, the objection has its point, too. Sophisticated religious believers have often sought to eliminate or deemphasize the rough-edged immediacy of particular convictions like D and E, substituting for them broader general principles that the rational found more easily applicable to all situations and that did not depend on controversial historical claims. Not "Jesus said . . ." etc., but the sterile "One ought to observe priorities." So the latter may become the form of the community's conviction. And yet in communities where such 'logical' refinements are widely adopted, haven't the faithful often become insensitive to the poignant demands of particular situations — situations upon which the concrete examples of the religious tradition, in all their particularity, might have reflected much light? Part of the point in the mid-century struggle over 'situation ethics' was the discernment, by moralists and plain folk, that general principles often fail in practice to convey the ethical urgency that the situation requires. The prophet Nathan's "Thou art the man" to King David, applying a story of greedy sheep-stealing to the marriage bed (2 Sam. 11 and 12), lacks explicit generalization, but it has provided a hundred generations of tempted men with a forceful particular conviction.[13]

Aleph's third conviction, J, "God was incarnate in Jesus of Nazareth," confronts us with a conviction at a different level of generality from D or E. It provides Aleph with some understanding of the importance of D and E and perhaps other stories: these words and deeds of Jesus are crucial because in them *God* was working. It provides him also with a theoretical explanation, or a condensed version of an explanation, of the power and the purpose of Jesus' action. Potentially, J offers an explanation and summary of an indefinite range of further particulars as well. We will call it, then, a *doctrinal* conviction, or sometimes, when the context permits, simply a doctrine. The Christian doctrine of the incarnation, as is well known, is open to a wide range of theological interpretations, and we do not intend to invent for Aleph a new interpretation or even to provide the details of an old one for his case.[14] Instead we content ourselves with noting that in Christian tradition J need not refer literally to a particular event or set of events, such as the events of the Christmas story as described in Luke's Gospel. When events like the Christmas story acquire convictional status in Christian minds, they may function merely as particulars (logically parallel to D and E) rather than what we are here technically calling doctrines.

To exemplify the distinction between particulars and doctrines, we note that within Christianity the former are often the stuff of popular devotions and serve as the texts of sermons, while doctrines are characteristically the building blocks of theological treatises. Thus when Thomas Aquinas says, "But in the state of corrupt nature a man needs grace to heal his nature continually, if he is to avoid sin entirely,"[15] he is enunciating what was surely his belief, was probably his conviction, and as his conviction is in our classification a 'doctrine.' The same classification would be made of Friedrich Schleiermacher's "The Redeemer assumes believers into the power of His God-consciousness, and this is His redemptive activity."[16] These are in their level of generality characteristically doctrinal.

We may make clear the relative distinction between these two levels of convictions and at the same time display some of the practical difficulties of such a classification by raising the question about the role, in Aleph's set, of G, "God led Israel across the Sea of Reeds." Grammatically G is similar to J, and this may incline us to classify it as a doctrinal conviction. Were we to provide Aleph with a richer set of convictions, these might include particulars that could be subsumed under G. For example, "God told Moses to lead Israel," "God opened the waters of the Sea," "God destroyed the pursuing Egyptians," might stand as particulars to G as D and E stand to J. As matters now stand, however, G seems to refer to a single event or a class of events, constituting the Reed Sea crossing, and it seems natural to classify it, with D and E, as a particular conviction. Indeed we might supply Aleph with a doctrine to preside over G — something like "God guided Israel's history." Besides G, other potential particulars would include "God led Israel forty years in the wilderness," "God led Israel into the Promised Land," and "God gave Israel prophets and priests." What becomes evident is that the particular/doctrine distinction is, like over/under or to-the-left/to-the-right, a relative one, admitting of variable application and possibly requiring still finer distinctions in practice.

Moreover, there are higher levels of generality than our 'doctrinal' level. To see this, consider the fifth of Aleph's convictions, T "(This) God exists." Even if Aleph is inclined to express his convictions freely, this last may seldom rise to his lips. It is, we shall say, a presiding conviction. In this case, the presiding conviction, T, is presupposed by J and G, but not all presuppositions of convictions are convictions; and certainly not all presuppositions of nonconvictional beliefs are of convictional rank. In each case the test of convictions must be applied afresh: they are, to repeat, persistently held beliefs that their holder cannot relinquish without being significantly changed thereby.

That T presides over J and G explains the point of our parenthetical "(This)." It is precisely the God of J and G whose existence T affirms. Some may feel that "God" in Western thought is so clear a term that "this" is somewhat precious, over-nice (hence our parentheses); our own view, however, is that "God" without further designation may not be precise enough to show the connection we have in mind.[17] There is a rough parallel between the relation of D and E to J, and the relation of J to T. As in the earlier case, holding the lower-level conviction (J) seems to call for holding the higher-level one (T), while the converse is not true. But we have to reckon here also with the paradoxical possibility that a believer might hold J and deny T, even though J apparently presupposes T. He might do this because he regards "exists" as an unworthy way to express the 'existence' or being of God (thus Paul Tillich), or because he does not in fact believe in the divine existence however described but does still find "incarnation" the most appropriate way of expressing something special or extraordinary about the role of Jesus, or perhaps because he is just inconsistent, an unstable but not infrequent case.

We have now briefly described a religious conviction set whose member convictions may be found within the Christian tradition. Conviction sets may be much more elaborate than this, or they may be even more fragmentary and less connected between members. In any case, it would be an empirical question to determine how nearly the actual sets of actual communities and persons displayed the schematism of particular, doctrinal, and presiding convictions here described. That the schematism is not completely without merit may be seen by the examination of the convictional structure displayed by such a document as the American Declaration of Independence. One will find in that instrument possible particulars, among them:

> The present King of Great Britain...has called together legislative bodies at places unusual, uncomfortable, and distant...
>
> He has dissolved Representative Houses....
>
> Giving his Assent....For cutting off our Trade....

That these were in fact particular convictions of all or some of the signers of the Declaration is a historical thesis, to be tested historically. The same is true of the possible *doctrinal* convictions of the signers, for example:

> whenever any Form of Government becomes destructive of these ends, it is the Right of the People to alter or to abolish it....
>
> A Prince whose character is thus marked...is unfit to be the ruler of a free people....

and of possible *presiding* convictions, such as:

> all men are created equal....
>
> they are endowed by their Creator with certain unalienable Rights....

Whether the last are indeed of highest rank or might better be classed among the doctrines concerning Nature's Creator whose existence was itself an (unstated) presupposition of the framers is partly a matter for classification, partly for historical inquiry. In any case, borderline classifications are likely and situations in which finer subclassifications may be required, just as there may be disagreements about the classification of the familiar sentences just quoted.

What seems important in the schematism is not its exactness in application to our examples, but the disclosure of the heterogeneous logical relationships of the several convictions contained in typical sets. For this means that the question of justification must attend both to the varied character of the convictions themselves and to the variety of the involved relationships between convictions. With regard to the latter, we are far from having exhausted the complexity of these relationships in even so artificially simplified a set as Aleph's. So far, we have noted that his convictions might usefully be arranged according to their levels of generality. If now some conviction, say, D, "Jesus said, 'One thing is needful,'" is *expressed,* the happiness of the resultant speech-act depends, as we have seen, upon conditions that might include, for example, the *loyalty* to Jesus to which the speaker, Aleph, is thereby committed, the *genuineness* of the reported saying of Jesus (did Jesus in actuality say that?), and the *intent* and attitude of Aleph in issuing his utterance (can these words be the speech-act that he intends to issue? what speech-act does he intend?). In other words, all the conditions that earlier (chapter 3) we grouped under the heads "primary," "representative," and "affective" will be at stake. And, with the proper adjustments, Aleph's conviction, his convictional belief, is subject to these very conditions. If *Jesus* said that one thing was needful, these words have special import for Aleph, given his attitude to Jesus. They are to some degree and in some way paradigmatic for his life, his singleness of purpose, his attitude to the task of the day and to the busy whirl of life around him. To make "in some way" specific, to understand the primary force of his speech-act (and the 'primary force' of the conviction it expresses), would require a fuller specification than we have yet undertaken of Aleph's view of Jesus. It would require knowing the types of situations in which he can find his conviction applicable; behind these lies the sort of "Jesus" whom Aleph contemplates. We have seen (J) that his Jesus is the incarnation, the human presence, of God. Exactly what effect has that doctrine upon his understanding of D? And what else does he believe about Jesus? Is his Jesus an ascetic? a revolutionary? a social reformer? In sum, we should require Aleph's "perspectival image"[18] of Jesus, in order to know how that picture affects the force of D.

Note then the interdependence of particulars D and E. The Jesus who spoke (D) is in Aleph's reckoning (we may assume) none other than the Jesus who acted (E). And among the conditions for the happiness of each of these convictions are the loyalties, attitudes, and deeds of Aleph himself. How intricate an account it would be that only took cognizance of all that was involved in the tension and interaction of D and E! D demands of Aleph in many a situation a certain detachment, while E demands in perhaps the same situations a certain intense expectancy. What will be the vital balance between detachment and expectancy, between D and E? If we recall the space required to set out in summary form the affects, states of affairs, and commitments demanded by a single (convictional) speech-act, G, how much more will two in combination and perhaps in conflict require? And what if Aleph had not two but two score such convictions? Then the calculus of the adjustment of their several demands would become too long for the telling. Like Tristram Shandy, it might take two days of writing to describe one day of living. But for Aleph, as for Tristram Shandy, it is the living, not the telling, that is crucial.

The upshot is that, while for analytic purposes it was necessary to consider the implications for Mr. Aleph of his single conviction, expressed in his single speech-act G treated in isolation, when it comes to the assessment, the evaluation, of a particular life or style of life and the convictions that form its backbone, it would be a fruitless task to attempt to assess the worth of any conviction in isolation. The convictions in Aleph's set do not occur in isolation; they cannot (normally) be tested in isolation; thus they are not accepted or reformed or rejected in isolation. The justification or rejection of convictions, we see, must often consist in the justification or rejection of *sets* of convictions, of conviction sets, that will stand or fall in interdependence and not one by one.

In the practical order, it must now be apparent that conviction sets as we understand them are seldom deductive systems or theoretical constructs. If they possess a unity, it is rather first of all the unity of their coinherence in the organic unity of a community of persons. Neither logical interdependence nor any other single explanatory feature will account for the occurrence of particular conviction sets. Logic, to be sure, is not debarred. The notion that some convictions preside over others suggests that logic has a role to play in most sets. But it may be associations of a contingent historical nature, or overt or subconscious emotive force of the sort explored by attitude research, or combinations of these and other, unnamed, elements, that bind our convictions together. We cannot, in general, say what these must be; they are surely as varied as life itself. What we can, definitionally, say is that the glue that binds convictions into a single set is their mutual relation to the life of the person or (normally) the life of the community in which he or she shares. The unity of conviction sets is the rough but vital unity of shared life, the narrative in which they cohere.

Why is it said that conviction sets normally belong to communities, not individuals? Zuurdeeg, our pioneer, held that convictions implied convictional communities,[19] but this seems to have been for him not so much a philosophical or a linguistic inference as a shrewd observation of the human scene. To see what sort of necessity may lie behind this observation, let us once more consider an old objection to our procedures. "You have spoken," the objection goes, "as if it might be quite difficult to sort out the meaning and force of Aleph's five convictions in their interrelations. However, you have underestimated the difficulty. The task is not merely complex, but hopeless; not simply a large task, but an impossible one. It is impossible because we can never surely know one another's thoughts or meanings; they are inextricably private. Aleph means what he chooses to mean, but who are we, who are you, to say what that is?"

Our response to such skepticism has been to invoke the public and convention-governed nature of language and of thought as well. Neither we nor he may at a given moment know what Aleph thinks or means, but he can find out, and so can we. The assurance that this is so lies in the nature of language itself. We were in position to say what Aleph meant by G because G arose within a community, within a religious tradition. Note further that the community that provided the context of the utterance was not merely a religious community, though it was that. It was also a linguistic community, not in the sense that it was confined to or defined by one of the natural languages (English, Hebrew, Chinese), but in the sense of using one or more of the natural languages in common ways in order to form and express its shared beliefs, including its convictions. It was precisely this communal feature of Aleph's (and of all) speech that made it possible (in chapter 3) to determine the force of G and test its happiness in utterance.

If this is the case, we may now see that linguistic communities as just described are convictional communities as well: that some convictions must be shared to give form to the community, and even private or rebellious convictions of members of the community can be understood only in view of their connection with the communal matrix from which they diverge or dissent. Therefore by speaking of convictional communities we do not imply that all persons therein must have identical conviction sets, nor that any two personal sets will be identical. Our convictions are what we are, and we humans are not merely or totally alike. Moreover there are (as far as the present writers know) no irreversible convictions — all may be challenged; each may be modified under pressure; any may in the extreme be overthrown. But when we later consider the possibility of convictional rebellion (chapter 6), it will become clear that even rebels can understand themselves, or be understood, only in terms of that against which they rebel. (One rightly distinguishes, for example, Catholic atheists from Jewish atheists.) It is just the existence of such linguistic-convictional community that makes the understanding of Aleph's five-member conviction set possible.

Aleph's own set need not, perhaps rarely will, be simply identical with the community's shared set. Even in his departures from the common store, however, the meaning and justification of his set are dependent upon the meaning of the common set. Since each of Aleph's convictions acquires part of its significance from all the other members of his set and since every member of his set depends for its understandability upon the language of the community, we cannot understand Aleph or justify his set of convictions save by reference to the community to which he belongs. If he participates in more than one community, then we shall have to consider each. The understanding and justification of Aleph's convictions, then, are dependent upon the understanding and (as we shall see) the justifiability of the community's convictions. It is the community that is logically prior, however keen may be our interest in the individual and his or her personal faith.

III. Pluralism and Justification

If there were only one convictional community, the human race, or if we lived, as perhaps humans once did, in a community so isolated that the convictions of outsiders made no impact upon us, we might have little more to say on this topic. As matters stand, we are just arriving in position to state and to investigate a central problem of the justification of convictions. This is the plurality of convictional communities. Today we can neither ignore communities other than our own, nor, given the imbedding of personal convictions in communities that generate the meaning and determine the conditions of the possible justification of a set, can we easily justify our convictions in universally satisfactory ways if the challenge to our convictions comes from a rival community.

Convictional differences are at once more serious, and harder to adjudicate, than other differences of belief (for example, differences of opinion). They are more serious because convictions are themselves more serious. They are more difficult to adjudicate because they are intertwined with our own lives and the lives of the communities from which we spring. To judge them within convictional borders is a kind of self-judgment — a notoriously difficult task that may yet fail to satisfy our convictional opponent. To judge them *across* convictional borders seems either question-begging and presumptuous or logically questionable: the former if we ignore the special problems involved, the latter if we acknowledge them.

How, then, are we to understand those whose convictions differ from our own? And for that matter how is any one of us (or any one community among us) to know that our own stance is justifiable, our own conviction set is right? Confrontation with these questions is likely to produce either dogmatism or cynical indifference — yet both dogmatism and indifference are to be seen as temptations rather than as solutions of these hard problems. Still, we must recognize that even to ask these questions in this form is rather different from the way in which some philosophers of religion have approached their task. These philosophers have assumed that at least they themselves (and perhaps their readers) have attained a grand cosmic neutrality, far above the strife of the systems. With their clean, convictionless slates they would set out on the quest, inviting the open-minded to come along and promising that at the end of the road there would be inscribed on their tablets nothing but the truth impartially discerned. Those who are satisfied with such a tale are not likely to have come this far with us, for we have made it clear that we possess no such higher neutrality, nor have we expected it in our readers.

Our approach implicitly challenges those who are blithely confident that their own conviction set is the only worthy one. To see my convictions *as* convictions is not to see that they are wrong, but it is to acknowledge the nature of my attachment to them, and thereby to be open, if only a crack, to understanding how someone else may see the world differently. Let us illustrate this from the contemporary debate about belief in God. In a perceptive essay, Paul van Buren once suggested that there was something odd about the demand that the talk of people who talk about God, or who "have trembled in a situation which they might later describe as being 'in the presence of' the gods, or God," should be explained in terms of the way people generally talk about other matters.[20] Perhaps there just *are* differences in folk, in the experiences they have, and perhaps the experiences of these few are not to be accounted for in terms of the general experience of humankind, or spoken of in ways that coherently report that more general experience. And if we acknowledge this, should we not be prepared to take another step: to concede that not all human religious experience is the same, that just as there are those who do not engage in religious talk, so are there those who do not employ certain *kinds* of religious talk? Some (Augustine, Tillich) place the emphasis upon the sense of limitation — the finitude, the guilt, the loss of 'meaning' in life — while others experience a sense of wonder rather than of limitation. "It is not *how* the world is, that is the mystical, but *that* it is," says Wittgenstein.[21] But van Buren comments that Wittgenstein was one of the minority, "one of the strange ones." He adds, "the decisive point to be made is that some men are struck by the ordinary, whereas most find it only ordinary."[22]

Now, asks van Buren, if some of us are "struck" when others of us are not, why should "contemporary secular man" become the measure for understanding his religious counterpart? Why in the world should we be interested in trying to justify religious language to this hypothetical person? How, for that matter, is such a one to justify *his* or *her* language to the religious? Isn't the issue between them precisely over what constitutes a justification? Will it do to say that there is a third way (the true way?) that sees both how the religious and how the nonreligious see the matter?

But if that were a way of seeing, would it not be *just* a third way of seeing, van Buren asks, alternative to the other two as they are alternatives to one another?

> It seems to be the case that there is no alternative to seeing things *as*. Every seeing is 'seeing as.' Depending on our purposes, what we wish to accomplish, the context, and many other factors, we shall have what we call grounds for seeing a situation in one way rather than in another. But seeing the 'ordinary' as extraordinary, as a cause for wonder, is no more and no less in need of justification than seeing the 'ordinary' as ordinary and as something to be taken for granted.[23]

And so there can be no more important a problem for theology than "that of sorting out the ways in which we do justify for ourselves and to each other our ways of seeing, our perspectives, our (to give them a more honorific title) metaphysical beliefs."[24]

Contrast that pluralistic enterprise with the much easier task of discovering the conditions for happiness of a belief or an utterance in a community in which we all participate. Take our diner Beth's speech-act requesting the bread, for instance. In that case, we were careful to specify that there existed a linguistic community or subcommunity, speakers of a dialect in which *certain* words (though not invariable, not indifferently chosen either) counted as the performance of that speech-act. Beth couldn't say just anything and be counted as requesting the bread.[25] And of course a linguistic subcommunity implies a communal ethos as well and a community of custom and institution, making any given practice (such as requesting or passing) possible. To put the matter another way, the practice of requesting is both a linguistic and a cultural institution, and the two are inseparable; *glossai* and *ethnoi,* languages and peoples, belong together and serve to define one another. Ethos works with language to specify the conditions of happy bread-requesting.

The reason we could specify so firmly and confidently (though not without considerable effort) the conditions of the happy performance of Beth's speech-act, the reason we could know whether the conditions for happiness *were* in fact fulfilled, is that the community to which she belonged is like our own — *is* our own, if we temporarily disregard the line between fiction and fact. We know directly the bread-requesting convention; it is our convention. Nor perhaps do we know anyone who lacks such a convention, anyone who construes the world of food at table radically differently than do we. If we do, a fresh problem at once appears. The reflection required to solve the problem, "What must we say, and what do, in what circumstances, in order to request the bread?" is then no longer the introspective what-we-would-say-when of ordinary language analysis, but (as J. L. Austin's investigations implied) *becomes a task of quite a different order.*[26]

We can see this shift of emphasis in the quest for happiness conditions in Aleph's utterance, "God led Israel across the Reed Sea." Aleph was specified as belonging to a community to which not all of us belong. Even if someone does belong to Aleph's community or one like it, he or she is very likely conscious of the pluralism involved, conscious of others who do not belong and of linguistic obligations to those others. Why is it that the very statement of conditions for the happy performance of Aleph's speech-act seemed more dubious than those of Beth's? And why would the claim that those conditions are or are not in certain circumstances fulfilled seem more dubious still? What is there *odd* about Aleph's utterance?

We can say at the outset that it cannot be the sheer novelty of "God led Israel across the Reed Sea" or of the practice of religious confession. Both are old, much older than the Christian era, much older, then, than the intellectual and spiritual tradition in which we live. Nor will it do to say that such confession is an exotic specimen in our culture, an Eastern import, in the way that (in 1995) joss sticks or temple bells are. On the contrary, some form of that confession is one of the foundation stones in the formation of Western culture. Many have suggested that the trouble is the use of the strange word "God," neither name nor common noun, which is the cause of our sense of discomfort or uncertainty. To be sure that word (or its predecessors in other tongues) has itself been there as long as the confession has been, or longer. Yet there is some merit in the suggestion that it is the strange "logic of 'God' " that is the scandal and stumbling block.

If however we follow the insight of more recent analysts, and our own in the preceding pages, we will prefer to say that the difficulty in understanding Aleph's utterance and appraising its happiness lies precisely in his convictional distance from us, or from others in our world, or in both of these. When a linguistic practice is one employed by everyone who speaks a language, there is relatively little difficulty in knowing what its conditions-for-happiness will be and in knowing to all intents and purposes what counts as the fulfillment of those conditions. One knows these things merely by knowing the language and culture in which the utterance is heard. For centuries many have confessed as Aleph confessed and have been understood and approved or challenged, the challenges directed mainly to the circumstances of each speaker, *his* or *her* fitness to utter those words, *his* or *her* being in position to utter that speech-act. But as a culture becomes more pluralistic, the status of the convictions conveyed in an utterance may shift from "generally accepted" to "disputed" or "accepted only within a subcommunity," and then we have the sort of circumstance that makes the process of examination for happiness similar to that in Aleph's case.

Readers should realize that we have now crossed the important watershed predicted in chapter 1. From here on, we are no longer going to be asking how the convictions of a community are justifiable (or how its speech-acts may be deemed happy) *within that convictional community.* From here on we are going to face this book's ultimate question: how in a pluralist world, a world in which one's own convictional community is not alone but exists alongside others — how in *this* world are convictions justifiable and speech-acts happy? Luckily, what we have so far done will be relevant, but there is more to do.

Ideally, how might this problem of pluralism be overcome? If conflicting subcommunities were members of a single overarching community, then the standards of the larger community (humankind?), subscribed by both sides, might serve as a convictional court of appeal. Indeed, it is partly by such means, we believe, that the perspectival fragmentation of the world may be mended. But we cannot with confidence indicate this procedure until we have fully examined the obstacle created by convictional pluralism. For example, what if a smaller community (even one person) chooses to challenge the prevailing assumptions of the world-community itself? Can we say that the convictions of the challenger *must* be justifiable in terms of the challenged convictions? Surely it is not self-evident that in every such case it is the challenger who is wrong. But this is no hypothetical situation — prophets, reformers, and revolutionary leaders have always been a minority, as the phrase *Athanasius contra mundum* reminds us.

One way to avoid the problem is simply to deny the necessity of adopting *any* conviction set. Why not be content (even delighted) with beliefs of a more limited, ad hoc, and provisional nature? But convictions, as we have said, are those beliefs that are central to the character of a person; a change in them would involve a change (would, indeed, *be* a change) in that person's character. So what would it be like for a person to have no beliefs that occupied this central role? It is not perfectly clear that we could survive without *any* convictions. Are not such beliefs as that I am the same person I was in the past, that some of my present experience is nonillusory, that I know my friends and they me, and perhaps others still more elemental, such as that nature is in general predictable and that our talk must be in general consistent, actually both necessary to our kind of existence and themselves convictions?[27] Thus, we can make a fair case for the proposition that the very concept of a person requires convictions, since to be a person is to have the sort of persistence through time that convictions alone provide. Again, some have argued that to be rational one must have some one principle that organizes one's choices. Such a principle would surely be convictional.

But apart from these subtle, difficult, and controversial arguments, there is a straightforward objection to doing without convictions or making out with only as many as survival seems to require. Our eighteenth-century predecessors would have called it a moral objection, an objection in terms of the kind of life such an abstinence would produce. To lack all persistent and central beliefs is, simply put, to lack character — not just laudable or virtuous character, but any character at all.[28] To be religious or sensual, ambitious or greedy, malicious or kind, radical or conservative, is (among other things) to have the sorts of beliefs we have called convictions. Lacking them, one may sporadically perform particular acts of kindness or cruelty, do conservative or radical things, act piously or irreverently, but these will be only reactions to particular circumstances, not expressions of settled or identifiable character.[29] One is thus, in a way, the victim of these circumstances, just as a boat having freeboard but no sail or anchor is the victim of every chance wind. We grant that life can be led in this way, or, rather, that one can be led by life in this way. One who still doubts whether such a life is satisfactory might consult Plato's *Republic* or *Gorgias,* where there are vivid portraits of men who always do as they wish, yet never get what they want. Nor is this merely an unfortunate but accidental fact about these men. For those without convictions do not know what they want in the settled way that would enable them to lead lives that might arrive at it.

How, though, can Athanasius (or the whole world) justify a set of convictions? In the remaining paragraphs of the present chapter we will introduce three elements of justificatory procedure, no one of which, taken alone, will prove adequate, but which employed together have in fact served humanity well in this regard.

In the first place, there are certain widely accepted considerations that go to establishing the adequacy of any belief. One may inquire, for example, whether one's convictions, so far as is relevant to them, are in fact *true.* Insofar as they are embraced by one community, one may inquire whether convictions are mutually *coherent.* Or if in particular cases these tests are inapplicable or indecisive, one may still raise more pragmatic questions: does the conviction in question contribute to living a good life, or, to ask a Greek question with a Greek word, does it make for *eudaimonia?* Is the life thus produced really the most *satisfactory* life possible, from the viewpoint of the owner(s) of the convictions under examination? Or, if these latter tests seem subjective, is the life that embodies these convictions a life of justice or *righteousness?* Are not such considerations as these (for the preceding list is by no means exhaustive) the criteria by which all people, of whatever convictional community, do judge and ought to judge their own convictions and those of others?

Those who accept this claim as it stands seem to have the support of St. Paul: "Finally, brethren, whatsoever things are true, whatsoever things are honest, whatsoever things are just, whatsoever things are pure, whatsoever things are lovely, whatsoever things are of good report; if there be any virtue, and if there be any praise, think on these things" (Phil. 4:8, KJV). There, but for a substituted or added term or two, is the very list we have produced, offered as a guide to the thinking of the Christian community by its chief apostle! However, the occurrence of such a set of criteria *within* a particular religious community may serve, if we were not already wary, to put us on guard. These terms in use may embody convictional elements. Appeals to them cannot be employed to settle interconvictional disputes because they have been preempted to assert the disputed claims. The "justice" of Jesus may not be the same as the "justice" of Muhammad; the "truth" of Aristotle may not be equivalent to the "truth" of Moses. Even if such terms do in a given language have a common content, that content may not be sufficiently precise to allay convictional misunderstandings and conflicts. The process of examining any one of them, say the term "righteousness," across convictional lines is then a means of reintroducing the very pluralist dilemma we have just delineated. Nevertheless there is a point in mentioning these considerations of truth, *eudaimonia,* and the others. The process of justification will in some way make use of such 'ultimate' appeals; they are, if not themselves the judges, at least indicators of the jurisdictions under which convictional judgments are formed; we may call them the *loci* of justification.

In the second place, we may again note the initial thesis of this chapter: the understanding of convictions can be correlated with the understanding of speech-acts, and the justification of the convictions with the happiness of the speech-acts. At the present stage of the investigation of speech-acts, we should not tire of reminding ourselves that these conditions include the affective setting of speaker and hearers (a point widely recognized already), but also the relationship between utterance and the wide world 'outside' the speaker (a point sometimes slighted by present-day analysts of religious utterance), and even more the primary relationship between the utterance and the linguistic-convictional community by means of which it is (if at all) meaningful.

We have claimed that fully to understand a speaker is sometimes to be in position to know whether his or her speech is justifiable, that the analysis of a speech-act is then tantamount to the justification or rejection of that speech-act. We are now in position to see the sense in which, and the degree to which, that claim is self-evident: if we understand Aleph, we can say what are the conditions for the happiness of his speech-act. The difficulty we now confront is that a convictional speaker's speech (including some of its conditions for happiness) may be locked into that speaker's conviction set, while in a pluralist world we have no ready means of transcending convictional barriers to transconvictional justification.

Perhaps the honest way to put the matter is that, since across these barriers we cannot know when convictional speech-acts are fully happy, we cannot (to that degree) even fully understand those who speak from beyond such barriers. (To understand the language of mathematics, one must accept the conventions of mathematics; to understand the language of Buddhism one must [in some measure?] accept the commitments of Buddhism.) The bright side of this dilemma is that if somehow we can, across convictional lines, understand Aleph, we *will* be able to say how what Aleph says can happily be said, hence how what he believes can be justified. But we grant that so far we have not shown the way to this transconvictional understanding, nor to overcoming the pluralism that creates the need for such understanding. We have only shown that understanding the *language* must be central to that task.

This brings us to *the third element* of the justificatory procedure. This element involves the recognition that the language of a community is never a hermetically sealed system, that it is never even static, but is in a constant process of adjustment to external as well as internal pressure. Therefore the same must be said of the community's formative convictions (for they can be expressed only in the language that is itself in flux). *Convictions make us what we are, but what we are does itself change.* What we said above about convictionless persons applies to convictionless communities as well. If the change is so rapid that the convictions are lost, the community is dissolved in the process. On the other hand, a totally ossified community is a contradiction in terms: in a changing world, an unchanging community acquires a new environment, natural and human, thus a new set of relations to the world.

Recognition of these truisms leads us to ask whether there are not now ways in which we change our shared convictions in our common efforts to survive in a changing world — ways that are at the same time the clues to testing and even justifying our convictions, or some of them, in a pluralist situation. Perhaps there are characteristic activities — we have in mind the work of the reformer and the revolutionary, the act of the rebel, the experience of the convert, for example — by means of which both single individuals and entire communities may be challenged to convictional shifts that succeed in meeting the challenges to justification that have arisen. These changes reflect the *social matrix* of justification.

Like the two previous elements (the existence of common loci of appeal; the nature of language itself) this last-named element is not adequate alone. Alone it cannot show how either Aleph, or Athanasius, or the whole world can (in principle) justify a conviction set. But what cannot be done by any one element may be done by three together, and in the two final chapters we attempt to say how this is possible. First, however, we must deal with some important objections to our procedure, objections that argue that plurality is not after all so serious a matter, that our procedures are therefore needlessly cumbersome, and that there is a simpler way to a world of justified convictions. Those objections will occupy us in the next chapter.

FIVE

Man is only a reed, the weakest in nature, but he is a thinking reed. There is no need for the whole universe to take up arms to crush him: a vapour, a drop of water is enough to kill him. But even if the universe were to crush him, man would still be nobler than his slayer, because he knows that he is dying and the advantage the universe has over him. The universe knows none of this.

Thus all our dignity consists in thought. It is on thought that we must depend for our recovery, not on space and time, which we could never fill. Let us then strive to think well; that is the basic principle of morality.

Blaise Pascal[1]

You will not find me inaccessible to your criticism. I know how difficult it is to avoid illusions; perhaps the hopes I have confessed to are of an illusory nature, too. But I hold fast to one distinction. Apart from the fact that no penalty is imposed for not sharing them, my illusions are not, like religious ones, incapable of correction. They have not the character of a delusion.

Sigmund Freud[2]

A Perspective on
Nonperspectival Reason

The claim of perspectivism is not merely that there are a variety of conflicting views in the world, but the immeasurably stronger claim that there is not among these views any that can be clearly established to be the superior of all the others; at least not in the short run. If there were such a conviction set, then its justification would require only an efficient organization of public relations and the passage of time. This might be expensive, time-consuming, and tedious, but it surely would not present the theoretical problems we have outlined in the previous chapter. Of course, any convinced community sufficiently isolated or dogmatic might make such a claim for its conviction set. But the vast majority of conviction sets — Christian, Marxist, Buddhist, materialist — are so hotly disputed that we are unlikely, if we are well informed, to take the claim seriously. There are two such putative sets, however, that seem to have such a wide appeal and impressive history of missionary success that we want now to consider the claim for demonstrability on their behalf. We intend first to consider the claim that mere *reason* can be relied upon to settle the disputes among rival conviction sets and establish itself as a principle above all convictions. Afterward we will consider a like claim made on behalf of scientific reason, or *science*.

I. Reason and Proof

Although we will finally reject the claim for 'reason' in some of its forms, we begin by confessing how much we are committed to rationality and reasonableness in our work, though we are aware that we may fail to live up to that commitment.[3] Our theses in this book are stated as clearly as we can state them and are supported, as well as we can support them, with evidence and argument. These are, of course, appeals to the reader's reason as well as the products of the writers' reason, and we know of no other way to support or criticize claims. Beyond this, we hold one form of the principle of fallibility, which is also (in a different sense?) a principle of reason. In its most extreme form, the fallibility principle shades over into a view we have already rejected: that one should minimize one's convictions, for fear of false belief. Though this may seem attractive at first, it has the unhappy consequence that we should always suspend our judgment. On the other hand, a softer form of the principle, the mere recognition that we can conceivably make mistakes, is so innocuous that it hardly deserves the name of principle.

There is, however, a form of the fallibility principle that is both significant and acceptable. It holds that even one's most cherished and tenaciously held convictions might be false and are in principle always subject to rejection, reformulation, improvement, or reformation. This principle has helped to guide our present effort and, indeed, to make it possible. Granting our desire to correct our errors and extend our knowledge, it follows that we should not only be open to criticism from others, but should seek it out, especially when we are criticizing others.

Nevertheless, the fallibility principle alone is not sufficient. A life of nothing but convinced self-criticism of loosely held beliefs would have little to recommend it. Even Socrates, for all his confessions of ignorance, roamed the streets of Athens striking at pretentious ignorance like a torpedo fish. Clearly, he was moved by something more than the fallibility principle. We cannot do without convictions, fallible though we are. But we cannot avoid error, convinced though we may be. We might summarize this point with a motto in Kantian form: conviction sets without the fallibility principle are blind; the fallibility principle without other convictions is empty. A minimal sort of rationality is therefore essential to our task (or any other in philosophy or theology). But the sort of rationality that is clearly necessary is clearly not sufficient.

Of course, one can add that "rejecting, reformulating, improving, and reforming" convictions are (or may become) rational enterprises. If they were also convictionally neutral ones, that would surely indicate a transconvictional status for reason that would, in principle, ease the task of reaching agreement among holders of rival convictions. Unfortunately, such tasks are not, and cannot be, convictionally neutral. For the work of criticism, evaluation, judgment, or justification requires a stance just as much as the convictions or confessions that may be under criticism.

Take *judgment* as typical of the classes of acts we have just mentioned.

It is obvious that utterances like "case dismissed" or "appeal denied" will not count as judgments unless their utterers have some legal authority, that is, unless they are judges. Anyone may say those words, just as anyone may say "time out." But only the referee can call time out in saying it, and only the judge can make a judgment in saying "case dismissed." In such highly formalized contexts it is clear that a special position or stance is required (one has to *be* a referee, or a judge) and also clear what are the characteristics of that stance (being a properly appointed referee or judge). But in informal contexts of judgment, the requirement that one have a proper posture is equally important, even though it is more difficult to say precisely what being in position now means. Still, if I say that Grofé is a better composer than Bartok and it turns out that I have never heard a composition by either, the suggestion that my judgment is poor will have to be taken as jocular understatement. I am in no position to make a judgment, even a poor one, about music I have never heard. Or, in a different vein, consider the utterance "It is easier to starve than accept a handout," where the utterer is the pampered son of the world's richest family. Can he really be said to have judged a situation so utterly alien to his own experience? Surely, it is only by attributing to him heroic powers of empathy and imagination that we can make sense of such a supposition.

A little reflection will show that evaluating and criticizing, like judging, require at least a minimal familiarity and understanding and even some special qualification in order to be distinguished from guessing, surmising, conjecturing, or posing. Of course much more is required of the utterer of these speech-acts if they are to be felicitous: the ability to cite evidence, to distinguish one case from another, and so forth.

In the same way the judge, the critic, and the assessor of a conviction set (including the convinced person) must at a minimum understand the convictions in the set. Even to judge their mutual consistency, one must know at least their representative force, and to assess the evidence for and against them requires much more. No less than the judge functioning within a particular legal system, the judge of convictions must get into position to make judgments. And that this latter "getting into position" can be achieved while having no convictions other than "be reasonable" is an arbitrary (and therefore an *un*reasonable) hypothesis. It seems more reasonable to believe that if a person has enough character or stability or selfhood to qualify as a judge, particularly a judge of such significant matters as the basic religious or irreligious outlooks by which entire human communities live, his or her character will necessarily be marked by some definite convictions, though of course they need not be the convictions currently under assessment. Without the requisite standpoint, without some convictions or other, there could be no such judgments, either for or against the convictions to be assessed.

These general conclusions regarding the rational activities of judgment, criticism, and the like apply as well to that more theologically and philosophically central use of reason, deductive proof. The history of theology and philosophy is dotted (some might say, littered) with proofs of the existence of God and to a lesser extent proofs of the nonexistence of God. Obviously, we do not mean all these 'proofs' are successful ("proof" is not a success-word), and in fact we are not primarily concerned with their validity or soundness, as many of our distinguished predecessors have been. We intend neither to criticize old proofs nor to construct new ones. Our aim is to account for the fact that such arguments are so ineffective in persuading those who initially disbelieve their conclusions, and to account for the related fact that even the validity of these arguments tends to be assessed or judged differently, depending on the antecedent religious beliefs of the assessor.

It is surely clear, by this time, what our general position is. The conclusions of such arguments are convictions and the proving of them — rational though it is — is a convictional activity as much as criticizing or judging is. Moreover, the construction of a proof requires a getting into position at least to the extent of establishing or assuming the truth of the premises. Now, to derive from premises that are themselves convictional a convictional conclusion may be of great interest and importance to those who share those convictions, but it can hardly be persuasive to those who reject them. To be persuasive across convictional lines, a proof would have to contain premises that were understood in the same sense and accepted both by those who accepted and those who did not accept the convictional conclusion. In our view theistic and antitheistic proofs fail to persuade because the premises of such proofs, as well as the method of proof itself, are neither convictionally neutral nor agreed upon by all in this way.

Since proofs are simply a special variety of rational assessment, the points we have made concerning the convictional nature of the general activity of assessment or judgment hold as well for proofs. Nevertheless, because proofs have played such an important role in Western thought, it is of some interest to show in more detail how convictional elements do enter into their construction, and how, having entered in, they affect the persuasiveness of the argument.

The *Summa Theologica* of Thomas Aquinas contains the *locus classicus* among theistic proofs.[4] But the proofs there lie under the double disadvantage of being imbedded in an antique worldview (so that they must be translated out of that view in order to become effective) and of standing under severe and probably justifiable logical criticism at the hands of Hume, Kant, and other subsequent philosophers. Fortunately for our purposes, Austin Farrer, a twentieth-century Oxford philosopher and Anglican theologian, once offered, in *Finite and Infinite,* a theistic proof that is both in the Thomist tradition and fully informed by the criticisms of that tradition.

Every argument for God's existence, says Farrer, must start from "the world of finites," that is, from the world as experienced. Yet it will not do to say, "The world exists, so God must exist"; that proposition carries no force. The world, then, must be examined, and in it certain "distinctions" must be noted. If these "distinctions" can be seen to be explicable if and only if God exists as their ground, then the existence of God will be required as the explanation of the observed distinctions.[5] Before we attend to these distinctions themselves, Farrer warns us to note that such an argument is unavoidably analogical — that is, the argument proposes only to show that there is an analogy between the relationship of God to the world, on the one hand, and certain familiar finite relationships on the other. To neglect the fact that we are dealing with analogy and to treat "divine causality," for example, as though it were a special case of a generally obtaining principle of causality, is to make a "formal false syllogism" or paralogism — the very error against which Kant has effectively warned us. What shall we do, Farrer asks, to avoid this pitfall? The only course is to present the arguments as analogical from the outset, for they present us with "a splintered image of God," and we can "treat the quasi-syllogism as analogical illustration . . . a challenge to us to recognize a genuine analogy."[6]

Now the form of theistic arguments, we are told, will be determined in any given case by the particular "finite distinction" that is to serve as its base. By finite distinction, Farrer means the sort of categorical distinction that can be made between "essence" and "existence," or between "actuality" and "possibility," or between "operation" and "interior effect." If one allows that there are such distinctions to be made in the world, one may then propose that the relation between God and the world is in the appropriate respect analogous to the observed worldly distinction. More, it may be argued that only on the basis of the God-world analogy is the this-worldly distinction at hand intelligible. If this is true, the analogy is not merely possible; it is, for the intelligibility of the world, really a necessary analogy. If, further, it is assumed that "relations of reason," insofar as they are valid, correspond to "real relations,"[7] then the admission of the analogy entails the admission of the existence of its terms, including, in particular, the Infinite Being or Activity, namely, God. An illustration of such an argument is found in the essence/existence distinction. We can distinguish the mere fact that things exist (existence) from any particular ways in which they exist (essence). But the relation between existence and essence is not that of belonging to one another as either constituents or properties belong to that which they constitute or qualify. Neither is there any form "which embraces both as constituents, or from which both follow as properties." Putting the matter differently, we quite easily imagine that things might not be as they are, or that as they are they might not have existed at all. Farrer's conclusion is that "every particular union of [essence and existence] is the work of a being in whom existence finds its own full possibility,"[8] that is, of God.

At once, however, Farrer moves on to criticize this argument. Whatever force it has depends upon smuggling in the assumption that whatever forms the union of essence and existence has or is a "form." But it was just the relation of form (i.e., essence) and existence that the argument was supposed to be explaining. "Thus the scheme of . . . causality in its widest sense, is simply an analogy, which points beyond itself to the inexpressible fact of creation,"[9] and why, Farrer implicitly inquires again and again, should anyone take that "inexpressible fact" to be a fact, why take the analogy to hold?

To understand his answer to that question, we must attend briefly to Farrer's exposition of the nature of "finite substance." By "finite substance" Farrer means roughly "selves" and "things." To say that there is finite substance is to recognize the actual existence of selves and things. However, as the use of the term "finite substance" indicates, Father does not take selves and things to have a merely phenomenal or haphazard existence. He argues, instead, that substance possesses very special qualities, a very special structure — a structure that can make the force of the analogies referred to in the preceding paragraph evident. Substances, more closely analyzed, are acts, such as the acts of a human being who wills to do this and not that; these acts, according to Farrer, constitute the human will; and the self and its central constituent, the will, then serve as all-important clues to the way things in the world in general are constituted.[10] For example, if it turns out that acts of the human will may properly be placed on a scale of being, if, that is, desiring is a kind of low-grade willing, whereas execution is a high-grade act of will,[11] one thing that follows is that there are degrees of substance. But if there are degrees, are we not prepared for a highest degree? And, if the will is 'free,' are we not obliged to give place to freedom or creativity in our understanding of the way reality in general is structured? And thus to an ultimate free creativity to which the human sort is analogous? And so forth.

If we are primarily concerned with the perspicuity of Farrer's terms or the validity of his arguments, our exposition of them would certainly have to include both an analysis of his doctrine of "finite substance" and an examination of his introductory exploration of the logic of theistic argument. We might find ourselves in that case quarreling with the appropriateness of this apparatus of metaphysical inquiry, as well as with the particular logical moves made through the maze of argument. Our goal, however, is a different one — it is to show that the first premise of Farrer's arguments, the "structure of finite substance," is taken by him in a way that cannot but express his convictions, or the convictions of those among his readers who find his argument persuasive.

For Farrer, substance is preeminently human substance, including his own substance. Is the self unitary? Is it free? Is the world it apprehends and acts on nonillusory? These are just the sorts of topics about which it is very difficult not to have convictions if one thinks about them at all. So to think, in Farrer's case, is to think not only about human nature but about the relation of all there is to God.

> For the theist, the reality of that unique object [God] and the validity of the construction by which all things are ordered towards Him are, of course, inseparable. To think theistically is both to recognise the being of God *and to construe things in this order.*[12]

And this is just the point with which we began: to think theistically (or deistically, or atheistically, we would add) is to see things in a certain way; in Farrer's term, it is to *construe* the world thus and thus.

> And therefore the theist's first argument [and last, we might fairly add] is a statement; he exhibits his account of God active in the world and the world existing in God, that others may recognize it to be the account of what they themselves apprehend — or, if you like, that others may find it to be an instrument through which they apprehend, for perhaps apprehension here is not separable from interpretation.[13]

To see the world as a theist sees it is already to see the world a certain way; to see is to interpret, at least in this case. The intention of theistic argument, then, says Farrer, is to bring a latent discernment into the view of the reader. The arguer must start with the scraps of cryptotheism that the reader (perhaps) possesses and show that they cannot be held consistently save in a full-blown theism. Thus argument will force us either to give up our latent cryptotheism (for example, belief in finite substance, including belief in a substantial self underlying each human person) or, alternatively, to incorporate it into a consistent theism.

What remains to be said? Well, we need to know that the beliefs that Farrer says theists and cryptotheists share with one another — such beliefs as the existence of finite substance, the reality of substantial selves, and the freedom of the will — are beliefs that are persistent and to change them would be to change their holders significantly, for it is such beliefs that we call convictions. In the preface to the second edition of *Finite and Infinite,* Farrer describes the circumstances in which his essay was composed: "Eighteen to sixteen years ago I sat down and wrote this book, because I was possessed by the Thomist vision, and could not think it false."[14] Now the "vision" is not the dialectic, not the argument — for in the dialectic section Farrer consciously assumes a post-Thomist, indeed a post-Kantian stance. The vision, then, must be just that view of God and the world, of "Infinite" and "finite," that occupies the second section of his book and forms the central premise of his theistic proof. There could be no clearer categorization of this "vision" as convictional than Farrer's phrase just quoted: "and could not think it false" — could not, that is, without becoming a markedly different thinker, a different believer, a different man.

If we are correct about this, then we have established all that we want to establish about Farrer's argument — that its premises, no less than its conclusions, are convictional. Nor is there anything shameful about arguing from premises that are convictions. Convictional ground *is* ground — the only kind of ground on which anyone ever stands. When, however, it comes to justifying all my convictions, the whole set that I embrace, it is an achievement of limited value to show that some of my convictions entail another, particularly when I know that some of my neighbors share neither the premise-convictions about how it is with the world nor the entailed-conviction, in this case, that God exists.

Proofs of God's nonexistence are not as readily available as some who disbelieve in God imagine. Very often arguments that are said to be against belief in God only call attention to apparent logical inconsistencies in a particular concept of God or in particular theistic proofs; sometimes such arguments claim an inconsistency between a concept of God (for example, that God is all-good and all-powerful) and the observed state of the world (which seems full of ills without number).

Clusters of such argument seek to persuade rather than to demonstrate. Our illustrative purpose might indeed be well served by examining one of these clusters of argument, e.g., the nature of evil and its relation to human happiness as these bear on the nature of God and God's existence. In doing this, we would seek to discover the convictional bases that the argument introduces or presupposes.

However, in a popular book, *Primary Philosophy,* Michael Scriven provides us with an antitheistic proof of the more ambitious sort, and we will consider it.[15] Early in his book, while discussing knowledge, Scriven defines rationality as the selection of "the most efficient available means to achieving a rationally acceptable end," where a rationally acceptable end is one that is not inconsistent with another end that is more valued.[16] Given this definition, it is not difficult to see the grounds for being, or trying to be, rational. As Scriven says, "we want certain things and being more rational is by definition a better way to go about getting them."[17] Scriven infers a corollary, important in the present context: "if what we want is knowledge or truth, we must believe those claims which are best and are well supported by the evidence."[18] It also follows from the definition that being rational cannot be the only aim one has. We can and ought to be rational about selecting and achieving our goals, but as Scriven puts it, rationality "can never be the only aim, any more than 'obey the law' can be the only law."[19]

Although there are undoubtedly convictional elements present in Scriven's general discussion of rationality, they are revealed more clearly when the results of this discussion are applied to arguments about the existence of God. Indeed, Scriven begins his discussion of the existence of God by observing that "no other problem has such important consequences for our lives and our thinking about other issues."[20] Certainly, Scriven agrees with Farrer and with us that whether to believe that God exists or not is (in our terms) a convictional question. Although Scriven's answer to this question is atheistic and based on argument, it is not an argument of the same sort as Farrer's argument for theism, that is, a set of premises about the nature of individuals or causes and effects or purposes that are intended to demonstrate that there is no God. Rather, Scriven regards atheism as the only rational alternative left once he has shown that all arguments for the existence of God fail. "All arguments" here does not mean merely all deductive or demonstrative arguments. Scriven is considering the consequences of failing to find any "evidence which supports the existence claim to any significant degree, *i.e.,* makes it at all probable.[21] If we assume that God is the sort of Being whose existence would make a difference and that our search for possible evidence has been thorough, then, says Scriven, we do not need a further demonstration that God does not exist. Atheism is "obligatory."[22]

As an illustration of his point, Scriven notes that belief in Santa Claus is a reasonable one only so long as we cannot explain the phenomena in question (the appearance of gifts in a locked house where everyone is asleep) without assuming the existence of a being with the supernatural powers attributed to Santa Claus. Once we find an explanation that does not require such assumptions, we need no further proof that Santa Claus does not exist. Just the fact that there is no reason to think he does is proof enough. Because the belief in Santa Claus involves the attribution of supernatural powers, it is in a less favorable position than belief in the Loch Ness Monster, or the Abominable Snowman, since neither of the latter are supposed to have supernatural i.e., wholly unprecedented) powers. If there were no evidence for their existence, belief in them would be irrational, but still a 'lesser sin' than a belief in a being whose powers contravene or go far beyond the powers that we know exist.[23] And in this respect, God is clearly more like Santa Claus than like the Abominable Snowman, Scriven thinks.[24] Thus, if we examine all the arguments for the existence of God and find all of them wanting, the only rational position to take is atheism. Even agnosticism is indefensible.

Now we are not concerned with examining Scriven's attacks on the theistic arguments or even to question the soundness of his argument for atheism. We intend, as with Farrer's case, to show only that its premises are convictional and that there are alternative premises (also convictional) that would yield an agnostic or even theistic conclusion. We now turn to that task.

Consider Scriven's claim that lack of evidence for a belief makes disbelief obligatory. Suppose someone should claim that next July in Seattle will be the hottest July in its history. Suppose further that she offers various 'arguments' in favor of this claim, none of which have any force (perhaps dreams she has had, astrological predictions, etc.), and suppose further that we find no meteorological evidence against the claim. What is the rational stance with respect to the claim? Should we simply give a Scotch verdict: not proven? Or should we *deny* that next July will be the hottest? If the criterion is plain consistency, surely either will do. Neither stance involves a self-contradiction, and either could be held in conjunction with consistent principles about how we should do all our thinking. One principle of rationality might be that whenever we are presented with a claim that lacks evidence for or against it, we should withhold judgment.

Another might be that under the same circumstances we should assume that the claim is false, that is, disbelieve it. If we adopted the first, we would accept fewer false claims (ones that later turned out to be false), but we would also accept fewer true ones.

Is consistency, however, enough? Which of the stances is the best one for getting what we want? There are two difficulties in trying to answer this question in the weather-prediction case. First, by hypothesis there are no observed phenomena that are explained either by the theory that it is or by the theory that it is not going to be the hottest July in Seattle's history. Second, in the limited context provided, there is no indication of any desires frustrated or fulfilled by the truth or falsity of the hypothesis. Thus there is neither need to adopt nor advantage in adopting any particular stance with respect to the hypothesis. Surely, in circumstances like those, the stance most consistent with the effective fulfillment of the goals I have — including the desire to understand, to know the truth about meteorological phenomena — is withholding of judgment.

Now the hypothesis that God exists is unlike this one in every important respect. As Scriven points out, the consequences of both belief and disbelief are (in William James's term) momentous, not only because of some possible afterlife, but in terms of our attitudes, decisions, and plans right now. Moreover, the sort of God claimed by Jews, or Christians, or Muslims, or Hindus (and denied by atheists of each tradition) cannot be ignored or avoided. If this God exists, the world is different than it is if God does not. Thus (again in James's term) the choice of hypotheses is forced. We cannot simply wait until some possible future date when the evidence will be clearer, for that is simply to adopt atheism on a provisional basis. Finally, as this chapter as well as the one on God in Scriven's book attest, both the affirmation and the denial of God's existence have broad current appeal, or, as James would say, they are live options.

James, of course, did in his day regard the hypothesis that God exists as a live, forced, and momentous "option." Because of that, James held that if the evidence both for and against it were indecisive, one had the right either to believe or to disbelieve it. A theist no more than an atheist is being irrational in this case. She is simply following her interest in circumstances where, in James's view, she has every right to do so since nothing else will decide a question that must be decided.[25]

In taking this position, James was directly responding to an essay by W. K. Clifford, which maintained that it was a serious crime against the intellect, a gross irrationality, and always wrong, ever to believe anything with less than sufficient evidence.[26] Scriven appears to be taking a position very much like Clifford's. We are not concerned with defending either James or Clifford. But in light of the enormous importance each assigned to his principle and of their lives lived in accordance with them, it is quite obvious that each principle is convictional and that anyone seriously maintaining one will be a significantly different person from one holding the other.

Can Scriven avoid taking a position in this evidently convictional dispute? In our view, of course, there is nothing suspicious or unfortunate about having a conviction and arguing from it. Indeed, it is inevitable in a self-directing adult. But it is inconvenient if one is attempting to prove to everyone of whatever conviction that some particular conviction should be adopted. Those who have significantly incompatible convictions will regard such an argument as unsound or question-begging, however sound and valid it may appear within its own conviction set.

There is the suggestion in Scriven's argument of another possible attempt to avoid a convictional stance. Though this attempt would not be successful, knowing the reason for its failure is helpful in understanding convictions and their function in argument. To make this attempt to avoid a convictional stance, Scriven might argue that while the failure of all theistic arguments leaves us with no evidence in favor of the existence of God, there remains one striking bit of evidence against God's existence, even if deductive atheistic proofs are ignored. For God is supernatural, that is, possessed of properties that contradict or go substantially beyond all the scientific laws we have. If we can account for all our experience without appealing to such a being, it would not merely be gratuitous to believe in God's existence — it would be irrational. Thus it appears that Scriven can show that atheism is the only justified position by appealing to nothing more than an empirical inventory of the universe and a definition of the supernatural. Surely that is convictionally neutral?

Now the claim that an appeal to empirical evidence is convictionally neutral rests on the assumption that we all have spread before us the same evidence. The only question that would then divide the theist from the nontheist is how to account for that common evidence. The atheist, it might be said, explains it parsimoniously and rationally by 'natural' means, but the theist gratuitously and irrationally insists on appeals to the 'supernatural.'

No doubt there are theists who have neatly divided their everyday 'natural' experiences and their 'supernatural' explanations of these experiences in this way, and to such theists Scriven's atheistic argument may be appropriate and sufficient. But there are also other sorts of believers, represented in the present book by one of its authors, by Farrer, and by van Buren, who differ from the nonbelievers not just in the explanation they give of the same facts, but in the facts they find to explain. Their world is a different world than Scriven's not because it contains miraculous signs and wonders (if indeed it does), but because it has pervasive characteristics that seem to require 'explanations' of a very different kind than the explanations provided by science. (Indeed, for some such believers, the success of science itself points beyond itself to the existence of God as much as does any other aspect of the world.)

We refer to the sense some people seem to have, both believers and nonbelievers, that the very *existence* of the world is itself a matter of wonder, a matter for awe. "For this is the truth we must reach to live, that everything *is* and we just in it."[27] It is not just that some believers *note* this phenomenon in themselves and others but the notice that they take of it that makes their world of facts significantly different from Scriven's. Thus we are not sure whether to say that they attend to different facts, or that they see the facts differently, or whether these two come in the end to the same thing. This sort of believer takes the world he finds to be itself 'supernatural' (to retain Scriven's term) and quite naturally seeks a 'supernatural explanation' and not just an unusual or unlikely natural one. He would agree with Scriven about the importance of rationality: consistency, examination of all the evidence, acting on the preponderance of the evidence, etc. He and Scriven would disagree, however, on how the evidence should be characterized and thus on what counts as a good explanation for it. Here, then, there is again a conflict of beliefs. And this belief, like the one about rationality, tends inevitably to be convictional since it determines as far as it goes one's stance toward the whole world.

We do not conclude from this that Scriven's conclusion is necessarily false or that his argument is invalid. We do find that certain of his premises are convictional. Not only his conception of what is rational but also his view of this world (about which, as noted, the present writers disagree with each other). The theist may be mistaken in the conviction that the world is 'supernatural,' and the nontheist may be mistaken in supposing it to be 'natural.' But just as Farrer will not convince Scriven with arguments whose premises contain claims that the world is contingent or that free and finite selves entail Infinite Being or that nature is designed, so Scriven will not convince such believers as Farrer with an argument resting on a presumption against the 'supernatural.' We are here faced with a convictional conflict that, while neither irrational nor in principle insuperable, will not be resolved by arguments that merely assume contrary convictions.

If we are right about Scriven and about Farrer, if our more general claim is true, and theistic and atheistic proofs *in general* depend upon premises that are the convictions of those who hold them, then the rational shortcut is at this point foreclosed, and we must return, in our search for the justification of conviction sets as wholes, to more gradual, roundabout, but we believe ultimately more satisfactory methods.

Another way of putting our point, perhaps terminologically more satisfactory, is to say, not that rationality or reason is unsatisfactory for establishing convictional conclusions, but that if reasonableness is to be the necessary and sufficient test of the adequacy of any conviction, we must gain an enlarged sense of what is reasonable, of the term "reasonable." Diogenes Allen has argued that one must distinguish between rationales for a given faith and the ground for faith that lies in the satisfaction by that faith of important human needs that cannot be so well satisfied in any other way.[28] In these terms, what Farrer and Scriven have been offering us in the part of their work we have considered has been rationales — reasons (extrinsic to the satisfaction offered by the beliefs for which they argue) to believe that these beliefs are true. An example of a satisfaction-ground, on the other hand, might be the experience of finding by faith the forgiveness of one's sins (Christianity) or the exhilarating discovery of liberation from an oppressive belief in God (secular atheism). Without exploring at this point whether these two kinds of reasons for embracing a conviction set can be separated, as Allen believes, we can note that his thrust is toward the effective enlargement of the current notion of reasonableness, so as to embrace not only questions of truth but also questions of satisfaction — the question of what makes life truly satisfactory. The considerations we have brought forward in the preceding pages seem to demand such an enlargement if there is to be any reasonable justification of anyone's convictions.

We have so far been dealing with proofs that (in our terms) have attempted to prove a presiding conviction by using doctrinal convictions (Farrer) or doctrinal convictions by using presiding convictions as premises (Scriven). Put in these terms, it is easy to see why such proofs would be convictional and therefore subject to the difficulties we have discussed. But suppose an argument could confront a presiding conviction directly. How would this affect our claim? To answer this question we propose an examination of the so-called ontological argument of St. Anselm.

We begin by noting a passing remark upon Anselm's argument made by a currently unfashionable British philosopher of the mid-twentieth century, R. G. Collingwood:

> What it proves is not that because our idea of God is an idea of *id quo maius cogitari nequit* therefore God exists, but that because our idea of God is an idea of *id quo maius cogitari nequit* we stand committed to belief in God's existence.[29]

At first reading, Collingwood seems to be saying that all that Anselm's argument can do is to prove that we think what we think — a particularly vicious subjectivism. Notice, though, that Collingwood speaks, not of proving that we believe, but of proving that we stand committed to believe: whether we believe it or not is another matter. Now, "stands committed" seems to be another way of referring to those deep convictions by which we live, to convictions that are foundations of the form of life of a human community.

In fact, Collingwood further argued that the quest for absolute presuppositions — those presuppositions that prevail in a culture or civilization at a given time and that are 'absolute' not in the sense of being unchangeable but in the sense of not themselves presupposing anything more fundamental still — was the proper business of that division of philosophy called metaphysics. "The analysis which detects absolute presuppositions I call metaphysical analysis."[30] Collingwood further believed that the metaphysics of Western culture, that is, the culture or civilization that replaced the Hellenic culture of antiquity, was ascertainably composed of fundamental *propositions* (which Collingwood, interestingly, sometimes called "convictions"[31]) not different from the "metaphysical doctrines" of Christian faith — the doctrines about the triune nature of God.

> A good deal of information about barbarians and Romans in the later Empire is now accessible even to persons who profess no special interest in the subject; and any reader who will spend a little time upon it can satisfy himself that it was not barbarian attacks that destroyed the Greco-Roman world. Further research will convince him that to this extent the Patristic diagnosis was correct: the 'pagan' world died because of its own failure to keep alive its own fundamental convictions.
>
> The Patristic writers not only saw this, but they assigned to it a cause, and proposed a remedy. The cause was a metaphysical cause. The 'pagan' world was failing to keep alive its own fundamental convictions, they said, because owing to faults in metaphysical analysis it had become confused as to what these convictions were. The remedy was a metaphysical remedy. It consisted, as they formulated it, in abandoning the faulty analysis and accepting a new and more accurate analysis, on the lines which I have indicated in this chapter.
>
> This new analysis they called the 'Catholic Faith.' The Catholic Faith, they said, is this: that we worship (note the metaphysical rubric) one God

in trinity, and trinity in unity, neither confounding the *hypostaseis* and, thus, reducing trinitarianism to unitarianism, nor dividing the *ousia* and thus converting the one God into a committee of three. The three *hypostaseis,* that is to say the three terms in virtue of whose distinctness they spoke of a trinity, they called respectively the Father, the Son, and the Holy Ghost. By believing in the Father they meant (always with reference solely to the procedure of natural science) absolutely presupposing that there is a world of nature which is always and indivisibly one world. By believing in the Son they meant absolutely presupposing that this one natural world is nevertheless a multiplicity of natural realms. By believing in the Holy Ghost they meant absolutely presupposing that the world of nature, throughout its entire fabric, is a world not merely of things but of events or movements.

These presuppositions must be made, they said, by any one who wished to be 'saved'; saved, that is to say, from the moral and intellectual bankruptcy, the collapse of science and civilization, which was overtaking the 'pagan' world.[32]

What Collingwood seems to be reflecting upon in these speculative lines is the connection between the leading ideas of a religious community, that is, its presiding convictions, and the presiding convictions of the civilization to which the religious community stands in creative relationship. If what he says is correct, then the 'necessary' utterances, beliefs, or presuppositions of a community are those that ground the beliefs of that community in the conviction set and thus in the 'necessary' ideas or presuppositions of the civilization in which it appears.

Perhaps we can to some extent test this view and to that degree understand Collingwood more clearly by noting the modern history of criticism of Anselm's argument. A. C. McGill has pointed out that in philosophy since the time of Kant this argument has been understood as attempting to move (illegitimately) from a purely mental concept to an existence that lies beyond the mental.[33] From the fact that we can think of a being than whom no greater can be conceived, and from the premise that such a being's actual existence would constitute that being to be greater than one who 'existed' as an object of thought alone, the argument tries to infer that the being than whom no greater can be conceived does in fact exist, or necessarily exists. And post-Kantian philosophers have in the main held that that inference is invalid.

Twentieth-century historical criticism, however, has argued that however correct these philosophers may have been in their criticism of the argument thus stated, its statement does an injustice to the argument of Anselm. (McGill, in fact, claims that the Anselmic form of the argument was not known either to Kant or to Thomas Aquinas, each of whom examined, not Anselm's work, but that of certain of his successors.) More particularly, twentieth-century historical critics have argued (1) that the Anselmic argument possessed a greater complexity than the philosophers have recognized, consisting at a minimum of three interconnected steps or stages, of which the argument cited above is but the first stage or step: the second stage is the argument to prove that the something-than-which-no-greater-can-be-conceived cannot be conceived as not existing, and the third stage (from *Proslogion* III, neglected, says McGill, by many philosophers) is to prove that this 'something' is actually the God contemplated in (Christian) theology, Creator of heaven and earth.[34] (2) The critics argue, further, that Anselm's motive in undertaking the argument has been misunderstood: his was not the rationalistic motive of establishing the existence of God by reasons that standing alone could refute disbelief, but was (in one view) the attempt of a believer to explicate for himself and his readers the content of his faith, or (in another view) the attempt of a mystical pilgrim toward God, Anselm himself, to use philosophical reflection as a kind of religious aphrodisiac, a means of arousing the religious vision, thus a means of finding God Himself.[35] This last view is supported by the fact that, as the name suggests, the entire *Proslogion* is offered by Anselm as a prayer, a cry to God. (3) Finally, the historical critics have attacked the philosophers in varying ways on the ground of their understanding of the rationale or logic of Anselm's argument. For example, one theory, widely held in the nineteenth century, is that the argument presupposes medieval or Platonic realism, the doctrine that ideas participate in the things that they represent, so that a real idea must represent reality itself. Thus, the historians argue, philosophic criticism cannot properly come to grips with Anselm unless it moves in the realm of such a doctrine of realism. This objection to the work of modern philosophers, however, seems not to take seriously the problem of truth. Philosophers will properly ask whether the realism that it is claimed Anselm depends upon is itself true.

When, however, McGill has surveyed in detail this and other proposed analyses of the rationale of Anselm's argument and has pointed out the difficulties in each, he finally concludes that "the traditional [i.e., rationalistic] view...has fallen out of favor, but no broadly accepted alternative has been found."[36] McGill has provided us with an interpretation of his own, which (he feels) overcomes that problem. He believes that the modern attempts to find a rationale are all "actually shaped by a common but unrecognized principle, and perhaps that principle is so alien to Anselm that no fully satisfactory interpretation can be achieved."[37] What is this principle?

In the first place, McGill calls attention to the stress that Anselm places upon the *words* that are used, particularly the words of the key phrase, "that than which nothing greater can be conceived." Thus, Anselm says, "However, when this very same fool *hears what I say,* when he *hears* of 'something than which nothing greater can be conceived,' he certainly understands what he hears."[38] And again, in the "Reply" to Gaunilo, Anselm is content to rest his case upon the meaning of the words, and the very *utterance* of them.

> [Anselm] argues that "something than which nothing greater can be conceived" must exist in reality, because otherwise it would contradict *the meaning of these words.* Since he makes no efforts to authorize and verify his phrase, Gaunilo directs some of his most vigorous attacks against this point. How can anything true ever be known simply on the basis of a word heard? In the face of this criticism, however, Anselm simply reaffirms his position. "In my argument nothing else is needed except uttering (*sonat*) the words, 'that than which a greater cannot be conceived.'"
>
> . . .
>
> The description of "conceiving what is heard" from the preacher is exactly parallel to the account of the atheist which Anselm gives in *Reply* VII. In the one case, the believer would never have faith if the preacher's *words* had not first communicated *their meaning* to him. In the other case, the unbeliever denies what is called "God" because he does not know the *meaning of this word.*[39]

However, modern interpreters (and here McGill means, apparently, both the modern philosophers and the modern historical critics) unanimously reject the principle that words can produce knowledge. Moderns, he says, regard language as an epiphenomenon.

> Men use it to *express* or *externalize* whatever lies within their minds. Words, they believe, do not produce thought — thought produces words and gives them whatever significance they may have. This means that if we want to find the meaning of any statement, we must discover what those who use it *have in mind.* We must penetrate their subjectivity.
>
> Every interpretation of the argument written during the last two centuries has been controlled by this hermeneutic principle.[40]

And McGill goes on to claim, against "this subjectivist theory of language," that an understanding of the *power and meaning* of language would overthrow the inadequacies of the last two centuries of interpretation and enable us to see how the Anselmic argument works in its own right.

Now, not all that McGill says here is clear. We do not understand how "thought produces words" or how "words produce thought," either. McGill seems to express himself concerning the "power" of words in almost an animistic or a mythical fashion. Yet what he says seems to be interpretable at many points in terms that we have developed. If we think of our "words" not in the sense of vocables or locutions, but as our utterances, our speech-acts, we too want to speak of their objective power. They have illocutionary force, or rather we exert such force with our words, our speech-acts. If we can understand Anselm's talk of uttering (*sonat*), not in terms of the production of physical sounds, but in terms of the production of linguistic acts; if, that is, Anselm's talk about something-than-which-nothing-greater-can-be-conceived can be accounted for in the terms that we have employed, then such language indeed has objective status. That does not mean that we merely shift from the claim that "thinking it makes it so" to the claim that "saying it makes it so." While the former is a distortion of Anselm's argument, the latter is a distortion not only of his argument but of all we say in this book. Rather the elements, the several sentences, of Anselm's argument are to be treated as speech-acts, and they are therefore subject to the sort of examination for happiness to which we have subjected another religious speech-act, Aleph's G. In particular, the conclusion of the Anselmic argument

T_a This God (the being than whom nothing greater can be conceived) necessarily exists

is subject to such analysis.

If the analysis is carried out, what is revealed? It appears that T_a functions for Anselm and for those who share his conviction set as what we have called a presiding conviction and that Anselm's argument is to show that T_a does function as a presupposition in that conviction set. That is why Anselm finds that denials of T_a issue in nonsense. Controversies over the validity of the argument, then, are not pointless; rather, they are efforts to discover whether T_a truly and consistently presides over this set. Thus, those philosophers or 'rationalists' who claim that Anselm's is a purely rational argument have a point. For it is rational in the only way the human mind can be, with not a wordless but a linguistic rationality.

However, there is also a point in the claim that Anselm's argument is a theological argument, which presupposes the faith of the community or the convictions that embody that faith. This is not negated by the fact that it sometimes takes account of the 'fool' who in a way does and in a way does not participate in that community of speakers. For in the argument the fool is one whose claim ("There is no God") is intelligible to the community, though it is necessarily false. Certainly, Anselm's is not an 'argument from authority' or 'from revelation' in the sense that Anselm was in any special or self-conscious way constricted or constrained in his rational inquiry. He was constrained by the conceptual or linguistic resources that were available to him in the conviction set that he embraced, but that is a characteristically human (rather than any special authoritarian) limitation. In saying that the argument is theological, then, we mean both to say that it is theological in the definitional sense that it is an exploration of the convictions within a conviction set in their interrelations and in their relation to whatever there is;[41] and theological as well in the narrower sense that in the argument Anselm is inquiring about the kind of God who is presupposed by the significance of the language that his linguistic community speaks.

This understanding of the argument and its conclusion T_a further suggests the role that the argument plays in intellectual and theological life today. It may be that Anselm lived in what Paul Tillich called a "theonomous" age. It seems evident that we do not. The existence of God is in no sense taken for granted in our times. Yet it is noteworthy that debate on the validity and force of the ontological argument is at least as lively in the twentieth century as that between Anselm and Gaunilo in the eleventh.[42] Both Norman Malcolm and Charles Hartshorne have put forward versions of the argument, and J. N. Findlay has written a kind of obverse ontological argument designed to show that on its terms God cannot exist.[43] As interesting as this debate is for its technical logical and semantic contributions and for its biographical disclosures concerning various philosophers, it also has a broader and more profound interest. Those philosophers and theologians engaged in it, like Anselm nine centuries earlier, are attempting to discover the foundations of their convictions, to set out the fundamental connections that give their lives the coherence they have. This is not a merely personal or subjective task. The logic and semantics involved are not Norman Malcolm's or J. N. Findlay's, but those of a language they share with each other and with us. And the convictions, if they are not so unequivocally shared, are the convictions of substantial portions of the world whose historical antecedents are Israel, Greece, and Rome. To the extent that we are in this world, we can hardly fail to be interested in the outcome of a dispute concerning its intellectual and convictional foundations. Even if one is separated from or alien to a world, to define one's stance in opposition to it requires a conception of what one is denying. If on the other hand one today wishes to share Anselm's faith, it is significant that such sharing is of a sort that requires restatement of the Anselmic argument in present-day terms.

In all the forms of the ontological arguments, it is either asserted or presupposed that there is a necessary connection among the ideas of goodness, coherence, perfection, and existence, while these ideas necessarily conflict with evil, incoherence, and nonexistence. Looked at in one way, disputes about the validity of the argument are really about one or more of these alleged connections. Those who hold that the argument is valid take these connections to be pretty much as the argument implies. Those who find it invalid take at least one of them (and usually all) to be contingent or even doubtful, so that the argument crumbles. But what is the basis for this finding of necessary connection or the lack of it? It must be the way in which these connections are related to the rest of our concepts, how they fit into the language of those who offer and criticize these arguments. Perhaps, then, the different assessments of these connections reflect different conceptual schemes. If this is so, each philosopher, both one who like Malcolm finds the argument valid and one who like Findlay finds it invalid, may be making a legitimate claim: what he says being faithful or true to the conceptual scheme or conviction set in which he participates. And the finding of validity or invalidity would then come to the same thing as the claim that T_a (or the like) does or does not preside over this (perhaps very general) set of convictions. If this is what he meant, Collingwood was right.

The argument at this point appears to lead to what in chapter I we called relativism: the view that those with a given conviction set are inevitably permanently foreclosed from assessing the beliefs of those with any other conviction set. In fact, as we intend to show, relativism is not a consequence of our view. But the convictional plurality we are here addressing, as well as our perspectival method, does make it a live option, which can be rejected only after some argument. At least in some way we must take account of the fact that what purports to be a purely philosophical argument (the ontological argument) seems to be appraised so nearly along the lines of the prior theological or antitheological beliefs of the appraisers.

We have been examining the content of one conviction that appears in some conviction sets, notably in Christian ones, with a view to discovering the role such a presupposition can play in the set and the way in which, if at all, it can be singly validated. The Anselmic argument for the existence of God has as its conclusion such a conviction. The point of the argument is to establish the conviction's presiding and presuppositional status. If the ontological argument is valid it does establish that status, and that is all the success it can have. What the argument cannot do is to establish the validity of the argument independent of the conviction set of its users; therefore if the argument is considered in a nontheistic conviction set, it will appear (and be) invalid. And what if it is considered apart from all conviction sets, apart from all linguistic frameworks? But what could such a question mean? To ask that question is to ask what our form of life would be if we had no form of life.

II. Scientific Reason

If pure reason, in the form of self-evident truth or deductive proof, cannot dissolve convictional barriers or leap over them, there is another candidate for these tasks, scientific reason, which may seem more promising to many a late-twentieth-century reader. Scientific methods are a subtle and powerful blend of experience (in the form of experiment and observation) and reason (in the form of constructs and theories), and their products, the special sciences, have performed so many wonders, from the early triumphs of astronomy to the latest exploits of microbiology, that we have become very cautious about setting limits to their achievements. This caution is especially evident among nonscientists, notably among religion scholars. Surely, some will hope, a sufficiently careful, subtle, and industrious application of the methods and results of the sciences could determine which of the various competing conviction sets are truly worthy of belief.

At the outset we need to make an important distinction between scientific results and scientific methods. Much of the discussion of the relation between science and religion has concentrated upon results. The leading religion in the West (Christianity), perhaps beguiled by earlier 'scientific' teaching, repeatedly favored what turned out to be unscientific views about the center of the universe, about the age of the earth, about the origin of the human species, about the role of Providence in human history. A series of conflicts pitted scientists who were destined for fame (Copernicus, Galileo, Darwin) against church leaders destined only for obscurity, and in case after case of conflict, religion ultimately saw that it had been on the losing side. In 1896 the first president of Cornell, Andrew Dickson White, published *A History of the Warfare of Science with Theology in Christendom* to establish the point: the relation between religion and science had been a war, and religion had lost the war. (Yet in his zeal to make that point, White often misrepresented the actual history.)[44]

Has spreading rationality been the key element here? For scientific results rationally to overturn religious doctrines (and thus challenge religious convictions), it is necessary for science to address the actual content of the doctrines themselves. And that may be easier said than done. Does (Christian) baptism wash away sin? Begin with a simplistic account. The scientist might observe a baptism and note its effects: the body immersed in water, the exchange of words, the emergence of the candidate dripping wet, and so forth. Such observations, together with what has already been established about water (chemical composition, boiling and freezing temperature, etc.) and about human psychology and physiology, will warrant a variety of conclusions about what can and cannot be cleansed away: soil and pollen can be, tuberculosis and cancer cannot. And what about sin? Well, we can't observe the sin; indeed, we cannot understand what "sin" means (what sin is) until we understand how it figures in the speech-acts of the community of users of the term. Consider the parallel in the case of promising: however clearly we hear the sound of Ann's promise to Bill and see the gesture of Bill's acceptance, we cannot at that level observe the obligation (to perform as Ann has promised) being created or assumed. The obligation, like the cleansing of sin, can be understood only by understanding the ways in which the language of the community of users (promisers or baptizers) functions. The situation regarding Aleph's G (chapter 3) was similar: whether God led the Israelites could be established only after we understood what those who confess this event mean in making that confession. "Sin" is observable, in other words, only when we know how the term figures in the speech-acts of the community of users of the term. Yet that requires going beyond empirical evidence narrowly construed and ourselves adopting (at least in imagination) the community conviction.

Thus a social science that undertakes to evaluate religious convictions cannot qualify itself for that task simply by claiming neutrality or indifference regarding the convictions concerned. Consider sociologist Vilfredo Pareto's scientific explanation of Christian baptism:

Christians have the custom of baptism. *If one knew the Christian procedure only one would not know whether and how it could be analyzed.* Moreover, we have an explanation of it: We are told that the rite of baptism is celebrated in order to remove original sin. That still is not enough.... But we do have other facts of that type. The pagans too had lustral water, and they used it for purposes of purification.... In cases where taboos have been violated, certain rites remove the pollution that a person has incurred in one set of circumstances or another. So the circle of similar facts widens, and in the great variety of devices and in the many explanations that are given for their use the thing which remains constant is the feeling, the sentiment, that the integrity of an individual which has been altered by certain causes, real or imaginary, can be restored by certain rites.... The human being has a vague feeling that water somehow cleanses moral as well as material pollutions. However, he does not, as a rule, justify his conduct in that manner. The explanation would be far too simple. So he goes looking for something more complicated, more pretentious, and readily finds what he is looking for.[45]

Pareto is here applying what he calls the "logico-experimental method" to the social and religious practice of baptism. But has he succeeded in giving an account of baptism at all? He has managed to indicate a class of similar phenomena, which includes Christian baptism, but only by ignoring (indeed, denying) the account of baptism given by its practitioners. On what basis does he do this? Not by showing the Christian account he mentions to be inconsistent, dishonest, disputed by other Christians, hypocritical, vague, or unintelligible (any of which might be true, but the proof of which would require Pareto to examine the account). Rather, he rejects it because the explanation the adherents offer does not meet his own previously established standards of appropriate explanation. Regarded thus 'from the outside,' the immersion of persons in water (or applying water to them in some other way) in ceremonial contexts may all seem similar. But *regarded from the outside,* can any sense at all be given to any of these apparently similar actions? Even in Pareto's account, concepts such as "lustral water," "pollution," "individual integrity," perhaps even "cleansing," rest on accounts given by those engaging in the practices.

Suppose we should remove even those references, since they are unobservable by Pareto's standards. Nothing would then remain beyond references to gross bodily movements and the utterance of now unintelligible words. That would mean removing all interest from the practices as human social phenomena. On the other hand, if we allow some part of the accounts given by adherents to those practices to govern our classifications, how are we to choose which part to accept? If the standard is amenability to explanation by our theories, that would not only violate the notion of independent confirmation central to scientific method, it would also make clear that the resultant explanation was based on our (scientific) convictions about the nature of facts, observations, explanations, etc. But the apparent alternative, examining each account on its merits, requires 'understanding from the inside,' that is, understanding that accepts the convictions of the baptizers (or pray-ers, or worshipers) and abandonment of the conceptual neutrality that scientists such as Pareto might have intended to maintain.

Pareto, writing as a sociologist, writes as if he had shown us that by reliance on sociology we can see that reliance on baptism is a mistake: it can't really wash away sin, and there isn't really any sin to wash away. The results of science (if he is right) challenge, correct, and in this case overturn the convictions of a religious community. That seems imperialistic and highly questionable. Yet what is the alternative? If we allow some part of the accounts given by the adherents, the practitioners of the practices, to govern our thinking, does that mean that whatever is practiced, merely because it is practiced, stands immune to challenge or correction from outside the community of conviction? We seem to be caught here in the dilemma with which this book began: that the alternative to convictional imperialism (in this case, the imperialism of Pareto's type of sociology) is relativism — the view that anything goes, so long as there is a community that sincerely believes it. In this view, no sense can be attached to the question (raised by outsiders such as Pareto) of what baptism means or whether it is justified: the very existence of a community that holds that baptism removes original sin shows that this is a reasonable or well-established conviction. At this point, we wish to postpone to the following chapter our constructive argument against rigid relativism. We merely note here the importance of remaining aware, in these cases, of the fact that multiple perspectives do exist.

There is also the question whether social science as represented by Pareto is the only, or the most suitable, sort of social science. We are not trying to prove that the social sciences are impossible. We do regard Pareto's errors as endemic to a particular approach to the social sciences, one that assumes that these sciences are nonconvictional and that also assumes that human actions can be reduced to bodily movements to which perhaps certain thoughts or attitudes or even words are added — rituals applied like so much decoration to bodies in ceremonial motion. The two assumptions are closely linked. For if the social sciences were conviction-neutral, their descriptions and explanations of human actions would be logically independent of the convictions held by the agents being investigated — in this case, the baptizers. But actions and convictions could be independent of one another in this way only if the convictions were irrelevant to the description or explanation of the action. In sum, the social scientist's results are not in the required sense conviction-neutral, because (1) they are logically linked to the scientist's own (social-scientific) convictions, while at the same time (2) they may rival or support the religious community's explanations of what it does, explanations that in turn are linked both with the practices being explained and with the relevant convictions of the community.

The only solution we have so far ruled out is a deliberately reductionist version of social science. Other versions, such as that represented by University of California sociologist Robert Bellah, are as sympathetic to religious convictions as Pareto's sort is unsympathetic.[46] Yet these versions take us no nearer our goal either, for such work only attempts an opposite weighting of the balances — convictional neutrality is not Bellah's intent. Theologians have been much taken with a lengthy and dense attack on the social science of the modern West by fellow theologian John Milbank. Well after the first edition of the present book appeared (but apparently in full innocence of its contents), Milbank launched his own account of the necessary connections between sociology and theology, showing that the methodological atheism of social science as it has developed in our era is not a neutral stance but of necessity a partisan one. American sociologists, from their presiding genius Talcott Parsons to such genial successors as Bellah and his associates, are censured by Milbank along with the rest for their marginalization of religion.[47] Similar difficulties attend the so-called "science of religion(s)" sponsored in some Western universities since the nineteenth century. Some versions of this discipline embrace a convictional stance that explicitly disqualifies it as the *umpire* of conviction sets, while other versions, by consciously eschewing such a stance, disavow any role as the judge of religious convictions.[48] That scientific *results* of this sort are irrelevant to this book's quest is all we mean to establish at this stage: we have still to ask whether scientific *methods* may lead on to our goal.

The changing face of scientific method in the half-century now ending is nearly as striking, to those aware of it, as the concrete scientific results of the same period.[49] School children three-quarters of a century ago were still being offered what experts call a Baconian view of the scientific task: confronted with persistent facts (Newton's apple tree forever shedding its apples downward, never sideways or upward) the scientist induces a law (in this case, the law of gravity) to account for the 'facts' thus haphazardly gathered, and science marches inductively forward. When some of those school children came to take up the tasks of the sciences, however, they found they needed an almost totally different set of methods. It has been the business of the philosophy of science to give account of these non-Baconian methods, and we must briefly treat them here. We recall from chapter 2 the rise of Logical Positivism, mainly in Vienna, between the two World Wars (1918–39). As we remarked there, this was a time of disillusionment; the 'Vienna Circle' philosophers who came to call themselves Logical Positivists had despaired of the inherited metaphysics, religion, and culture of their day, finding it all empty and in particularly sharp contrast to the achievements of science. We remember that they sought a linguistic distinction between the emptiness (as they saw it) of sentences such as "God is in heaven" and such positive assertions as "the electrons are in the cathode." Grammatically, these sentences look alike, and neither God nor electrons are gross physical objects, yet a *principle of demarcation* might nonetheless distinguish which sentence was and which was not scientific. This was the *verification principle of meaning:* if an assertion indeed asserted anything, its means of verification was its (only) meaning. For electrons, this verification was perhaps found if a bright spot appeared on the cathode ray tube when voltage was applied; for God — well, nothing would do. The sentences of religion only expressed emotion. The Logical Positivist view thus neatly dismissed religion; its dismissal required less than six pages in British Positivist A. J. Ayer's *Language, Truth and Logic,*[50] although Cambridge philosopher of science R. B. Braithwaite attempted to turn the position into a commendatory account of religious belief within a scientific worldview.[51]

In due course, the Logical Positivist program was undermined by its own rule of demarcation, the verification principle of meaning. For that principle could not itself be verified, nor was it analytic, i.e., self-evident. Perhaps then in all their careful work the Positivists had only been expressing their own sentiments? However that might be, philosophers of science wished for a better rule to guide scientific work. This was provided by Neo-positivists such as Karl Popper, another Austrian. Popper suggested that it was not verifiability but *falsifiability* that marked the demarcation between scientific assertions and all else. The theories of science, unlike those in other fields, are falsifiable, and a theory rightly survives (is accepted as true) until it is itself falsified by the data. If rival theories appear, the one most falsifiable (most vulnerable, we might say, to empirical attack) that nonetheless still stands (has not been falsified) is the winning theory. Light as waves versus light as particles was to be decided by inventing experiments that would test each and eventually produce a (falsifiable but unfalsified) winner. As philosopher of science Nancey Murphy has pointed out, falsifiability as a theory of scientific demarcation took one very important step that was little noticed at the time (1950s) of its appearance: Popper's theory marked "the beginning of the end of the Logical Positivists' *foundationalism.*"[52] Science began to perceive itself, not as resting upon logical deductions and indisputable evidence, but as a body of theories hovering over a swamp of shifting data. The various scientific theories were pilings driven into that swamp, stable enough for scientific purposes, yet resting on no ultimate bedrock of certainty. The 'facts' were those recognized by the community as facts. They were thus not self-evident, but always awaited further testing.

The first reaction of many philosophers of religion to the new falsificationism in science was highly favorable. They contrasted the splendid falsifiability-in-principle of science with the stodgy (often dogmatic) persistence of religious beliefs — persistence that this book has identified with convictions. Scientists under Karl Popper's guidance put forward rival theories and tested them, that is, attempted to falsify them by experiments suggested by the theories themselves, while religion stubbornly continued age-old practices such as prayer or baptism whose 'truth' seemed unfalsifiable and thus by this standard empty. A good illustration of a discussion of religion carried on in these terms is the "Theology and Falsification" chapter of *New Essays in Philosophical Theology* (1955), edited by Antony Flew and Alasdair MacIntyre. It represented an important new question in the philosophy of religion: was there any factual occurrence, even a hypothetical one, that could count so decisively against a religious belief such as "God loves us" as to lead believers to abandon that belief as a falsified hypothesis? Flew's contribution was a parable of two explorers who come to a clearing and argue whether there is a gardener who tends it. The 'believing' explorer says there is, but that the gardener is never seen because he is invisible — indeed, undetectable by any means (cf. "unfalsifiable"). But the other explorer objects that such a 'gardener' is no different than no gardener at all.[53] Translating the parable, if in actuality no event, not even being abandoned to a cruel death, could make believers give up belief in God (and generations of the faithful from Job in antiquity to religious martyrs in our own time seem to suggest that nothing could), does it not follow that "God loves us" has no claim to our assent since it could not be falsified? Is "God loves us," in the term of the original Logical Positivists, meaningless? Perversely, the falsifiability rule, when applied to religion, made the faithfulness-to-the-death of the martyrs' count *against* the meaningfulness of their faith! Perhaps, then, the falsifiability rule was inappropriate for religion? Yet surely religion made a real difference, as Flew demanded that it must.

To this point, the parallel between religion and the methods of modern science seemed mainly to work to the disadvantage of religion. Let us not forget, though, the larger question we are addressing at this stage, which is whether *on nonconvictional ground* anything could assess and rule in or rule out a set of convictions — either a religious set or a scientific one. Even if philosophers had been able to propose a suitable falsifiablity test for "God is love" that made that religious belief evidently falsifiable and still not falsified (such a test was in fact proposed by Basil Mitchell, one of the essayists just mentioned), we would not have reached our goal. Commitment to the falsification rule in science already presupposes some deep-seated (scientific) convictions that lack the neutrality we seem to need. An excellent account of the commitments entailed by the practice of science is Alastair McKinnon's *Falsification and Belief.*[54] In brief, McKinnon argues that some scientific beliefs, such as "the world has some order or other" lie beneath scientific work and yet are themselves unfalsifiable: no one can propose a test to falsify "the world has some order or other," yet it is (undeniably!) meaningful. McKinnon goes on to show that the same logic applies to religious belief and language; here again 'unfalsifiable' sentences appear.[55] These 'unfalsifiable' beliefs look to us very much like the convictions of their holders. In the preceding chapter we identified "presiding convictions," which seem to play the role that McKinnon's ultimate scientific beliefs do. Are convictions, then, unfalsifiable? We do not draw this conclusion; we only point out with McKinnon that falsificationist science is formed around its own *empirically* unfalsifiable convictions.

Doubts about falsification as a rule of demarcation provoked dissent among philosophers of science as well. We have already noted that Popper's work had begun to erode the foundationalism that the Logical Positivists had brought along, perhaps unawares, from their own philosophical roots. Popper's science did not rest upon indubitable foundational truths that nothing could shake. Now came the generation of the historians of science, including Stephen Toulmin, Paul Feyerabend, and Thomas Kuhn. The best known of these is Kuhn, an American who taught the history of science at Princeton University and whose book, *The Structure of Scientific Revolutions,*[56] is as familiar to workers in its field as T. S. Eliot's poetry is in his. Because he was by discipline a historian, Kuhn was in better position than his predecessors to see that the actual development of scientific thinking inconveniently failed to follow the logical patterns laid down by his more rationalist predecessors — or even Popper. In every science, Kuhn taught, a given experiment, learned and repeated by students in the course of their training, served as a current paradigm. Work was judged truly scientific not simply when counterexamples or anomalies (the stuff of Popper's theory) were curried and counted, but when that work conformed to the paradigmatic example that currently presided in its field. Thus the name "paradigm" might be given to the whole course of each "normal science" whose method followed that of its model experiment. Scientific revolutions (one of Kuhn's examples was the shift from phlogiston to oxygen as the component of air crucial to burning — see chapter 6 within) came when a new group of scientists (usually belonging to a new generation), ignoring the boundaries of the previous model, invented a new model and thereby achieved results their predecessors could not. Science was ordinarily 'converted' from an older to a newer paradigm mainly by the retirement and death of an older group of practitioners. Kuhn's historicist view of the progress of science was disquieting. Some called him an irrationalist. Others found his account liberating; among these were philosophers of religion and theologians such as Basil Mitchell, Ian Barbour, Hans Küng, and Nicholas Wolterstorff.[57] From our own point of view, it seems that while Kuhn with a wealth of examples helpfully described the actual workings of scientific rationality, he did not provide any reliable standard by which we might choose among competing conviction sets, unless the message addressed to older conviction sets is simply "Die off!" — a threat that, however realistic it is, still leaves our concerns unmet.

We come now to the most recent and for us the most challenging of the century's developments in the philosophy of science. Building on the work of Popper and Kuhn as well, Imre Lakatos, a Hungarian historian of science, produced a theory of scientific progress that has gained widespread acceptance in the field and has induced at least two prominent philosophers of religion to follow up his methodology in their own work.

Lakatos's contribution to scientific method is summarized in two lengthy research papers.[58] He deliberately stood upon the gains made by Popper and Kuhn and found ways to incorporate some of the work of each. Rather than paradigms, Lakatos refers to "scientific research programs." A research program is constituted by a cluster of related theories addressing a given body of data. One of these related theories, the "hard core," is essential to everything else in a given program. (The theory that light is transmitted in waves of measurable wave-length might be such a hard-core theory for some physics research program.) Yet the program cannot consist in a hard core alone; there must also be auxiliary theories — "theories of observation or of instrumentation and lower-level theories that apply the core theory in different kinds of cases."[59]

A research program does not abandon its defining hard core. When challenged by anomalies (falsifiers, in Popper's scheme) the program modifies, abandons, or adds additional theories (the "protective belt") in order to sustain the hard core. They prevent the entire program's being falsified as it seeks to take account of new data. A key insight was Lakatos's recognition that these modifications could either add to the program's empirical power, or they could be ad hoc — mere face-saving qualifications. In order to rule out such ad hoc modifications, he developed his criterion of "empirical progress." Empirically progressive programs were those whose new auxiliary hypotheses, not ad hoc ones, allowed for the successful prediction of "novel facts," i.e., facts, ultimately confirmed by experiment or observation, that would never have been noticed or would have been thought insignificant had it not been for the research program that yielded them.

For Lakatos, the history of science is best presented in terms of competing research programs — programs each with its own, different hard core. Headway is made as one or another research program makes empirical progress, providing more and more knowledge on the basis of its own theories and data. Headway is lost, and a particular research program (for example, in physics the research program that centered on the luminiferous ether) degenerates and is eventually abandoned when it ceases to make empirical progress.

There are further components in Lakatos's rationalizing account of the history of science (the so-called negative and positive heuristics, for example) but this brings us far enough along to attempt a summary statement for our purposes: Lakatos's answer to the problem of 'demarcation' (when do we, and when do we not, have a science?) was that a science is present whenever a series of related theories (as in a research program) yields increased empirical content over time. Astronomy, by that definition, is a science; its methods yield ever increasing knowledge of the cosmos; astrology, for all its deathless persistence, is not.

Our quest in this half-chapter is twofold. How can the work of some science apply to religion (this is the question about results, or to use Lakatos's phrase, empirical progress within a field), and second, does science offer a rational method that will permit us to choose between rival sets of religious or other convictions? It will be useful to return briefly to the question about results in light of Lakatos's contribution before concluding with this chapter's basic question: have we here an understanding of rationality that can resolve convictional disputes without a (circular) appeal to convictions? Does Lakatosian science (the most helpful scientific proposal available, as far as we can see) provide a tool for the conviction-free assessment of conviction sets?

Consider then the question whether there can be a *science* about religion (even if we retain for that science the old name "theology"!) that will, measured by scientific standards, be truly scientific — a bearer of knowledge about the concerns of religion fit to set alongside chemistry and geology and anthropology in science's hall of fame. That was the old dream of Catholic theologians, renewed by Protestants after the Enlightenment, and perhaps it has been that of theorists in still other religious bodies. Certainly it is the project of Nancey Murphy, a Berkeley philosopher of religion and science currently teaching at evangelical Fuller Theological Seminary in California. For Murphy, the rules and definitions of progressive science laid down by Lakatos apply equally well to historic Christianity on its theoretical side. If today's theologians would take those rules seriously, their work would become as scientific as Einstein's or Feynman's, as empirical as Crick's and Watson's.

Following Murphy, let us recall Lakatos's demand upon any real science: competition is of the essence of scientific thinking. So it would count *against* Christian theorizing being scientific if Christianity were intellectually all of a piece, with all its beliefs and practices laid down once for all by some inflexible authority. So far, Christianity passes the test very well — while convinced Christians often wish theirs were the only view of Christianity around, this is never the case, not even within old established Christian communions. If anyone objects that while theoretical conflict indeed characterizes modern Christianity, historically it was not so, this is easily shown to be wrong. Of course one remembers the Middle Ages, which saw both a Great Schism between East and West and also the series of sixteenth-century 'reforms,' consisting partly in profound doctrinal disputes that historians call the Reformation. One can turn still farther back, to the history of Christianity just after the New Testament was produced, a period in which 'sects' and 'parties' (including the self-styled Catholic 'sect' or 'party') abounded, to the dismay of the orthodox.[60] And recent study has confirmed that the New Testament itself reflects not a single theology or convictional viewpoint but a variety of such theologies, some of the main ones being the Pauline, the Petrine, and the Johannine. These are facts of which the discipline called New Testament theology has long been aware.[61] Murphy's contribution is to show that certain modern theological projects (she uses the Anabaptist tradition, the work of Jonathan Edwards, that of Ignatius Loyola, and especially that of the Roman Catholic Modernists Alfred Loisy, George Tyrrell, and Ernesto Buonaiuti, as well as the Swedish Lutheran Lundensian school and the work of Wolfhart Pannenberg as extended examples) fulfill not only the demand for competition and diversity, but severally the other requirements of a Lakatosian research program: one and another displays hard-core theories, protective belts of subsidiary theories, empirical data, and (at least potentially) progress including the discovery or production of 'novel facts.'[62] And they do all this, as Lakatos demanded science should, in competition with one another within the field.

Since the part of Murphy's work that may seem least credible to religious outsiders is her claim that the 'facts' to which religion attends are empirical, we had better see what count as empirical facts in her book. These are in general facts in the historical sense — events and circumstances from the broadest to the most personal scale in human history that demand explanation. Jonathan Edwards, facing a religious crisis in New England, wrote careful and extended accounts of human behavior observed in contemporary New England; these behavioral facts were selected in light of the theories Edwards advanced (for example, that God works by way of authentic conversions); other of his theories came into play to permit (empirical) distinction between authentic and inauthentic conversions.[63] George Tyrrell, Murphy's Catholic Modernist example, dealt with what he originally named "experiments": these were practical situations faced by individuals who cumulatively saw their own life situations working out in one way or another (perhaps obedience to Christ resulting in satisfaction to the experimenter and disobedience issuing in dissatisfaction instead). Such 'experiments' were cumulative, Tyrrell argued — the cumulative facts of collective society "pieced together into a mental construction of the spiritual world which is communicated by tradition to each member of society, to be received and modified."[64] A third example, D. C. Macintosh, a Baptist theologian at Yale, taught that the facts of religion were discovered when individuals and communities made a "right religious adjustment" to the empirical environment. When human beings did so, they found that "what the religious speak of as the 'promises' of God" were promises being kept.[65] A fourth example, German Lutheran theologian Wolfhart Pannenberg, has consciously attempted to weave historical data (including the historicity of the resurrection of Christ) into the fabric of his systematic theology in the manner of a research program that competes with contemporary secular interpretations for the explanation of "all reality."[66] In sum, the empirical facts of history and experience constitute a substantial part of the 'research programs' of Christianity on its intellectual side; such facts form the data of this surprisingly this-worldly religion. Murphy presents three of these theorists, the Lundensians, the Catholic Modernists, and Pannenberg, as each displaying all the features of a full-fledged research program.

However, Murphy wants more. Not only does the (Christian) theology that interests her do its work in "an age of scientific reasoning"; it should do it by more strict adherence to the methodology of Lakatosian scientific research programs so that theology would show itself in the fullest modern sense a science yielding knowledge. She sets out the requirements:[67] (1) Any scientific theology must have a hard core. This might very well be an irreducible account of the God Christians turn to in Jesus Christ; perhaps this will be a trinitarian account of God, God's holiness, and the revelation of God in Christ. (Pretty clearly, Murphy's is not a *reductionist* hard core!) Perhaps more generally a suitable theological hard core would be some central conviction or convictions of a community that are logically related to all the other convictions of the community addressed by a given theology. (2) Scientific theology must stick to its chosen hard core (in Lakatos's jargon, have a "negative heuristic"). From this it follows that theology, so far from simply accepting damaging counterevidence against its claims, must have an aggressive theoretical program in place as well: supposed disproofs of Christianity are in this way to be empirically shown as not that at all. So alongside the negative or defensive heuristic goes also (3) the positive heuristic: theology must embrace (within its 'auxiliary belt' of theories) a set of doctrinal teachings (doctrines, dogmas) that maintain the broad integrity of the teachings of the religious body envisioned by that theology and that lead to some 'novel facts.' This 'positive' task is easier conceived in religious settings that place a strong value upon constituted authority and its pronouncements (Roman Catholics, Lutherans); with church bodies formed on a more radical pattern, the 'positive heuristic' might instead be a "plan to treat all the traditional loci [of church teaching] in a way consistent with the teachings of Scripture." A third 'positive' approach might be (with a Schleiermacher) to relate everything to the sense of utter dependence he posited in all believers. In any case, the 'auxiliary hypotheses' or doctrines must be strongly related (in one direction) to the hard core that explains them, and in the other direction to the data (facts and experiences) that these doctrines themselves explain.[68] Murphy for her part would wish the data to come mainly from Scripture and from "the varied results of discernment" — a concept she explains in detail. Other approaches to theology as research program will doubtless select differently than she, *and the best program will win.*[69]

Here, then, we have a proposal to treat religion (on its theoretical side) scientifically. It is not the only such proposal,[70] but its logical integrity and the informed care with which it is worked out alike commend it. How far does this move us toward our present chapter's elusive goal — the discovery of a conviction-free standpoint from which to assess rival conviction sets? Not far enough. So far from showing how without convictions we can know what is worth knowing, the work of the most recent generation of philosophers of science, and centrally Lakatos, rather shows them to be even more deeply committed to (some) convictions than we might have expected. Our point is not to disparage scientific theology — we will have our own analogous suggestions to make in the two following chapters — but to remind ourselves of the limits science, and certainly scientific theology, face if the goal were to find a conviction-free basis for convictions. Paul Feyerabend, a well-respected senior member of the historicist school of philosophers of science, seemed to recognize this when he remarked (in a letter to Murphy) that since science was so highly regarded in the present world, it was probably "an important propaganda move" to show that theology, too, could be scientific.[71] If we see that "propaganda" is not here used in the sense of wicked falsehoods, but in the sense of rational argument based on what the propagandist hopes are shared convictions, the value (and the limits) of this work come at once into view.

One of the necessary characteristics of convictions is that we live by them — not just live our private lives, our home lives, but the whole of our lives including our intellectual lives. Consider, then, such presuppositions of today's science as the value of *simplicity* (simpler explanations are preferable to more complicated ones that reach the same result), the expectation of *empirical progress* (science advances, and today's science is correspondingly better than last year's), and *replicability* (nature responds uniformly to uniform experiments). If someone, whether a professional scientist or not, governs his or her working conduct and determines the acceptability of his or her intellectual beliefs by such presuppositions, then they play a central role in that person's life — the same sort of role that the Marxist, or New Age, or anarchist presuppositions play for their holders. They cannot themselves be justified by the use of scientific methods, for the methods depend on the presuppositions.

The apparently nonconvictional claim that the methods of science (or the methods of pragmatism) 'work' is not really nonconvictional at all. For what counts as working, and what they work for, are determined at least in part by one's convictions about what is valuable and one's (convictional) criteria for rationality, reliable experience, and the like. The consequence is that scientific utterances and those that logically depend upon them are in the same situation as utterances belonging to other activities. To understand a particular scientific statement — for example, "Water is composed of two gases" — we must understand the sense of the theoretical terms as well as the relations the statement has with other parts of scientific theory and with observations. It hardly needs to be added that the same is true of reports of religious discernment. As Lakatos emphasized, what we consider to be the facts is determined in part by our acceptance of theories linked to relevant scientific presuppositions. If in a particular science we count telescopic sightings, photographic plates, and radar blips, but not dream reports, drug-induced visions, or astrological charts, one reason is the compatibility of counting the former and the incompatibility of counting the latter with the particular scientific theories then engaged. As a Lakatosian might put it, the auxiliary belt determines whether proposed data qualify for acceptance. On the other hand, the fact that statements are understood and even accepted within a science does not provide sufficient ground for assenting to them unless we have grounds of some sort for accepting the convictions (or presuppositions) on which they are based.

None of this, as we see it, counts against the worth and integrity of the scientific project as a whole, or against the worth and integrity of theology or religious theory carried on by such scientific methods. Whether such a project in religion is good "propaganda," as Feyerabend suggested, or a somewhat loftier task fully worth a lifetime of effort, it is in any case the sort of work that a community of conviction (such as the Christian or alternatively the Buddhist one) needs to engage in. And Lakatos (via Murphy) provides help to such community theorists facing rival theological traditions. Although the grounds they offer are not conviction-neutral, they are, it should be remembered, very widely shared, at least in the West. As we sought to show in chapters 3 and 4, community-justifiable beliefs, like happy speech-acts, make for the authenticity of persons in community and for the authenticity of the communities themselves. What we had sought, though, was a shortcut — a way to address those outside our own communities in terms of a common rationality that would not merely propagandize others to our own faith but speak to them in terms they could not (rationally) refuse. Science standing by itself cannot attain that goal in the wide world because it is a convictional enterprise. It follows that scientific theology, that is, a given convictional community's theology that adopts strict scientific methods in its work, cannot do so either, and that for two related reasons: the convictional nature of the methods of science and the convictional content of the doctrines and presuppositions of the religious community itself.

In the Middle Ages and again in modernity, thoughtful theorists who were distressed by the quarrels of rival religious communities turned back to a mode of thought as old as Plato and Cicero — natural theology. What could be known of the gods or God if the knower gave up all claims to particular revelations via Moses or Jesus or Muhammad, all ideas of contemporary churchly authority, and asked the questions of theology in light of 'nature' alone — sun, moon and stars, the appearance and growth of life on earth, human reasoning capacity and its reach?[72] In the late nineteenth century, a lecture series in the Scottish national universities, the Gifford Lectures, was founded to continue to pursue these questions. By that time, much of the ground addressed had been worked beyond productivity: Hume and Kant had already showed that (according to the presuppositions of their age) the positive results to be obtained were minimal. The first half of this chapter, written in light of these earlier philosophical discussions, has displayed once more how fruitless is the attempt to validate (or invalidate) just one widely shared religious conviction (the reality of God) on conviction-neutral grounds.

Some have argued, though, that the terms of 'natural' theology were artificially constricted if they omitted from consideration the content of human religions. Never mind the claims to revelation made for the contents of the Koran or the Bible. Did not the actual human religiousness — the faith — to which these books witnessed have its claim to lay upon every natural theology? A recent example of such argument is Wilfred Cantwell Smith's *Towards a World Theology*.[73] Smith believes that each religious community (as we have seen in chapter 1, he eschews the word "religion") can make an informed, theological approach to all of the others, so that there will appear after much labor a 'Christian' theology of comparative religion, a 'Muslim' theology of comparative religion, and so on. These may converge, finally, toward a "faith" that will embrace all — not to exclude the 'faith' of the atheistic protest against any and all religion.[74] Smith's proposal is not to eliminate convictions but to discover their convergence. Something like it will occupy us in the remaining chapters.

Meanwhile, we have found no single, swift solution to the problem of convictional justification. But why should we expect to find one? Convictions, being those beliefs that govern all our lives, must be judged in the court of all our experience — and that of our ancestors and progeny as well. Nevertheless, our discussion of these problems has yielded results that will help us to delineate the task of justification to which we now turn afresh.

S I X

If good or bad acts of will do alter the world, it can only be the limits of the world that they alter, not the facts, not what can be expressed by means of language.

In short their effect must be that it becomes an altogether different world. It must, so to speak, wax and wane as a whole.

The world of the happy man is a different one from that of the unhappy man.

Ludwig Wittgenstein[1]

It is my impression that many philosophers do not like Wittgenstein's comparing what he calls his 'methods' to therapies; but for me part of what he means by this comparison is brought out in thinking of the progress of psychoanalytic therapy. The more one learns, so to speak, the hang of oneself, and mounts one's problems, the less one is able to say what one has learned; not because you have forgotten what it was, but because nothing you said would seem like an answer or a solution: there is no longer any question or problem which your words would match. You have reached conviction, but not about a proposition; and consistency, but not in a theory. You are different, what you recognize as problems are different, your world is different.

Stanley Cavell[2]

The Process of Justification

We have now brought into sharper relief the discordant state of affairs presented in chapter 1, our existence in a plural world whose inhabitants disagree about many things that matter most. It is not merely that we do not agree: *we cannot even clearly disagree.* The preceding chapter explored the claim that by pure science or pure reason, plurality, so far as it is a problem, can be straightway overcome. We saw that such claims do not take convictional disputes with sufficient seriousness — a fault of all the shunt proposals for justifying or rejecting convictions. The examination of these shortcut solutions has not been time wasted, nor merely the disposing of objections to our own thesis; we need such enterprises as science and reason in the justificatory task, and even the drive to eliminate convictions may be fruitful in some circumstances.

We now turn our attention to a challenge from those who take pluralism not too lightly, but too seriously. These see plurality not merely as a cause for concern, but as a reason for surrender. They embrace pluralism either with skeptical satisfaction or with slothful despair: "We are all in convictional prisons; we cannot escape them if we would." Such hard relativists would hold that "I am my convictions" (that tantalizing motto) means that we are no more able to adjudicate our convictions across convictional lines than we are able to jump out of our own skins. To refute this position will be a hard task if, as they claim, it is immune to external argument in this way.

But there is a general argument against relativism if taken seriously: it is paradoxical to the point of self-contradiction. For it holds, first, that one can view reality only from one's own perspective, and, second, that they know perfectly well that interconvictional justification or criticism of convictions is not possible from *any* perspective. If as relativists claim they are so enclosed in their own perspective, how can they know what is

149

impossible to all others? If on the other hand they retreat to the claim that at least transconvictional criticisms cannot penetrate *their* perspective, we can respect their testimony about their own view of the matter without assuming that this view is correct. For if they acknowledge that they may be wrong about the convictional prisons in which others are confined, may they not also be mistaken about possible ways of escape from and access to their own outlook? If all this is conceded, relativism seems a shaky theory indeed. Yet if we are to reject it, we need assurance that transconvictional criticism and justification can indeed occur. We must now show the possibility of this occurrence, or (to speak more accurately) the possibility of this process.

I. The Language of the Process

Both imperialists and relativists tend to judge the possibility of justifying religious convictions, or disputed convictions of other sorts, without recognizing the historical contingency of the state of affairs they are judging. The present state of religion in the Western world is a historical novelty. For a very long time the Western intellectual and spiritual heritage, Hellenic, Hebraic, and Christian, was not seriously challenged by any outside tradition. There were, of course, Jews as an implicit challenge to Christians, and Christians as an explicit challenge (or threat) to Jews, but that controversy, like the party struggles within the Christian religion itself, could be understood as a family quarrel within a single convictional community. (The more terrible the outcome of those quarrels, the more apt the analogy, for it is ever our kin whom we murder.) The Muslim threat to the West was ended by the end of the Middle Ages. From then until the nineteenth century, encounters of voyagers and traders, explorers and missionaries with those outside the Western tradition were regarded more as oddities and marvels than as problems for justification across convictional lines.[3] To the degree that convictional differences within the Western family *did* appear profound, they tended to be settled by means of spatial separation — *cuius regio eius religio,* "as goes the sovereignty, so goes the worship," sufficed to define Protestant-Catholic relations, and the ghetto sufficed for the Jew — rather than by anyone's justifying beliefs in terms others could comprehend, and so the question of interconvictional adjudication did not forcefully arise.

Thus the pluralist consciousness that is characteristic of contemporary culture is a relatively recent arrival in our intellectual tradition. If we have not found ways to handle the problems it presents, this may be a function of the novelty of the situation. We hold that our solution of these problems is sure to be a time-consuming task, more likely to be measured in centuries than in shorter seasons of time. It will take time to show that secular atheism (or Anabaptist Christianity, or Maoist Marxism, or Vedantic Hinduism) is or is not an adequate conviction set, or the adequate conviction set. Present confusion in these matters, then, is not necessarily hopeless or pointless; time may well yield satisfactory changes in our state of convictional disorder. But the passage of time, though it may be necessary, is rarely sufficient for the resolving of serious problems, any more than it is for producing maturity in a newborn infant.

Indeed, our theory of speech-acts and their relation to convictions suggests that this analogy is worth more attention. Consider the situation of an infant learning its 'native' tongue. The earliest cooings, gurgles, and blurts of sound give way, ever so gradually, to primitive speech-acts: "da da," or "go bye-bye," or (perhaps least mistakable) "me!" So crude are these at the outset that listeners are not sure whether the linguistic level, as opposed to mere imitative cries, has been attained: in any case the child's progress depends in part upon very generous appreciation of every success. Part of the learning of a language is saying it the wrong way; that is, issuing speech-acts that are in a variety of ways and degrees unhappy. Yet there is promise in precisely these unhappy utterances: once past the threshold, they are indeed functional speech-acts, and the loving family makes even the most ludicrous beginner's talk the occasion for congratulation and shared joy as well as for merriment. Nor is this congratulation in any way ironic; the technically unhappy utterances are stages on the way to happy ones.

Are such circumstances in any way like the circumstances of folk of diverse convictional communities living through a time of learning how they may in their pluralist age happily talk together or justifiably embrace some set of convictions? The illustration is, of course, inept; it presupposes the established linguistic world of adults as a norm that measures the present unhappiness in the speech of the infant learners. But if we can imagine a race of babes on its own, groping to know what to say, disagreeing with one another in many ways, and struggling toward a language in which to express their disagreements, the analogy acquires considerable strength. In that way, this infant race represents our own.

As a second suggestive analogy consider a time of political upheaval in which a traditional monarchy is seized by a fit of republican fervor. Royalty is deposed, denied its divine right to rule, denied all monarchical rights. There *are* no kings among us, it is said. But the discarded 'king' lives on in his country. Was he once a king? To say that he was is to admit a term that is denied all status in the new egalitarian theory. On the other hand, to avoid saying that he once was king makes it difficult to explain what the revolution has achieved. The time of linguistic uncertainty has come. Neither "we once had kings" nor "we never had kings" seems quite adequate to the situation. But with the passing of the years, remembered (and even surviving) kings, no longer a threat to republicanism, are again mentionable. "Look, there's old King Julio; I remember when he was the king." Has "king" acquired a new meaning then? It seems more accurate to say not that the *word* has changed but that everything has changed, including those words once so unspeakable. If anyone believes that this story of kings is a parable, we shall not disagree, only adding that similar stories could be told of institutional change inseparable from linguistic, using "property," or "slaves," or perhaps "witches" in the place of "kings."[4]

Similar crises appear in other fields. Thomas Kuhn records one in connection with the discovery of oxygen.[5] Who discovered it? Of the two principal candidates for this honor, one, Joseph Priestley, collected gas released by heated red oxide of mercury and identified it in 1774 as nitrous oxide and in 1775 as "common air with less than its usual quantity of phlogiston." The other, Antoine Lavoisier, started later, but held by 1775 that the gas thus obtained was a distinct species, one of the two chief constituents of air, a conclusion Priestley never accepted. So far Lavoisier may appear the winner, since Priestley never knew what he had found. Yet Lavoisier's claim, too, must be questioned, for throughout his days he held that oxygen was "an atomic 'Principle of acidity,'" while oxygen gas, he thought, resulted only from the union of that 'principle' with caloric, the 'matter' of heat. Was oxygen then not yet 'discovered' in 1777? Perhaps not, but, says Kuhn,

> the principle of acidity was not banished from chemistry until after 1810, and caloric lingered until the 1860's. Oxygen had become a standard chemical substance before either of those dates.[6]

What the history of science requires, Kuhn argues, is a changed understanding of what scientific discovery in such cases amounts to — a new view of the role of anomalies, of scientific paradigms, and of the respective roles of 'theory' and of 'fact' in science, for "until the scientist has learned to see nature in a different way (i.e., acquired a new theory) — the new fact is not quite a scientific fact at all."[7] For us the story of the problematic 'discovery' of oxygen affords another illustration of the barriers to understanding raised by changing conceptions (and, Kuhn would add, changing scientific commitments), barriers at once conceptual and linguistic.

No one of these illustrations, the speech of infants, the linguistic crisis of a social upheaval, or the language changes involved in scientific revolutions, is a full analogue of the crisis of the justification of convictions confronted in contemporary convictional pluralism, but each suggests that the temporary unhappiness of language, or temporary unjustifiability of convictions, may be a necessary and thus desirable state on the way to long-run justifiability and happy utterance. In this view, we humans are a classroom of children learning to express happily our deepest prehensions — our generation (in Lessing's metaphor) a single school-day in the education of the human race.

Such a way of viewing the matter is not inimical to religion, or at least not inimical to all religious traditions. We spoke above of long periods when the shared convictions of our civilization faced no external challenge. It is helpful to remember that during these very periods the chief Western mystics flourished. Some philosophers like to point out that classical mysticism regards all talk about the mystical, including its own, as unsuitable. Often this fact receives ironic treatment — for the mystics nevertheless write such long discourses! But if there is irony here, it lies, according to the mystics, at a somewhat deeper level, not in the fact that they do speak, but in the very situation whereof they speak. For speak they must. Their talk, they feel, is at once inappropriate and unavoidable; in our terms unhappy but not meaningless, not mere babble.

Such a strand is even more deeply imbedded in the biblical tradition. Thus the Apostle Paul characteristically speaks of (what we would call) religious knowledge as somehow flawed, obscured, partial. "For now we see through a glass, darkly; but then face to face: now I know in part; but then shall I know even as also I am known" (1 Cor. 13:12, KJV). And he employs the illustration we have given a few paragraphs above: "When I was a child, I spake as a child, I understood as a child, I thought as a child" (1 Cor. 13:11, KJV). In the realm of convictional utterance, Paul believed, he was still 'childish,' still inept; he awaited an eschatological time when this ineptitude would be removed.[8] Similar instances can be found in the speech of Jesus according to the Gospels and in the prophetic books of the Old Testament. Indeed our earlier remarks about a stable period when convictional speakers knew perfectly well 'what it was in order to say when' in matters of faith may have been misleading. The history of religions, or at least the history of prophetic religion, is the history of turmoil. The normative periods in such turbulent communities are not eras of stable continuity, but revolutionary times when talk of the gods is challenged from within (often in the name of the gods or of God) by the prophets.

In this view, it might appear that no authentic utterance can ever be acceptable to more than a prophetic minority to whom their own speech, however compelled they may be to utter it, will seem perplexingly at variance with recognized norms. Confessing that one's convictions are absurd, 'impossible,' or foolish is not, in the view of such saints, mere hyperbole. But while the apostolic message may seem foolish, it is "God's foolishness" and therefore wiser than conventional human wisdom (cf. I Cor. I). While the apostle now speaks "as a child," he envisions a day when his talk will be mature, when he will know as he is known by God. Thus even the inspired minority appeals to 'wisdom' or 'knowledge' or 'mature speech' *in the long run.*[9] Since this is so, we may do well to move on from our examination of the imbedding of speech in communities to see how these considerations of justification may be affected by the appeal to what are usually called 'ultimate criteria.'

II. The Loci of the Process

Justification, as we have used the term, is not a once-and-for-all yes-or-no achievement but an ongoing task of any who have convictions. That task includes attempts to meet current objections and to present evidence to show that the conditions for happiness of one's convictional speech *can* be satisfied. We have already observed that claims for the adequacy of conviction sets have very often involved broad appeals to considerations like truth, consistency, rationality, *eudaimonia,* satisfaction, and righteousness. These considerations cannot be regarded as neutral, for they themselves are convictional in practice; nor are they universally accepted bases of justification, for they are the perennial battlegrounds of convictional warfare. Only their generality and vagueness makes it possible for them to be used so widely as appeals.

To argue here for a particular significance for these considerations or a particular use of them in debate would be an exercise in what we shall (in the final chapter) call theoretics — the assumption of a particular convictional stance and the offering of an *apologia* for it — rather than our present philosophical task of asking how such justifications can in general go. In any event, the appeals we have listed are not mutually exclusive nor is our list exhaustive. For example, it omits the compelling concept of *beauty,* though there are those who might allow it to do duty for all the rest, while others might insist on *peace, love, justice, holiness,* or still others. Moreover, anyone can refrain from appealing to any one of these considerations without being inconsistent or absurd. So we cannot argue that any one of them must be accepted as a criterion for a happy conviction set. But if there is no logically necessary member of the list, and no single list that will satisfy all comers, we think it better to regard the possible terms of all such lists not as criteria but as possible loci of justification. To the traveler negotiating the traffic of justification these will appear as main intersections, junction points of reflection, criticism, debate, and correction. No one justifies his or her convictions without crossing some of these intersections; many find that they have to negotiate all that we have mentioned and others as well. That this is so is a contingent fact about our world — but it is about the only world, the only form of life, with which we have to do. What we will do here is to consider one important locus of justification, namely, *truth,* in order to show how it plays the role we ascribe to the loci. We will then leave to the reader the task of applying our remarks to other loci.

Disagreement about the desirability of truth is extraordinary. Those who, like Braithwaite, hold that religious principles are themselves neither true nor false nevertheless regard it important that their own overall *account* of religion should be true. Conversely those who reject scientific investigation generally do so not because they question the goal of truth, but because they doubt the efficacy of science in attaining it, or because they see the work of science as conflicting with some other goal that they hold to be equally, or even more, important, or because they hold that another method than the scientific attains truth that disproves the 'truth' (as they say) of science. The widespread commitment to 'truth' implied in these examples has suggested to some that truth is an empty concept. Even in its high generality, however, a term like "truth" is not devoid of meaning: adoption of it as a goal, as Aristotle saw,[10] does limit the range of choices one may consistently make, though it does not sufficiently narrow that range. We will understand, for example, the person who in the search for truth puts more weight on 'correspondence' between statement and fact or on 'coherence' among statements, and we can be prepared for one who is more interested in 'performative' or in 'pragmatic' features of truth. Yet the failure of such specialized theories to carry the field suggests that the locus truth is broader than any one of them can show.[11]

It is not a part of our plan to engage in a systematic analysis of "truth" and "true." But it may be illuminating to call attention to the way in which one religious theorist, Wilfred Cantwell Smith, has employed the concept and to point out some of the assets and liabilities of his account. Smith notes some disparate uses of "true" in religion. Some speak of a particular religion's being true: "Christianity is true"; "Islam is true." But the difficulty here, he holds, is that it is not at all clear (except in very specialized contexts) what is meant. One possibility is that "Islam is true" means that present-day Islam conforms to prototypical Islam, Islam as revealed by God to Muhammad. Here "true" means "genuine" or "authentic." But to claim that the prototype is true in the sense just indicated would then be meaningless. Is there any other sense? Smith doubts that there is. Religions, he holds, are not just statements or sentences; they are living historic realities and as such no more to be judged true or false than Mt. Everest is to be judged true or false — it is just *there*.

> Like Mt. Everest, you may like them, or you may not; you may decide to climb them, or you may not; you may feel that you can trust them to bear your weight or not, or the weight of those who, unlike you, have pitched their tents on their slopes.
> Yet whatever your attitude to them, they are more like Mt. Everest than they are like a proposition in science. The latter may be true or false, but historical facts and social institutions are existent actualities.[12]

So in this view we cannot speak of a "true" religion (save in the sense of "authentic" or "genuine"). Yet Smith claims that we can speak of "true religious life," or "the truth of *my* Christianity (Islam, Buddhism)," and correspondingly of the "truth" of this or that person's Christianity (etc.), and that we can speak of this one's Christianity being "truer than" the Christianity of that one. By such use, he means to distinguish between those whose religion is mere outward form or show and those whose religion is inner life.

We have no quarrel with this use among others, but we note that there remains a difference, which Smith's account cannot make clear, between sincere attachment to a false belief and hypocritical profession of a true belief. The convictional protestations of a fraud or hypocrite need to be marked as faulty, but they need to be so marked without confusing the issue of the truth or falsity of that about which he or she is hypocritical. In the assessment of Aleph's speech-act, *one* kind of unhappiness (representative) was liable to arise through the failure of Israel to have crossed the Reed Sea, or God to be God; *another* through Aleph's failure to take up the appropriate stance of one who was issuing such a confession, and to witness thereto, or to fail in the intentions and behavior that are the affective implicates of his speech-act. It was in the latter that questions such as sincerity and hypocrisy were examined, while it was in connection with the former that questions of truth arose.

But it may now be objected that we have argued in a circle. When the justification of individual convictions was at issue, we remarked that in many and crucial cases convictions would stand or fall with the set in which they inhered, the total outlook to which they gave spine. Now we are discussing in summary certain considerations that enter into the justification of whole sets, yet we refer to the earlier discussion of the representative aspect of *particular* speech-acts. Is the reader then in the position of someone handed a card, on the front and back of which is printed merely "See other side"? Not quite. For the interconnected justification of many related convictions, though more arduous, may not be so barren as would the assessment of any one of them while disregarding the others. The assessor of the truth of conviction sets may be like the interpreter of an unclear photograph, composed of many blurred spots and indefinite blotches. Attention to the spots alone (the several singular convictions) may never yield results. Yet the interpretation of the whole photograph cannot be achieved save by bringing each blurred part of it as sharply as possible into focus.

Take this question about the 'truth of' a theistic religion such as Christianity, or of a meta-historical theory of history such as Marxism, or of a typical Western convictional outlook such as free enterprise economy. In such systems, there will be beliefs having representative dimensions relatively easy to examine for truth value and other representations much harder to bring under such assessment, as our earlier examples have shown. To be sure, religions are not mere sets of beliefs — recognition of just this led us to the notion of convictions, beliefs that are crucial clues to life and character. Thus we showed a connection between belief and life even while providing for a discriminable central set of beliefs that could be assessed and found worthy or unworthy. In doing this, moreover, we were prepared to give up the idea that *truth alone* could discriminate worthy from unworthy convictions. So the considerations besides true or false that Smith urges may enter into the assessment of the religion of a given tribe:

> beautiful or ugly, edifying or wicked, rational or grotesque, poetic or prosaic, helpful or obstructive, cohesive or disruptive; ... the opiate of people, or the form of social progress; the channel through which they know God insofar as they do know Him, or a totally human contrivance ... [13]

are all ones that we would regard as potential canons of the adequacy of the conviction set that the tribal religion embodies and reflects, the canons being applied either directly to the convictions themselves or to the life with which they can be linked by the rules of meaning we have investigated. It seems reasonable that the process of justification should take hold where it can as it can, seeking to know the truth of those convictions capable of direct assessment, the coherence with these of others, and seeking to apply to all the convictions the further relevant considerations — *eudaimonia,* righteousness, and the like.

While the sort of inquiry represented in these pages by Scriven and Farrer produced, we showed, no knock-down, conviction-free results, yet the considerations to which they respectively appealed are certainly relevant to belief in the existence and nature of God, and similar considerations would be relevant to the truth of other religious (or metaphysical) conviction sets. But "true" and "false" are not the only possible assessments. Very often someone will say of a conviction that it is "truer" than another or that it is the "truest" available, without wanting to claim that it is "true" *simpliciter.* At the same time, "true" and "false," as Austin and others have reminded us, are members of a class of terms that includes also "accurate" and "careless," "rough" and "exact," "fair" and "hasty," and a host of others.

Keeping the preceding cautions in mind, however, we can reiterate our insistence that truth may indeed appear among the loci when religion is at issue. We have recognized that such beliefs as the Christian belief in the existence of God are much more than mere beliefs; they are obliged to be convictions if they are to be felicitous. Our report on several recent theories of religious language in chapter 2 shows how difficult it is for any theory to display the sense and reference of *all* religious talk. The conviction that the world is created (and thus that there truly is a Creator and a world) and the conviction that its Creator is Lord of all and active Redeemer of all are just what provide in traditional Christianity the grounds for the claim that the agapeistic way of life is (alone) satisfactory, that the sacrifices it demands cannot be in all senses vain or empty, that whatever the limits and failure of human effort, there is assurance that the poor, the merciful, the seekers of righteousness of whom Jesus spoke are indeed blessed. Likewise Mahayana Buddhism cannot in fidelity to its tradition be merely the inculcation of the Bodhisattva ideal; there must also be the real Manushi Buddhas, whose attainment of the ideal is not a mere tale, but the truth that must be told. These are obvious illustrations, but other, more agnostic styles of conviction also have their representative element, even if these are convictions about what is *not* the case — e.g., no hell in Universalism, no soul in Theravada Buddhism. Although our discussion has throughout insisted on the necessity of recognizing the other elements in convictional language, we have also been at pains to emphasize the widespread importance of this representative element. Without it, religious belief of the sorts we have studied here comes close to justifying the charge made by one of its concerned critics: it becomes only a "retreat to commitment."[14] We have argued above that there is no easy appeal 'to the facts' in questions of convictional difference: our apprehension of facts, the very kinds of facts there are, will be determined in part by the convictions we hold. Yet this does not free us from the task of referring to the discoverable facts or adjusting our convictions themselves to the way things really are. To seek to do so is to take truth seriously. And if truth or falsity is irrelevant to the most important commitments we make, it will be difficult indeed to insist on the importance of truth in less momentous questions.

We can consider now more briefly the place of consistency among the loci. In a sense, it could be regarded as part of the locus truth. For an inconsistent conviction set is certain to have a false conviction. Consistency, on the other hand, can hardly stand alone. For hardly anyone will consciously embrace false or empty convictions on the mere ground that, being false or empty, they are (therefore) consistent. On the other hand, if someone is genuinely unconcerned with logical consistency, either in the use of her words or in the avoidance of contradictions, then all attempts at justification addressed to her are futile. But this concession in no way constitutes a victory for the irrationalist over his opponents or even a standoff between the two. The irrationalist can't *have* victories, not ones consistently so described; he never knows, is never in position to tell us, when defeat may be victory or victory defeat, for he has renounced such consistencies as knowing that. So they can't be victories from his point of view — he hasn't a point of view — and that hardly constitutes a defeat for the rest of us.

If on the other hand someone takes the position that while logical consistency is necessary she is perfectly content with practical inconsistencies in her life, we are on more intelligible and familiar ground. It is, however, no more comfortable ground for the skeptic. For to be unconcerned about consistency of this kind is tantamount to rejecting the idea of having any convictions other than whatever minimum is necessary to logical consistency itself. And this takes us back to an earlier argument (chap. 4), where we conceded that a person could set out to minimize his

or her convictions, but argued that those people who seek to make rud-
derless boats of their lives (1) do after all have *that* (apparently needless)
conviction, and (2) turn out to be people who, not knowing what they
want, are unable to plan their lives so as to get it, and thus seem especially likely not to live well, not to be happy folk. In any case, they are
in no position to justify their way of life, since they forfeit every form
of those appeals (such as to consistency and happiness) that are the very
marrow of justification.

On the other hand it is not a logical necessity that one must have more
than a minimal set of convictions. It is just that in general folk do, and
even more generally they are unhappy when they do not. This conclusion
may be disappointing for those who hoped for some logical necessity on
which to rest, *ne plus ultra*. It is important, however, to see that this hope
is ephemeral. It is the contingent fact that human beings agree as much as
they do that makes it possible for them to disagree and argue intelligibly.
Men and women are not content with overt inconsistency; they prefer satisfaction to frustration; they are uncomfortable being ignorant or doubtful
about the future. If there were not agreement on such matters, there would
be no considerations to offer to incline others in one direction or another,
and a shared life (in which justification and attempts to persuade and convert play an important role) would be impossible. There might not have
been areas of such agreement; this shared life itself might not have existed; both these are logical possibilities. Given the existing agreements,
appeals to these and to consistency are practical necessities in the task of
justification, but they are not sufficient appeals; they do not enable us to
discard other loci such as righteousness or justice. Influenced by different
circumstances, different ones of us may take our stand upon different loci.

To call the appeal to any particular locus no more than a "practical necessity" and to acknowledge that our common fund of agreement is only
contingent may seem to concede too much to unreason. If the loci are not
logically required criteria, is there any hope of an acceptable justification?
But this complaint forgets or ignores certain features of the complex task
we call justification. Remember, first, that utter neglect of such a locus
as truth has been seen to be extremely rare, to say the least. Remember,
further, that any particular disagreement, even about which loci are to
be considered, implies some sort of agreement as well. We should recognize, too, that not every difference in action (including speech-action)
rests on a disagreement. Here we invoke in another way the temporal
considerations with which we began our discussion of justification. Two
persons living in different circumstances may act very differently, even

though they have common convictions. A convinced Marxist living in an advanced industrial society will have very different tasks than one living in a rural, semifeudal society. Similar considerations evidently apply to Jewish or to Christian conviction sets. Thus diverse actions may express shared convictions and count for the justification-in-practice of the same convictions.

But if circumstances differ, so do human beings. No two people are exactly the same, and none at a given time is exactly as he or she was or will be at other times. It is surely not effete skepticism, relativism, or irrationalism, but common sense both to recognize individual differences within our common humanity and to admit our own changes over the period of our lives. We may be equally devoted to health at seventeen and at forty-seven, but that does not mean that we eat, sleep, and exercise in the same ways at both ages. If, as we are arguing, justification in its broadest sense is a life-long process, we must recognize that fact when we are called upon for justification in its narrower sense of confronting current challenges and meeting them, and we must qualify our claims for justifiability accordingly.

We change, and our circumstances change. In the next section we will consider some of the things that, facing certain challenges, humans *do* to justify their convictions. There we will see that any device for justifying a conviction set must include some method for making it and its lifestyle intelligible. Often this will require a reorientation, a redefinition of terms, even a change of stance on the part of the one to whom the justification is offered.

In a pluralist world, a conviction set for which changes cannot be induced will fail and deserve to fail as a long-range candidate for commitment. It is essential, however, to having convictions that one does not give them up lightly or in the face of short-run adversity. Indeed, of the most important convictions held by a person or a community we may say (definitionally?) that they are maintained even in face of death. A just person, a faithful person, an honest person must be prepared to be just, faithful, or honest even at the sacrifice of personal advantage, or lose claim to the title. It does not count against a certain style of life merely to say that the convictions it embraces are held dearer than that life. A readiness to sacrifice one's life may even be necessary to the justifiability of such convictions. It will, however, count as a criticism of a sacrifice that it is unworthy, or that the demand for sacrifice is unjustly distributed, or that the good achieved is not that satisfaction at which the sacrifice was aimed.

Within a community an appeal to one or more of the loci may answer a challenge regarding the justifiability of a single conviction: it may even effect a convictional change in those ripe for change. Within Aleph's community, for example, appeal to the facts (the truth) about the sea that in the Hebrew Bible *Yam Suph* designates effected a shift in G from "Red Sea" to "Sea of Reeds." A more momentous theological revision in that community might lead to a changed view of the truth about God, and hence to a changed sense of "God" in some not yet expressed G. Where challenges to justification cross the lines of sharply differentiated convictional communities (Marxism versus classic liberalism, for example), appeals to truth or justice do not lack importance, but the canons of adjudication may be obscured by convictional disagreements over these loci themselves. In these cases, something more than a simple appeal to 'ultimate criteria' is therefore required. In such pluralist situations we can clearly see the function of the social matrices of justification, which we must now examine.

III. The Social Matrix of the Process

To see the role that the matrix may play, we remind ourselves that convictions are persistent beliefs, beliefs for many if not all seasons. A belief that cannot serve as a guide to other beliefs or actions through changes in time and circumstances simply will not have the persistence to recommend itself as a conviction. One of the recurrent problems faced by religious convictional communities is that many members of the community have identified the action appropriate to a conviction at a particular time and place with the whole meaning of that conviction for all times and places. Of course, if that identification is accurate, if the conviction's application *is* thus restricted, then as times change it will sooner or later cease to attract anyone's commitment. Those who continue to profess (or confess) the conviction will become hypocritical, which is not only unhappy but inherently unstable. Those who cannot or will not become hypocrites will reject the conviction so construed and will be regarded as modernists or heretics, especially by the hypocritical.

An illustration may be drawn from early Christianity and another from early Marxism. Both these communities were at the outset apocalyptic. Their earliest adherents thought that dramatic changes, soon to take place, would overthrow the Kingdom of Satan (or selfish capitalism) and usher in the golden age, the Kingdom of Christ (or the classless society). Both were disappointed by the actual course of history. The disappointment was a threat to community existence. Rigorists held unyieldingly to their outmoded view. But both movements showed their vigor by their refusal to be destroyed as convictional communities by the localized disappointment. Surely, they said to themselves, there is *something* right in these beliefs of ours. What is it?

If the convictional community is fortunate, at this juncture a reformer will show by example and by argument how one can live an acceptable life (and perhaps die an acceptable death) guided by the (reformed) convictions of the community. Thereby he or she enables the community once again to enjoy a justifiable set of convictions. We will examine *reform* as our first example of a matrix of justificatory activity, then a contrasting social phenomenon that we label "interconvictional encounter," and finally, more briefly, some other matrix types that may lead to the challenge and to the justification of convictions.

When we speak of the reform of convictions, we imply a convictional distance between the reformers and their own community, although neither need be aware of this gap at the outset. Such reformers cannot be mere good housekeepers, asserting the community's fundamental convictions and urging conformity to these. For, if convictional reform is needed, it is precisely the relevance of those fundamental convictions that is in question. On the other hand, an appeal to a conviction inconsistent with or radically different from those already recognized is not reform at all but rejection (though obviously we are not dealing with an all-or-nothing question here). A common way of speaking about a conviction set that stands in need of reform is to say that it has 'lost its meaning,' just as one says that a conviction set 'has no meaning' to those who reject or ignore it.[15] Reformers are thus confronted with the task of showing that the conviction set is *or can become* meaningful.

How is this to be done? One method employed by reformers as well as others is what modern philosophers have called the persuasive definition.[16] Briefly described, persuasive definitions propose a (more or less covert) shift in the descriptive force of a term or phrase while maintaining its affective force unchanged. If being a Jew is not, or is no longer, to be understood as entailing circumcision and the acceptance of dietary regulations, but is instead having faith like Abraham's faith in God, then those favorably disposed toward Jewishness can maintain that disposition without being bound to circumcision and diet, though they will be bound to faith. If a 'real Christian' ("real" is a characteristic adjective of persuasive definitions) is not so much one who goes regularly to church and believes in the divinity of Christ as one who sides with oppressed peoples and who believes in sharing their fate, then the attachment that Christians formerly felt for the old pattern is now to be given to the new.

How radical may such shifts be before the would-be reformer becomes instead a stranger and outsider? We must address this question, but first it will be helpful to examine still other techniques reformers may employ. Clearly a part of the problem confronted by any reformer is that of being correctly understood. If the justification of beliefs is inseparable from their understanding, being understood is not an optional aspect of successful reform, even though the reformer's convictional distance from his or her community is a crucial barrier to such understanding. In these cases, reformers may turn to paradox or parable.

Any examination of the teachings of Socrates and Jesus reveals an extraordinary use of paradox and (especially in the case of the latter) parable. These devices have been the subject of much discussion by both philosophers and literary critics.[17] While we cannot provide a full investigation of their significance, parable and paradox share several features that are of special interest to us at this point. Most obvious is their ability to bewilder, puzzle, and silence their hearers. How could it possibly be that those who save their life shall lose it? Or that it is better (more profitable!) to suffer rather than to do injustice? Those who have ears, let them hear. But the listeners cannot believe their ears. Can those who are cursed and reviled be *blessed?* Can all those leaders of Athens be *ignorant?* How could a *Samaritan* be my neighbor?

Yet the discomfort produced by these stories and puzzles, even when it issues in silence, is not a stultifying or barren discomfort. Those who understand even a little of what Socrates and Jesus are saying are driven to find resolutions to the paradoxes and points to the stories. And — here is the crucial point for us — almost any resolution or point will mean some shift in the meaning of key terms like "ignorant," "blessed," "neighbor," and "justice." Conventional uses are no help, since they led to the puzzlement. Furthermore, often many resolutions are possible, and which one listeners adopt will depend on their openness, their imagination, their sensitivity to nuance, the hardness of their hearts, the state of their souls ('hearts' and 'souls,' if you like).

Thus the community may find its reformer demanding of it a reformation in the form of a self-discovery, a revision of convictions that is a recovery of authentic community, a re-formation that is also a justification. Is it a justification of the old set? Clearly there is a sense in which it is not, but if in some sense it is, this is because justification is finally the justification of persons in community, and by no means of beliefs apart from persons (or of persons apart from one another). If we grant, however, the newness as well as the historicity of the reformed conviction set, this does not count against our long-range purpose. For we are not seeking in the present book to show how any *particular* set may be justified, much less every set, but how some set may be. If such justification via reformation entails change, so be it.

The similarity between reformation and the next matrix we shall examine, the *interconvictional encounter,* will be evident. While reform seems to be strictly an insider-to-insider affair and encounter seems to involve groups external to one another, that distinction is too sharp to fit the facts. To the extent that those inside the convictional community are like those outside, apart from their convictional differences, a successful reformation will provide the basis for a successful missionary appeal as well. In making the conviction set the object of (or vehicle for) a renewed or revitalized commitment by those who were nominally convinced, the reformer also makes it a possible object of (or vehicle for) commitment by those who have previously been uncommitted or committed to a different conviction set. If, for example, both Jews and non-Jews fear death, then, to the extent that a Jesus can show that this fear can be overcome with a Jewish conviction set, he offers an inducement to the non-Jew to consider and perhaps accept that conviction set. Again, to the extent that both convinced scientists and nonscientists share a desire to control their environment, a Bacon will be able to attract converts to science at the same time he invigorates the interest of scientists. Thus, these modes of justificatory action are not so much exclusive categories as they are types, distinct timbres that social history orchestrates in a variety of ways.

As we have seen, convictions conflict not only within and between communities, but within the same person. Severe cases of such conflict can be found in prisons and mental hospitals, but most of us have experienced less serious conflicts of this sort at one time or another. Choices of career, of love and marriage, of political or religious allegiance are often painful, not merely because I cannot get my own way, but because I cannot *discover* my own way, cannot discover which of my conflicting convictions is to be surrendered in the interest of the other. It is such dilemmas that make Polonius's maxim "This above all, to thine own self be true"[18] an empty one, save when offered to perfect saints (who will not take it) or perfect knaves (who already believe it). Sometimes the dilemma ends in the wholehearted adoption of one and the giving up of the other conviction (conversions often take this form). Or we vacillate between the choices for a time, trying in some way to reconcile them. More rarely we try to isolate the conflicting sets in our thinking and acting and thereby ignore the conflict. (In the nineteenth century, many intellectuals of religious bent tried this form of solution of the science-religion controversy.) In the long run, however, conflicts between convictions cannot be disguised or ignored: God and Mammon decline a joint appointment, and even the most skillful hypocrite is rarely consistent.

What cases, then, do we characterize as interconvictional encounters? Ones in which representatives of distinct convictional communities meet one another in such a way that one or both parties are thereby convictionally changed. Such encounters range from the relatively benign meetings of the classroom and campus, through the clash and interplay of the social, ethnic, and religious groups in a wider society, to the deadly interaction of cultures epitomized by the meeting of East and West in twentieth-century Indochina. Not least, they include the friction, the fire, and (sometimes) the fruitful engagement in the meeting of diverse religious communities.

An interesting model of such encounters is provided by the Christian ecumenical movement, a movement marked by the successive appearance of 'correct' mutual disdain, of icebreaking courtesies, of a baffling inability to characterize disagreements in mutually acceptable ways, of the emergence of suppressed areas of agreement, and of the discovery of unknown realms of disagreement.[19] Following this model, it appears that a prime element in fruitful encounter must be the location of actual belief differences. As we know, this is a prime element in the work of justification as well. To understand an utterance or a belief is to know how it can (conceivably) go wrong; to hold it justifiable is to hold that it does not in fact go wrong in those ways. To this degree, at least, the work of meaningful encounter and the work of justification go hand in hand.

This may be seen more clearly by examining, with William Christian, the transformations we may effect in utterances in order to bring them into direct disagreement with one another.[20] Suppose a Christian issues the confession, A, "Jesus is the Messiah." Now it makes sense to say that a Jew may not directly disagree with that utterance, even though he issues as *his* conviction "Jesus is not the Messiah." Not directly disagree, because the speakers do not mean the same thing by "Messiah." For the Jew, "Messiah" means a nondivine being who will restore ancient Israel, making a new nation of it, and bringing about a golden final age of history. For the Christian, "Messiah" means the promised Savior, who will save people from their sins. Since the two speakers mean different things, they have not yet directly disagreed, though of course they have not agreed either. Doctrinal systems may seem hopelessly cut off from one another by such considerations, but there is a way in which the Jew and the Christian can talk on the same doctrinal topic. This involves the reformulation of the Christian's confession into B, "Jesus is the one whom God promised to send to redeem Israel." On this, Jew and Christian can significantly disagree. To be sure, problems may remain. Do the Christian and the Jew have different concepts of Israel? Of God? (Perhaps even of "promise" and of "redeem"?) Still, their concepts may overlap enough to permit disagreement. If not, further reformulation may be needed whereby common elements in the two differing concepts are joined in a new predicate. This should become clear enough in the next illustration.

Suppose, says Professor Christian, there had arisen a dialog between the Apostle Paul and the Stoic philosopher Seneca. If Seneca were confronted with utterance B above, he might respond that B is neither right nor wrong — it simply makes no sense. For God does not send people or promise things; God does not act in history. Yet it may be that Seneca's concept of God and Paul's concept of God overlap. Both might think, for example, that God rules the world. If (and only if) that is the case, Paul and Seneca might disagree on the following utterance, C, "The being who rules the world acts in history." Thus we have moved from an apparent disagreement between Paul and Seneca to a real one. And via C, they may discover that they indirectly disagree about B and A as well.

If we are prepared to revise again we may widen still further the circle of those who are indirectly engaged over the original utterance, A. Suppose Paul encounters a Neoplatonist, say Plotinus. Plotinus may be as perplexed by C as Seneca was by B. For he may say, "The source of all being (to which I suppose you are referring) does not rule the world in any way at all, much less by acting in history.... What you are saying does not seem to make good sense."[21] If the game is to be played, then, C must be revised into D, "The source of all being rules the world," and about this the Neoplatonist on one side, and Jew, Christian, and Stoic on the other, can disagree. At first sight it may appear churlish for religious speakers to seek, or for philosophers to seek for them, ways to *disagree*. Yet as we indicate here, and as Christian goes on to show in a valuable concluding chapter of a second book, the logic of disagreement is an indispensable clue to the logic of agreement.[22]

It appears, then, that the participant in encounter can clarify her own convictions for the other by such transpositions, and this is surely a part of the practical logic of encounter. Justification would proceed as each member of the dialog sought to discover and to show how their original convictions were related to their other convictions and to whatever each knew to be the case about the world.

However, there is more to be said about this procedure. Suppose it is desirable to transform A into B, C, or D; it is then likely that the champion of A will spend more energy upon the justification of B, C, or D (depending upon who his or her opposite number is) than upon the justification of A. These may call for different sorts of backing, may interest their champion in different ways, call attention to different facts, than did A. B brings a seeker, say, to a study of the Hebrew Scriptures, C to an inquiry into the quality of human history, D to metaphysical explorations. To be sure, one might have come to all these inquiries in solitary intra-confessional doctrinal exploration of A, but in practice the procedures will be different. Not only does one engage in a wider range of inquiries; one does so against a different backdrop — that of one's counterpart in the dialog.

Missionaries of the 'higher' religions such as Buddhism, Islam, and Christianity sometimes expect that an encounter between religions will result in mass conversions from one to the other. While individual conversions do occur, world history has not borne out the wider expectation. The main instances of mass conversion seem to be the conversion of 'primitive' peoples to one of the advanced religions. The missionary who seeks converts from advanced religions has had to be content with more modest achievements. On the other hand, some philosophers believe that the encounter of the world's religions will produce a single, syncretistic world faith.[23] While our investigation neither favors nor opposes such an outcome, it suggests that overt syncretism is not the inevitable result of dialog. Convictions being what they are, the convinced do not yield them readily with integrity. But the attempt to justify our convictions in the dialog does produce a reformulation and reclustering of convictions not unlike the renewal involved in the work of the reformer. It is natural that such renewal be aimed at making the reformulated convictions more attractive to both partners in the dialog.

We have been investigating the logical character or structure of actual justification procedures; in order to do this we have examined some characteristic matrices of this process. From our examples it appears that the acquiring of a conviction set and the justification of the set are often simultaneous and always interrelated — not to be understood apart from one another. To speak of choosing one's conviction set is not necessarily wrong, but it may be misleading unless we recognize that "choosing one's convictions" is a shorthand way of talking about many choices made over a period of time, reinforcing one another, accumulating, developing in more and more definite directions until we find ourselves with a conviction set that we acknowledge as our own, as being the way of life, the outlook, that we have chosen.

The apparent counterexample to the preceding generalization is *conversion* or *enlightenment,* for in these matrices one finds oneself dramatically introduced into a new realm, as if a new creature. It would seem appropriate, then, to inquire how strongly such an apparent exception counts against the general rule just formulated and how different the problem of justification of new convictions may be for the converted or enlightened one. "Conversion" can refer in a derivative way to any new formal attachment to a party, sect, or community. The primary sense, however, is broadly synonymous with the religious terms "enlightenment," "regeneration," "new birth" — phenomena that appear in many cultures and communities. In this sense, conversion may or may not involve a change in church membership or party allegiance; if it does, the importance of the external change is its signifying the internal — the new way in which the enlightened one views self and world and god. What does surely characterize conversions is the radical reorientation, occurring dramatically in a few hours, days, or months, of all that is most important to the convert.

All — or is it all that is changed? It seems so. Consider, however, the paradigmatic cases of the conversion of Paul on the road to Damascus and the enlightenment of Gotama under the bo tree.[24] Surely these are as radical cases of conversion as occur in the literature of religion: Saul the rabbi, persecutor of Christians, becomes Paul the chief Christian preacher, theologian, apostle, martyr; Gotama the young Hindu prince and seeker becomes the Buddha, the Enlightened One, founder and teacher of the Way of the Lotus. Could there be more profound and sudden reversals? Yet in both cases, we must acknowledge, there were certain continuities as well. Saul/Paul had the same God before and after his conversion, however his conception of this God may have been modified. He revered the same Scriptures, kept the same feasts, worshiped (until ejected) in the same synagogues. One way of understanding the contribution of Paul to Christianity is to say that he brought the background of a broader, more Hellenic, more universalist Judaism to bear upon the narrowly Judean Jewishness of primitive Christianity. However sharp the contrast between Paul's pre- and postconversion convictions is made to appear, there is still a great tract of continuity. The conversion itself cannot be grasped save within a *certain* context, and that context is Paul's earlier convictional orientation. Thus, when he set out, after his conversion, to explicate and justify the new convictions (as in Romans), his method was to relate these convictions to Hebrew Scripture, to the history and hopes of the Jewish people, to the outlook of the Hellenic world in which he had grown up (since he was not a Palestinian Jew), and to Paul's own preconversion struggle with 'law,' sin, and the meaning of death.

With allowance for changed circumstances, the same points can be made about Gotama. After the Enlightenment, his first disciples were the intimate friends of the years of his preceding quest. His teaching, the Four Noble Truths, consisting in the formulation of the question that the quest had implied as well as in the answer to the quest provided in his enlightenment, was governed by the religious texture of the Hinduism from which it sprang. For example, the Buddha's steadfast refusal to give an (acceptable) answer to Hindu questions about God and the soul can be understood as first of all an attempt to correct the distorted other-worldliness of Hindu religion (distorted, of course, from the convictional viewpoint of the Buddha) without rejecting the doctrines of karma and rebirth that he saw as central to that outlook.

Summarizing, we may say that dramatic conversions do indeed contain new convictional elements, but that (1) these are imbedded in a changing body of convictional material; (2) the previous convictional history of the convert contains the seeds of the new material that flowers in the conversion process; (3) in many cases, the conversion is a symbolic concentration representing changes that either precede or succeed it, as well as the changes of the luminous moment itself. And it is in this longer process of change that the convictional revisions occur that justify, as well as being justified by, the concentrated changes of a 'second birth.'

What conversion is to the individual convictional pilgrimage, *revolution* is to the journey of a whole community. We call attention to only one side of revolution, disregarding both its violence and its role as arbiter in the struggle for social power. Our interest is in revolution as the revision of a community's understanding of itself and its place in the world. Seen in this way, revolutionary vision may be described as judging the present world by the canons of the world that is to be; against present and (by his lights) reactionary values, the revolutionary pleads the values of the future about to be born. Thus, unlike the reformer, the revolutionary cannot appeal to the authentic tradition of the community against current deterioration of that tradition; the justification he offers is to be found not in the past but in the unattained revolutionary goal. This futurity is at once the lure and the liability of his program viewed in its justifying power, for what he is attesting to is by definition not presently available. This goes far to explain the difficulty and perhaps also the attractiveness of convictional revolution.

> The *revolutionary* wants to change the world; he wants to project into the future, to an order of values which he invents.... The *rebel* has a need to maintain intact the abuses from which he suffers in order to be able to rebel against them.[25]

That Sartrian aphorism suggests our next matrix of change, that of *rebellion*. It also suggests that the rebel is sometimes unfavorably compared with the revolutionary. Even petulant rebellion may be understood in convictional terms: the cartoon of a white-bearded old man in Confederate uniform, holding the Stars and Bars and snarling, "Forget, hell!" represents a legion who are convinced that the present is insufferably wrong. Such a conviction, however, is not necessarily unworthy. It may be supported, as it is in Sartre's aphorism and in the cartoonist's parody, by the self-deception of an idealized and thus irrecoverable past; on the other hand, it may be a stance that is more clear-eyed and realistic than that of the revolutionary. The latter rebel appeals neither to the past nor to the future, but says of the present order simply, "This is wrong."

How justifiable convictional rebellion may be depends, then, as much upon the unsatisfactory state of the community's current convictions as upon any alternative that the rebel may have to offer. In the worst of all possible convictional worlds, the rebel's singular conviction is justified by that world itself. However, not every rebellion occurs in such a world, and perhaps Sartre and Camus are right to typify the rebel in unflattering terms.[26] For the rebel may be one whose significance is found almost wholly in terms of that against which he or she rebels, while the complete failure of that establishment would be the end of his or her own convictional existence. Professional anti-Catholics, anti-communists, anti-Semites lead a convictionally precarious existence, which may help explain the ardor of their protestations and the venom of some of their actions.

Finally, we mention one matrix that has perhaps played a larger role in philosophical works on religion than in real life justificatory activity. This is the *quest* for the best or best possible set of convictions. The quester goes tentatively from outlook to outlook, from stance to stance, testing each and finally adopting none, until the fully satisfactory, or most satisfactory, is discovered. This may seem to be the course of some personal histories — Gotama to his enlightenment; Justin Martyr to his Christian conversion — but we doubt that it is a fully accurate characterization. For if the quester maintained a continuous selfhood he or she could not have been free of a continuing (though perhaps ill-realized) set of convictions all through the quest. And the idea of tentative exploration of alternative life commitments would seem to preclude the seriousness that would make justification of certain of those alternatives possible. There are today a few religious eclectics who roam over the world of religious knowledge and experience trying on theologies, religions, outlooks, myths, rituals as a shopper tries on hats. Some have approvingly dubbed such gourmet eclecticism 'pluralism,' but it seems to us that this misunderstands the roamers. Religious (or irreligious) convictions, in the present sense, are not a decoration to be added at will to human character; they *are* human character brought to expression. The culture-taster or the religious role-player may be doing something of personal or of sociological interest, but he or she cannot be trying on and discarding *convictions:* we *are* our convictions.

On the other hand, there may be more serious quests, and two of these are worth mentioning, though they are in some tension with one another. Though the quester cannot (purposefully) make a conviction-free pilgrimage, one may on a quest enrich one's prior set in such a way as to make it justifiable, or more justifiable. So one sort of quest may be a deliberate and open search for interconvictional encounters, and these may even produce the sorts of enlightenment or conversion referred to above, in which belief and life seem to tumble together into a happy new pattern.[27]

The second serious sort of quest is of even more general interest. The quester may be at bottom a questioner or *skeptic,* whose present convictions include the determination to challenge every possible conviction, retaining only the refined set that survives such examination. We have spoken of the move to eliminate all conviction, and of the absurdity to which that leads and have urged instead the general usefulness of a principle of fallibility in any conviction set.[28] In this way we have given special endorsement to the place of skepticism in the justificatory task.

Mention of the principle of fallibility and of others' viewpoints reminds us of our earlier controversy with relativists and leads us to conclude this section on the social matrices of justification with a fresh reflection on the question, In whose eyes must a justification be effective in order to be acceptable? The only possible answer is that a justification must be effective in the eyes of the community or the individual holding the conviction. If it is *not* justified in their eyes, in what sense is it a justification at all? (If I cannot see that my conviction is worth holding, it matters little that someone else thinks it is; if Muslims cannot see that they are right convictionally, it matters little that some non-Muslims think they are.)

"In their eyes alone, then?" Yes, but that requires qualification. The relativist envisions a world composed of people who, looking each from his or her own perspective (singular or communal), can neither move nor be moved from that perspective to any other — and who is to say who is right? In this view, there is no truth in general; only "truth to me" or "to her." The relativist reads "in their eyes alone" to mean that no one can transcend his or her own perspective by any means. But the honest perspectivist, as we may now call ourselves, takes these words in a different way. Here one does not deny the logical necessity that *I* shall confirm my beliefs, but one holds that people may be conscious of their convictionally plural existence in such a way that that consciousness contains the possibility of transcending the singular perspective of its owners. To the perspectivist "in their eyes alone" means here "in the eyes of those who see that theirs are not the only eyes."

That is, though we define the limits of justification as justification within (in the eyes of) the community of the convinced, that is not so rigid a limit as it would be were there not ruptures of the convictional barriers. If, for example, I am convinced that there is one God (or none, or two) the justification of that conviction is my business, mine and that of my convinced fellows. But the process of justification cannot be altogether the same for me if I so much as know that there are those who dissent; if, for example, I know that "the fool hath said in his heart, 'there is no God'" (Ps. 14:1). And it will be quite different if I come to see those who differ with me, not merely as 'fools' or 'barbarians,' but also as folk with flesh like my flesh, brain like my brain, soul like my soul. To that extent, though the justificatory task is still my own, it may draw upon sympathies, correspondences, insights that are not merely private or partisan. And therein lies our hope of transcending the convictional cellblocks to which we might otherwise be confined.

To continue the illustration, if I believe in God (am convinced of God) in a pluralistic world, a world in which I know there are people of good will who do not so believe, then my faith, if justified at all, must be a faith that takes account of that very pluralism that in part denies my faith. It must be faith justifiable (I must be justified by my faith?) *in a world that includes unfaith.* Conversely, if I disbelieve, believe in no God, am convinced no God exists, in a world in which I know there are those who do so believe, then my conviction, if justified at all, must be one that takes significant account of that fact: it must be atheism *in a world that includes faith.* The pluralism that we envisage, then, does not obviate justification nor require narrowness of outlook, but it does require that the pluralism itself shall be internalized, so that it becomes a factor that my convictions take into account.

IV. Retrospect: Aleph's Task in a Plural World

The role of this chapter has been to expand the idea of justification of convictions with which we began.[29] Just because convictions are ongoing beliefs, their justification in a changing world must be an ongoing task rather than a once-for-all achievement. If having a (relatively) fixed character is one aspect of having convictions, then even the talk of 'choosing' or 'picking' a conviction (or conviction set) may be misleading. Such talk conjures up a picture of our standing on some neutral point with the various alternative convictions spread before us as we demand of each its credentials. But we choose our characters, if we can speak of doing so at all, in a much different way. We begin life with a certain minimal set of biological and psychological characteristics. By the time we can be said to make any choices (as opposed to reacting in certain ways) these characteristics in interplay with our environment have already produced in us dispositions with some degree of persistence. (Although recognition of this fact may induce deterministic *Weltschmerz* in some, we believe that this reaction is demonstrably wrongheaded.) These dispositions are reinforced, modified, or weakened each time we observe, deliberate, hope, choose, and reflect on the consequences of our choices. Thus while it is true in a way that our dispositions determine our choices, it is also true in a way that our choices create our dispositions, not all at once but over a period of time. And of course if we do not deliberate and reflect on the consequences of our choices they will remain more like reactions, and we shall turn ourselves into the desperately unhappy people portrayed by Plato and others.

What we have said of our relatively practical dispositions applies to our relatively theoretical ones as well. As we learn to talk and think, we have initial inclinations to make various statements, guesses, conjectures, judgments, and the like about how the world is, and these inclinations are reinforced, modified, or weakened as we consider them and reflect on the evidence. So our inclinations determine our beliefs, but only at the same time that our beliefs are determining our inclinations. What follows is that having convictions is as 'natural' as having human life itself — a naturalness that consists neither in sheer fortuity nor in sheer grit, but that is the natural product of being or becoming human, the world being what it is. In the broadest sense, one tries to justify one's conviction set (or one's life) by living it. Yet life includes talk, and persuasion, and reflection, and certainly change, and thus it can include the special dynamics of justification we have been describing in these pages.

Seen in this perspective, the justificatory techniques that we rejected in chapters 4 and 5 must have their role to play in the task. While we rejected there the skeptic's simple-hearted faith in the elimination of all convictions, we have seen that the principle of fallibility may play a useful role in the selective thinning of a set. While we have denied to 'science' the role of supreme judge of all convictions and to 'reason' the claim that it occupies conviction-free ground in offering proofs of God or the like, we have not foreclosed the possibility that some science or sciences may play a more modest role in convictional explorations or that a modest reasonableness can inform even interconvictional justificatory activity. (One way to characterize the present book is as an attempt to redefine "reasonable"; to discover how a not disinterested reason may yet justify its convinced interest.)

Readers might well be reminded here of Alasdair MacIntyre's work — work that appeared since the first edition of the present book.[30] For MacIntyre, rationality (and justice) inhere in narrative traditions, whose claim upon their adherents lies in part in their enduring capacity to withstand new shocks and confront rival rationalities, accounting for their rivals in their own terms better than they can account for themselves, thereby displaying rational superiority. In a metaphor MacIntyre does not himself employ, rationally superior traditions establish their superiority, justify themselves, by rationally devouring their rivals.

Before comparing it with our own, we may note two or three prominent features of MacIntyre's solution. First, "rational" in his neo-Hegelian scheme is necessarily an equivocal term. As we have seen, that is not a fault, but we do well to keep it in mind: Nietzschean rationality is not simply Thomist rationality. Second, MacIntyre trades upon the concept of tradition, where this means not simply and literally a handing on across time (the sense in which everything existing in this instant of time is traditional, having emerged from the previous instant of time), but instead implies a unity best described, according to *After Virtue*, as *narrative* unity.[31] What holds the beginning, middle, and end of a story together?

Surely not that the story says the same thing again and again and again —
that would make it no story at all — but the linking of its parts into one
narrative.

In all these ways MacIntyre addresses the problems and often closely
parallels the paths this chapter had already taken. The divergences,
though, are as instructive as the convergences, and we must look at
both. To begin, we can agree from our standpoint that if the Enlightenment project (what people today still call modernity) works from shared
convictions, it must work as an *ongoing* set of convictions — which is
entailed by the very nature of convictions themselves, for they are by
definition *persistent* beliefs, resisting change, not easily relinquished, and
not relinquished at all without significant change in their holders. To have
a conviction is to be engaged over time, and (at this point MacIntyre
puts the matter better than we had) this must be a narrative engagement:
*the narrative of the convictional community is the glue that binds its
convictions into one set.*

To see the differences as well, consider the three elements that we
have picked out as vital to the justificatory task. First there is the appeal to standards, our *loci of conviction.* MacIntyre does this when he
argues for *rational* justification. Just what is rationality? It would be convenient if rationality (or logic, or truth, or justice, or all of these) meant
the same across the lines that divide convictional communities. So convenient that the problem of relativism would not arise. Regretfully, that
is not the case, for these terms themselves embody convictional elements
(see sec. III of chap. 4). Clearly rationality falls among these disputed
considerations; hence no univocal appeal to it alone can prevail in a the-
ater of conflicting convictions. Recognizing this, our project named these
disputed elements — truth, beauty, fairness, and the like — simply *loci,*
arenas, of justification: each locus designates, not a criterion that could
settle an interconvictional dispute, but an arena to be entered by anyone making such claims. Rationality is one such locus, and the task of
interconvictional justification will often enter that locus as well as others.

This brings us to our second element. In justificatory work, one thing
at issue is the transparency of the medium of communication. Traditions
take form, express themselves, in words as well as in (wordless) deeds;
to justify a tradition must be to justify its speech — and to do this across
convictional lines. Is this even possible, though, if language is already
in itself the bearer of convictions? Is language ever a transparent (or, to
change the image, ever a translatable) medium?[32] Is there finally just one
language, or are there only languages? This is not the only element in the

problem that gives rise to relativism: fellow speakers of English, even fellow speakers of Irish-accented English, may remain convictional enemies, and it is said of British and American speakers of English that we are "divided by a common language." Yet in practice the language that divides is also the language that joins. Our argument in this chapter has been that in successful justification, the joining or union comes in the course of time to predominate. Value-laden terms such as "witch," like the term "centaur," progress from being terms for debate (are there really centaurs? really witches?) to being terms that in use answer the question if it should arise. "Centaur" is clearly such a case; perhaps "witch" is. For yet another example, "redneck" passes from being (1) principally a descriptive term of derision to (2) an impolite pejorative applied to those with different tastes in music or politics to (3) a self-ascription of praise: in time, we suggest, some football team will without vilification be named the Rednecks. In the passage, the question whether there 'are' rednecks will receive more than one true answer.

These references to the passage of time and to social process lead to a third element in the machinery of justification, which we have continued to call the social matrix of justification, listing a number of possible matrices: the radical *reform* of an existing community, the *encounter* between convinced rivals, and still others (conversion, enlightenment, revolution, rebellion, the quest). We are so accustomed to seeing some of these in exclusively religious or exclusively military terms that we may fail to recognize the convictional, rational, and self-involving character of each process. It is out of place to enlarge upon these here further than to note that in each the contest over the *loci* (what counts as justice or truth or fairness?) is likely to be a part of the justificatory process and likewise that in any of them the changing *language* of convictions has a contribution to make to the process. It is this third element that MacIntyre has stressed in his concept of *traditions*. His *Three Rival Versions of Moral Enquiry*[33] effectively illustrates the encounter of his own (Thomist) tradition of moral enquiry with that of Nietzschean genealogy and Scottish Enlightenment encyclopedia. Does he with equal realism recognize the other matrices we have listed here? We think not, yet to recognize them is to acknowledge (even more fully than MacIntyre) the story-shaped or narrative character of the justificatory process: a "tradition" must in the nature of narrative itself be open to the vicissitudes of time and change in all these forms. As Miroslav Volf correctly reminds us, traditions are necessarily impure, and part of the promise of each lies in its (present) impurity.

Justifying religious or other convictions, in short, is a historical process, complex in nature, involving contested loci of support and the
progress of language, all within a matrix of human engagement and action. This original analysis is supported by that portion of MacIntyre's
work in which he takes on the referee role; it is then illustrated in action
by his partisan positions. Positively, he has improved our account by iden-
tifying more clearly than we the traditional or narrative glue that binds a
convictional community into one.

It may be helpful, before enlarging these themes in the remaining
pages, to mark our conclusions so far by considering their application
to Aleph's convictions as represented in chapters 3 and 4. Our task is
not to attempt the justification of his hypothetical set but to show what
might be involved in such a justification. Aleph, it will be remembered,
uttered his confession as a member of a conservative, traditional religious community. When for convenience we furnished him with a related
set of religious convictions of just five members (one of which was expressed by G), we left open the question of Aleph's relation to the wider
set shared by his community. Is God triune? Is God's nature summed
up in self-giving love? Are all people sinners by nature? We did not define Aleph's position on these matters or his relation to his community's
position. Yet it may be that his confessional/convictional attachment to
a historic community (cf. G and J) shows our list of his religious convictions to be artificially limited. Perhaps Aleph can be understood and
his set justified only by an *understanding* of *all* the shared convictions
of his community. This is not to say that, in order to be justified, Aleph
must go along with each and all of the defining (or orthodox) convictions
of his community. If his community's set is at some points infelicitous,
his own felicity may require dissent at those points. It is to say that the
understanding of his speech and his belief involves understanding of the
community or communities of speakers and believers in terms of which
his own life is formed.

Though such understanding is necessary to justification or rejection,
it is sufficient for either only where judgments of truth or falsity, consistency or inconsistency, righteousness or unrighteousness are so immediate
as to go unnoticed. In a convictionally plural world, though, these judgments are often conscious and sometimes seem imponderable. Did Israel
cross the Reed Sea? Does God act in history? Does God exist? In such
cases, Aleph inevitably enters the arena represented by our (partial) list of
loci, risking the convictional disputes that such loci may stake out. Historical inquiries (the Reed Sea; the Jesus of history) and rational arguments

(the theistic proofs; the bases of ethics), while quite relevant to his task here, cannot by themselves settle his convictional questions on grounds independent of the convictions themselves. In any case, if Aleph's set is justifiable, its justification will require implicit or direct appeal to one or more of these common loci, for example, to the claim that life lived in his way is a truly *happy* life. Failing to make (or make good) such claims, he will have failed to justify his set.

If the preceding activities prove inadequate for justification, Aleph may be aided by a third element. We remember that justification is a demand to meet a finite number of actual objections (not hypothetical, not innumerable). Sometimes these objections are suggested by outsiders, but the important thing is that they arise for Aleph himself. Such crises are at once challenges to justification and occasions of justification. To show how Aleph will justify his set if he does justify it is thus dependent upon a contingency: what challenge, what matrix will form for him an occasion of justification? Will Aleph become, or will he meet, a reformer, a revolutionary, a rebel? Will the form of his justificatory activity be a profound interconvictional encounter or an internal pilgrimage or quest? As these matrices differ, so do the form and content of the justification to which they may give birth. And so will the time that they may require.

If such a summary of one hypothetical justification appeals to some as displaying the 'crooked lines' of actual life, others will be distressed at its chanciness and disorder. Can we convinced human beings do no better than this? Is there no highway to order in the convictional wilderness, no return to reasonableness, no science of convictions? The present writers share to some degree both the delight in jagged veracity and the desire for greater order in this work. While we cannot in the present pages give full vent to the latter desire (having indulged the former) we will now say something more about a science of convictions and its relation to philosophy.

SEVEN

Here as elsewhere in philosophy, analytic techniques help to answer the penultimate questions, while the ultimate ones, being incapable of answer, must be come to terms with in some other way.

Joel Feinberg[1]

In its defense of truth against sophistry, philosophy has employed the same literary genres as theology in its defense of the faith: against intellectual competition, Dogmatics; against Dogmatics, the Confession; in both, the Dialogue.

Stanley Cavell[2]

Give me somewhere to stand and I will move the earth.

Archimedes

Theology as a Science of Convictions

It has often been the role of philosophy to break the ground for the construction of a new science. Many previous philosophic proposals have seemed to suggest the possibility of a convictionally neutral science of convictions. Let us look at two such proposals, one classic and the other contemporary, as prelude to our own suggestion. William James, toward the end of his *Varieties of Religious Experience*, suggested that the old dogmatic theology was about to be replaced by a new, philosophically pure "Science of Religions," to which the *Varieties* itself was making "a crumb-like contribution."[3] James must have had the development of experimental psychology, with which he had so much to do, in mind as a model. The "science of religions" would be impartial and would "presuppose immediate experiences" as its subject matter. The fruit of this science, James hoped, would be a common body of conclusions about religion. To this common body each scientific inquirer would add, according to his predilections and faith, his own (more dubitable) superstructure of "over-beliefs." James thought, for example, that the new science might be able to conclude from the facts of experience that each of us is continuous with a wider self, a "more," through which saving experiences come, while James's own corresponding over-belief was that the "more" was on its higher side to be denoted "God."[4]

James's early-twentieth-century view seems far too uncritical, far too sanguine about the possibilities of a science independent from what we have called conviction sets. Against his scheme, so briefly presented, there seem to arise all the objections to a sovereign role for science in convictional matters that we raised in chapter 5. Indeed James was conscious of the difficulties: while the science might be "impartial" to any one of the several religions (as theology was not), it would have its "internal difficulties"; notably, it would be biased against the claim that "the

181

essence of religion is true," a bias James sought to overcome partly by argument, partly by assigning an ultimate role to the over-beliefs.[5]

Two elements in James's program, however, seem commendable still. (1) If there are indeed religious data that can be brought into view by a scientific suspension of some of our convictions, then this is one set of facts that any conviction set in the modern world worthy of adherence must reckon with. It may not be enough for present purposes, but it cannot be ignored, either. One thinks of the present-day discipline of history of religions in this connection. (2) It is noteworthy that James makes no hard and fast distinction between the methodology which yields the over-beliefs and that which yields the common core of conclusions in his science of religions. Both spring from empirical investigation and from reflection and are subject to correction from either of these sources; nevertheless, they may contribute to the sum of our knowledge. (It would be a mistake, James holds, to say that all should have identical religious views, pending any final resolution of our differences in one harmonious system.)[6] Perhaps, then, the science of convictions that *we* envisage might make room, not only for common empirical data, but also for those aspects of convictional belief in which folk are (and so far ought to be) separated. There may be a *scientific exploration of convictions* even in a convictionally pluralist world. (Murphy in chapter 5.)

Consider, second, the argument made by a contemporary analytical philosopher, Kai Nielsen, for "the primacy *of philosophical theology*" in settling the questions both of religion and theology.[7] Philosophical theology, in Nielsen's view, analyzes fundamental religious concepts and claims. Once one has completed one's analysis, one can judge the religious convictions that rest on these claims. The judging standard that Nielsen seems to favor is the concept of coherence. He says that opponents of Christian claims may with reason argue that the concept of God central to Christianity is incoherent. Christian theologians may well reply that belief in Christian revelation excludes the recognition of any point of view external to revelation that can understand and assess the truth of the latter. Offering these as appropriate moves in "philosophical theology," Nielsen then leaps into the demonstration himself, arguing in response to the last move that the concept of revelation is itself incoherent.[8] And so forth.

We can heartily agree with Nielsen that certain elements intrinsic to religious belief and discourse are subject to philosophic examination — indeed such examination is the stuff of the present book. Even those teachers of doctrine who, like Karl Barth, consciously eschew philosophic discussion continually take up positions on matters that philosophers discuss in their own way. If we disregard those cases in which (it could be argued) philosophers are actually engaging in tasks theological not philosophical, still there are other cases where theologians tread on historic philosophical preserves. For example, theologies sooner or later make direct or indirect appeal to one or more of the loci, such as truth and consistency, for which philosophy has always held itself responsible. Nielsen reminds us of this fact.

It is not clear, however, in what sense we should speak of a "primacy" of philosophy in such cases. The loci, for example, are arenas of combat, not realms in which philosophy as such can somehow settle theology's business, or anyone's business. We have pointed out in chapter 5 the inability of 'rational theology' *or* philosophy to settle fundamental convictional disputes on nonconvictional grounds. Nielsen seems to us another of those philosophers whose arguments against religious convictions are based on contrary convictions.[9] It is significant that he finds religious talk of God, or talk of God's self-disclosure, not so much mistaken or unproved as "incoherent" and "utterly opaque," "Language seems to have gone on a holiday."[10] Is this a nonconvictional assessment?

Have we not come far enough to see, though, that there is no escape from convictions? That all our serious thinking, exactly to the degree that it is rational, is deeply convictional, and that some or all of the involved convictions are likely to support or to clash with the convictions our proposed 'science' is meant to assess? That was the outcome of chapter 5, where the argument led us to conclude that rationality was never conviction-free. What we are looking for now, then, is a way to proceed *with* convictions to create an honest science of convictions. We will not pretend to begin without convictions — that is the Enlightenment dream of some universally available foundation on which all learning can effortlessly rest. Instead, our work will be a scaffold alongside which a structure of justified convictions can (with hard work) be raised. What we have learned from Nielsen (and from a tradition as old as pre-Christian Greece) is that such a task may legitimately use whatever philosophical methods offer promise in the inquiry. From William James we have the suggestion that the investigation of convictions can proceed simultaneously down many corridors (the several sorts of over-belief). Combining these two, we begin to envision a discipline that is consciously convictional, plural in form, responsive in many ways to many sorts of empirical data, and open to the rational modes of adjudication (the role of language, the loci of appeal, the social matrices of encounter, reform, etc.) that we catalogued in the previous chapter. More than any rival candidate we can envision, such a discipline would deserve to be called a "science of convictions." Or for a less novel but still provocative name we would call it *theology* (or *theoretics*).

By theology or theoretics — terms to be distinguished in what follows — we mean *the discovery, examination, and transformation of the conviction set of a given convictional community, carried on with a view to discovering and modifying the relation of the member convictions to one another, to other (nonconvictional) beliefs held by the community, and to whatever else there is.*[11] We intend this as a descriptive definition, singling out the characteristic activity of most if not all of those who call themselves or are called theologians. (Our definition could thus be faulted if it merely defined a task nobody was attempting or, like some definitions we have seen, merely identified our own theologies to the exclusion of everyone else's.) While we think our definition does function in dictionary fashion to refer to the work of actual theologies and theologians, we recognize that not all theologians will immediately recognize it as a description of their own work. So our first task is to show how it is. In doing so, we will be showing that no small part of what is now called theology (and philosophy, when we come to that) is already constructively engaged in solving the problem this book addresses, that is, the plurality of human convictions. What is most needed, we think, is not an utterly new approach, but a reconceiving of a cluster of related approaches already on hand. Theology or theoretics, with philosophy, *is* the scaffold, it is already in place on the construction site, needing only modest reformation, and thereby the understanding or justification of at least some convictions, religious and other, has already begun.

It is traditional to say that theology is about God, or about God and the world. Yet that is a somewhat misleading idea of what it usually attempts. Thus one contemporary theoretician, Michael Novak, writes that theology is "critical concern with alternative images of human identity, human community, and the relation of man to his world."[12] To generalize more broadly, theology as we observe it is not usefully characterized by its subject matter any more than convictions are: convictions can be about any and everything; so can theology. For that reason, the definition we provided above does not restrict theology to 'God' or to 'religion' or to 'religious' topics however conceived. (Indeed, historically "theology" is a much older and longer-honored term in communities of faith than is the neologism "religion" — see chapter i, page 14f.). But if anyone finds it unsuitable to refer to the exploration of the conviction sets of secular or 'nonreligious' or atheistic communities by the name "theology," we have at hand an acceptable synonym in "theoretics." Indeed "theoretics" (or "theoretic") is already in the language in this sense — as in "Communist (or New Left) theoretics," or the expression "Marxist theoretician." In what follows we will normally use "theoretics" to refer to every investigation and transformation of the shared conviction sets of convictional communities, while using "theology" to refer to the theoretics of religious convictional communities. Theology, in other words, is religious theoretics; theoretics is convictional exploration, whether 'religious' or not.[13]

A more ambitious (more Germanic?) project than ours might attempt at this point to list, classify, and correlate all the world's theologies, or at least all its present ones. Mercifully, we have no thought of attempting that. Instead, we want merely to indicate a few better-known theological projects of the present or recent past that illustrate our claim. Our choices are of course selective, the more so because most of the examples we choose do display interest in a 'universal' or 'public' or 'world' theology. These specimens are continuous in style with more particularistic theologies, though, and we must leave it to the reader to see whether and how projects not mentioned here fit our description.

Our first example is the work of the early-twentieth-century school of theologians associated with Sweden's University of Lund. The Lundensians held that their own work was purely historical. They said that theology is merely a descriptive science. Philosophy in the style of Immanuel Kant must precede theology by guaranteeing a priori that religion is a possible mode of human experience. Theology is then left with the task of exploring the historical forms of the experience thus legitimized. Buddhist theology (in this way of thinking) would discover and explore the organic whole that is Buddhism; Christian theology the organic whole that is Christianity. And all this is to be done in strict historical fashion.[14] The motive in this division of labor between philosophy and theology seems to have been twofold: on the one hand, Lundensian theology was relieved of an intolerable burden of apologetic prolegomena to its doctrinal inquiries; on the other, the importance of theology's fidelity to history was underscored.

Clearly there is a close connection between this understanding of the work of theology and our own. We part with the Lundensians in our belief that theology not only is but ought to be prescriptive as well as descriptive; it must propose as well as describe. Evidence that theology is ordinarily normative can be found in abundance on any shelf of theological works; not only radical revisionists but reactionary conservatives are constantly telling their readers what to believe. Even the excellent theological works of the early-twentieth-century Lundensians display this normative feature.[15] This is not because the Lundensians forgot their principles and lapsed into adjuration, but, we think, because of the convictional nature of the material that theology has to address. It is part of the meaning of a conviction that its holder wants others to share it in appropriate ways. Lundensians could hardly provide sympathetic accounts of "organic wholes" such as Christianity without thereby providing a more or less effective argument for the adoption of those wholes. And in line with what we say in chapter 5, part I, the very identification of convictions *as* convictions involves judgment, insight, and interpretation, tasks from which 'normative' considerations cannot be effectively filtered out. Nor, by our reckoning, should they be. With that caveat, we honor the historical-theological work of the Lundensians as a part of the task we envision here.

We come next to the American exponents of 'public' theology, that is, theology that professes that its evidence and arguments are available not just to the insiders of a religious community, but to any or all in the wider intellectual world. A major proponent of this 'public' approach, University of Chicago theologian David Tracy, calls his own version of it 'revisionist' theology.[16] For Roman Catholic Tracy, a public theology must have just two sources: "common human experience and language" and "Christian texts," notably the Bible understood not as sacred Scripture but as a humane classic. To be brief, these two sources (when understood by way of a metaphysical analysis that Tracy provides) are to yield "fundamental faith in the ultimate worth of our life here and now." Tracy argues that this basic faith is "common to the committed secular thinker and the committed Christian alike."[17]

Aspiring to a 'public' theology seems too attractive a proposal to refuse. Harvard Divinity School dean Ronald Thiemann, whose own orientation is toward Chicago's rival, Yale, has published a collection of essays that borrows the "public" motto, and still others have found it an effective slogan.[18] Yet there are aspects of Tracy's own project that make us deeply uneasy, at least at the outset. His programmatic statement of the common ground to be established by public theology seems to disregard most of what the present chapters have been at pains to establish: to begin, that we must take seriously the capacity of convinced speakers, whether committed secular or committed Christian or committed anything else, to say what they mean and mean what they say. It seems remarkable, for ex-

ample, that Tracy could understand the Apostle Paul (surely a good case
of a committed Christian) to have expressed faith in the *ultimate* worth of
life here and now. ("If in this life only we have hope in Christ, we are of
all men most miserable. But now is Christ risen from the dead" [1 Cor.
15:19f, KJV].) Such a question of interpretation turns toward the other seg-
ment of Tracy's theological source material — "Christian texts." And that
brings up afresh the hermeneutical task we pursued in chapters 2 and 3:
Are inscriptions and utterances to be interpreted by Wittgensteinian, or by
post-Saussurean, or rather (as we have argued) by Austinian methods? It
seems neither of Tracy's "sources," neither human experience nor classic
texts, will permit anyone to avoid the hard questions faced in the preceding chapters. Yet we delight in the goal of the public theologians, however
necessary it may be to challenge their methods. In particular, we note that
theologians such as Thiemann, just mentioned, and William Placher, to
be considered next, accept Tracy's challenge without commitment to his
(questionable) philosophical foundations.

Placher, a Yale-trained theologian teaching at Wabash College in In-
diana, in 1989 published *Unapologetic Theology,*[19] an entertaining and
sharp-edged picture of the contemporary American theological scene.
Following a pattern developed also in the first chapter of this book,
Placher contrasts the philosophical "foundationalism" of an Enlightenment approach to rational thinking (what we here call imperialism) with
the pluralistic starting point (what we call perspectivism) that he favors.
Like ourselves, Placher contrasts both these positions with relativism —
whose threat he, too, seeks to defuse. Using these familiar categories,
Placher shows how not a few theologians and philosophers in the past half
century (though not David Tracy) have moved from the assumption that
there is some one set of beliefs, some shared faith, that all thinkers have
and must have in common (foundationalism, imperialism) to the recognition that there is a plural variety of starting points, methods, sorts of
evidence, and goals.

A central chapter of Placher's argument is called "Conversation." If
there are no starting points, no foundational assumptions, that all thinkers
must assent to, how can we understand one another enough to converse?
In the spirit of our chapter 6, he shows that rational conversation in fact
always proceeds "ad hoc": We find that we have this or that or the other in
common (though not everything), and the conversation begins there. We
also discover where and how we disagree, and our agreements and disagreements together furnish the matter for particular conversations with
particular partners. Nor would this version of public theology exclude

from such transconvictional conversation those who adhere to particular traditions — since to do so would be to match their 'prejudices' with a more severe prejudice of our own. As Placher writes, "Enlightenment can become totalitarian too."[20] Yet Placher has not himself provided us with an example of the sort of theology we need, but only, as he somewhat self-deprecatingly says, a "discussion about discussions" about theological method — "Prolegomena to prolegomena! Worse and worse!"[21] In fact his survey is not only winsome but useful, yet we need now to find concrete examples of such theological conversation at work.

It seems natural to turn to the work of comparative religionists, or, as they usually prefer to be called, historians of religion. Not so long ago, these scholars were busy overcoming their confessional heritage (hence the low esteem in which some of them held 'comparison' — your religion is not as good as our religion). Accordingly, most of them have not attempted theological construction. Yet as we have seen (chap. 5), not even 'scientific' work can or should avoid convictional commitments, and more recently some historians of religion have turned to the theological task. We mention three. Kees Bolle, teaching at the University of California at Los Angeles, argued that the phenomena of comparative religion can be usefully approached from any one of several ideological standpoints: Catholicism, Marxism, and the one Bolle favors: "cultural creativity." The last recognizes (as the others do not?) the involvement of one's own tradition in the attempt to understand the religion of another people. It is plain, Bolle thinks, that no religious symbol from the past can without loss or remainder be translated into the language of the modern West. What is instead possible is "bringing the symbol" into the life of the investigator so that it functions creatively in his or her own life. "Cultural creativity" is thus not mere originality; it is "the establishment of human order out of chaos on the basis of the (re)discovered coherence of a symbolism."[22] Yet Bolle himself provides no extended example of the theology of "cultural creativity."

A historian of religions who may better fulfill this goal is Ninian Smart, a Scot who spent much of his teaching career at the University of California at Santa Barbara. Like some other students in the field (and in harmony with the argument already put forward in the first edition of the present book), Smart came in time to believe that no general demarcation between religious and nonreligious outlooks was possible, and one of the books produced later in his career was therefore named *Worldviews* — since so-called 'world religions' are prominent but not preemptive among the more successful worldviews to which human beings are committed.[23]

Of immediate interest, however, is Smart's *Christian Systematic Theology in a World Context.*[24] Here the worldview analysis of the previous book is employed to inform and explain Christian theology. Smart, a Scottish Episcopalian, and his writing partner, Steven Konstantine, who is Orthodox, use a framework of Christian theology to explain, to embrace, and even to absorb the teachings of other 'world religions.' As they say,

> We draw from all this the conclusion that the transforming and saving power of divine grace is operative widely in other faiths. It is true that the atmosphere of such religions may be very different: thus in the Theravada [the Buddhism of Southeast Asia] there is no sense of being alienated from a personal Lord and holy God; and the theory is propounded that one can attain a kind of self-salvation. But such theoretical and theological judgments, though at variance with the vision which we here present, are not the only vital features of such nontheistic religions. Looked at more widely such religions can be seen to produce fruits which are signals of the transcendental contact which, on our view, is contact with the Trinity herself.[25]

Such eclectic and synthesizing moves are certainly interesting, perhaps even strongly reassuring, to Christians who fear their own community's teaching may be arrogant: is Smart's not an appropriately humble (and thus more Christian) approach to other religions? Yet from the standpoint of the present book we sense that Smart and Konstantine move too far too fast. Is it really suitable to assume that all other worldviews (no longer to be confined to religions) are about salvation? And about salvation understood as reconciliation to a transcendent God, whether alienated from humanity or not?

Having such doubts, we find more compelling the approach to theology made by another historian of religion, Wilfred Cantwell Smith, whose analysis of the term "religion" proved helpful in chapter 1. Smith, a Presbyterian Christian whose comparative studies have focused upon Islam, has developed an approach to the relation between the major religions of the world summarized in lectures titled *Towards a World Theology.*[26] Here he repeats his warning that the word "religion" has changed radically over the centuries and urges that students focus not upon the "religions" of the world but upon the various ways of being "religious." This "religious" focus enables one to see what is the same in the various religious communities, while that sameness goes some distance to explain how elements of religions (for example, prayer beads or rosaries) are found in a number of world religions, performing similar though not identical functions.[27] This substitutability of elements, together with a theory about human solidarity ("we human beings on earth are diverse but not incongruous"[28]) is offered to justify a radical proposal: there can be a "world theology," one theology for all humanity, though this must be approached step by step, along several tracks, from the standpoint of the several traditions.

Wilfred Smith's approach is based on his own Christian identity. It incorporates three main elements: faith (which he takes to be a common human trait), revelation (not confined to original divine disclosures, but a generic name for the continuing access to truth in each religious community), and God, or the transcendent.[29] By taking an extremely flexible view of what is meant by "God," Smith finds it possible to include within the theological view of God even atheistic Buddhist and humanist understandings of *dharma* or truth, so long as these are seen to be transcendent by the community that believes in them. So far, we seem to have a proposal not unlike that of Smart and Konstantine, save that this is based upon a more Protestant approach to Christian thought, theirs upon a more Episcopal or Orthodox one. The distinctive feature of Smith's work is his attempt to respond, from the points of view of a typical Muslim, Hindu, Jew, Buddhist, and secularist, to the 'universal' proposal he has put forward, thus incorporating some of the elements of *conversation* (remember Placher) into his theological proposal. The present authors, with our own strongly differing conviction sets, have found such conversation so helpful that we are heartened to find it appear again in Wilfred Smith's project. Yet (in our own Christian and secular names, if not in the name of Buddhists and others) we have to ask if a theology based upon faith, revelation, and God or the transcendent can truly and successfully incorporate the diverse convictional communities of the world. The proposal seems ideally suited to Wilfred Smith's mild Calvinism and to the Islamic world he has so long studied, far less, though, to the rich broth of convictions, Marxist and materialist, polytheistic and profane, that the human world at present displays.

So we turn for our final illustration to a theological project already surveyed in chapter 5, the 'scientific theological' scheme modeled upon the philosophy of science of Imre Lakatos and put forward in Nancey Murphy's *Theology in the Age of Scientific Reasoning*.[30] That book argues that theological reasoning, to be effective in an age dominated by scientific thinking, must adopt the reasoning methods of science, which according to the Lakatosian model involves the adoption of 'research programs' whose 'hard cores' would persist while various theoretical adaptations were adopted by the researchers to accommodate new possibilities — and to avoid blind alleys. At the conclusion of our earlier account, it will be remembered, we bracketed Murphy's scheme, together with all other scientific proposals, if these were to be understood as nonconvictional shortcuts that avoided the costly work of justifying convictions — a work we have now sketched in chapter 6. Yet if we recognize (with Murphy herself) that such shortcuts are of necessity illusory, can we yet find a better role for the scientific theological reasoning she advocates? Does it offer a clear description of theology as a (convinced) science of convictions — the very sort of theology we advocate in this concluding chapter?

We cannot provide here a more compact summary of the Lakatos-Murphy project than we did in chapter 5, and readers are asked to review that summary as needed — indeed, to consult the concise account in Murphy's own elegantly brief volume. We want here only to recall the demands that she places upon any theology that would be truly scientific: it must have a "hard core" — a central conviction or convictions logically related (perhaps as their presupposition?) to the other convictions of the community; it must retain the hard core against refutations — the "negative heuristic"; it must have a positive doctrinal program (a "positive heuristic") that maintains its integrity and makes possible empirical progress. Murphy offers examples, drawn from the history of Christian theology, that fulfill these requirements. Her implicit demand is that other theologies, and those of other communities than the Christian one, take up the competitive task in the scientific trust that *the best research program will win.* So like William James's earlier project, hers envisions a pluralism of inquiry. No solitary theology can be in this sense scientific, exactly because it will lack competitors. And like Nielsen's, Murphy's envisions the use of philosophical method as required. It is not unlike the "public theology" proposal of David Tracy in finding two possible sources (or sorts of "data") for theology, namely, 'experience' and 'Scripture,' though it recognizes that data are theory-dependent so that they necessarily vary as the several theological theories vary.[31] It differs significantly from the *theological* proposals (as distinguished from the history of religions research) of Kees Bolle, Ninian Smart, and Wilfred Cantwell Smith in making no requirement that theology somehow already embrace all the religions (or all the convictional communities!) of the world. In Murphy's account, theologies can be scientific although addressed in the first instance to particular communities of reference — even communities so particular as the heirs of Luther, or the Council of Trent, or the Radical Reformation.

We have two final comments, in the form of questions, to put to Murphy's scientific theology. We ask, first, whether its present account of the data or sources for theology recognizes the role of convictions in forming human communities? There can be no rehearsal here of that role, which has occupied us in all the preceding chapters, but readers may recall that we found in convictions a bond between the objects of a faith (God, the Party, the Scientific Enterprise) and the sharers of that faith. Thanks to convictions the world that a science of convictions investigates can be one world, neither purely subjective experience nor coldly objective targets of faith, but annealed of both together. Might not scientific research programs investigate *sets of convictions narratively linked,* and indeed find in them ready-made bodies of data for inquiry? And second (here returning to a point raised first in chapter 5) does the logic of scientific investigation itself, as rationalized by a Lakatos or a Murphy, potentially stand not as an ally but as a rival to some (otherwise justifiable) set of convictions? To put the matter as a question, what justifies the logic of science when it comes to investigating (the truth of) scientific *or* religious convictions? Yet perhaps that is a philosophical question not properly part of scientific inquiry itself.

It is surely plain by now that we hold that philosophy is subject to the same convictional restraints and has the same kinds of opportunities as other disciplines dealing with convictional matters. There is considerable resistance within the philosophical community to this view of philosophy. Before we turn to the implications of our theory for the practice of philosophy, it is worth investigating the grounds for this resistance.

Philosophers have claimed independence of convictional barriers on two main grounds: One is that true philosophical thinking transcends mere cultural or historical barriers and is, in that sense, "pure." The other is that philosophical thinking does not rise to the importance of convictions, being merely an underlaborer, a brush-clearer for science or theology or some other discipline. To the first we have already responded. Philosophy is a human activity, and if it confronts fundamental human problems our previous arguments show that it cannot do so without being convictional. Purity or transcendence can be purchased only at the cost of emptiness. As for the second ground, it is not altogether false. Certainly much that is called philosophy (in professional journals, for example), while it may be of technical interest, has little to do with convictions. No doubt philosophers could resolve to limit themselves to such concerns. But the probable result would be that others less devoted to standards of clarity, precision, and rationality would seize the field of convictional inquiry. We would do well to remember that some of those who have announced the most modest aims for philosophy have also spoken most readily of convictional matters: Locke, who aspired only to be an underlaborer, wrote the *Second Treatise on Government,* and Wittgenstein, who characterized philosophy as (a very special kind of) nonsense, could nevertheless make remarks like the one used as an epigraph for chapter 6.

But there is another, more practical ground for resisting convictional restraint and we have considerable sympathy with it. No philosopher, conscious of the life and death of Socrates, Spinoza, or Russell, and cherishing independence, will readily consent to making himself or herself a partisan of a particular class or culture. Unlike theology, philosophy seems to have no institutional identification to begin with; therefore it is tempting to elevate this appearance into a necessary truth and assert the freedom of philosophy from all intellectual restraints — including convictional ones.

To yield to this temptation, however, is to misunderstand convictions and the restraints they impose. As we pointed out in the case of theology (and this point is equally valid for politics, economics, history, etc.) convictions need not be conservative or orthodox or tailored to the dogmas of any given group. A philosopher can be as radical or heterodox as one likes. But to be intelligibly radical or to have a point of view recognizable as heterodox requires that one take a position with respect to what is understood as orthodox or conservative. This is likely to be convictional in two ways: First, since it is the taking of a position, it involves the adoption of standards of rationality, coherence, morality, and so forth — and such standards are almost necessarily convictional. Second, in taking one position over another, the philosopher is opposing views that are likely to be convictional, and in doing so, proposing logical homogenes to them. Socrates, Spinoza, and Russell were radical and independent not because they lacked convictions or identified with no community, but because the smaller community out of which they grew (and which grew around them) was devoted to standards of rationality and rigor that the hostile larger society could hardly understand.

As these examples show, the restraints produced by the holding of convictions are not barriers to independence or intellectual freedom in any intelligible sense. Test oaths, censorship, and other legal threats are barriers to philosophical development. Convictions, on the contrary, are the result of philosophical development as well as a standard for further development.

In our discussions of Scriven, Farrer, James, and Nielsen, we have suggested some of the limitations our theory implies for philosophy. But it would be more accurate to speak of limitations on the claims made for certain philosophical techniques. We have produced no basis for calling into question either the interest in or the validity of philosophical proofs or disproofs of the existence of God, free will, or any other convictional matters. We *have* argued that such proofs, insofar as they employ convictional premises or appeal to convictional standards of rationality or coherence or significance, are incapable of settling those convictional conflicts that have been the focus of this book. Proofs may nevertheless be (as we think) indispensable for establishing and exhibiting the internal coherence and significance of a conviction set and for indicating common ground with other conviction sets. They may certainly lead to an appreciation of the complexities and profundities within a conviction set. And the aesthetic appeal of such proofs — like many proofs in mathematics — is obvious to any who have taken the trouble to follow them rigorously. We regard these as enormously important and interesting properties of convictional arguments, not to be ignored or deprecated. To be disappointed because they cannot settle convictional disputes is to weep because the jet engine is not a perpetual motion machine.

But this is not to say that philosophy is useless in convictional disputes. That would not be true even if philosophical techniques were exhausted by the proofs and disputes we have been discussing. The exhibition of conceptual connections in a precise and perspicuous way is an aid — perhaps an indispensable aid — to the self-understanding that precedes a fruitful dialogue on matters as fundamental as convictions.

But philosophical techniques are not, in fact, exhausted by deductive argument and the application of established or a priori standards of significance, rationality, coherence, and the like. Another technique (on which we have depended heavily) is the patient searching out and exhibition of the distinctions revealed to us by common speech, including, of course, the speech of adherents of rival convictions. It was this technique that Austin believed offered the "fun of discovery, the pleasures of cooperation and the satisfaction of reaching agreement"[32] (and we can testify to the accuracy of his belief). As our own efforts show, this is neither a mechanical process, nor one guaranteed of success. Indeed, to understand fully the speech-acts of a community requires no less (but no more) than understanding its corresponding beliefs and convictions. Speech-acts, however, have an immediate availability that convictions (traditionally conceived) lacked. If our thesis concerning the relation of convictions and speech-acts is correct, that traditional conception is in error, and the significance of speech-act analysis is broadened all the more.

The speech-act analyst may be denied the pleasures of cooperation and agreement precisely because of the linguistic convictional barriers that in fact exist. If so, there remain the variety of devices for redefinition that have as long a philosophical history as deductive argument: whether the philosopher proceeds by paradox and Socratic *elenchus, de more geometrico,* dialectically, or through depth grammar, he or she will not lack for models. Indeed, there is considerable ground for claiming an enhanced role for philosophy if we are correct about the nature of convictional pluralism. For philosophers since Thales have perennially dealt with convictional matters, and they have been made unusually sensitive to the dangers and opportunities in convictional conflict. What may be obscured by narrow concentration on *one* kind of philosophical approach may be revealed by patient and imaginative use of the variety of alternatives philosophy has provided through its long history.

What contribution is to be made by the philosophy of religion? Much philosophy of religion is clearly what we call theoretics — the assertion and reasoned defense of a point of view. The same is true of philosophy more generally. When a Scriven or a Farrer sets out to prove that God does or does not exist, we think he is engaged upon a theologian's task. Since not all convictional exploration concerns religion, we prefer to say that the work thus undertaken is theoretics. It is no criticism of philosophers to say that they are sometimes theoreticians as well. But in other cases, the philosophers merely come to the aid of the theoreticians in the untangling of puzzles or the checking of work. In these cases, the philosophers clearly cannot replace the theoreticians, though their advice may be indispensable. How easily the theoretician's job may shade over into the philosopher's and philosophy into theology again is a matter for philosophical attention itself.

The present work, with its interest in just such distinctions, represents another strand in philosophy than that described in the preceding paragraph. Our work may be called philosophy of religion, not because it sets out to decide religious (or convictional) questions, but because it seeks to show what kinds of speech-acts religious speakers perform, what sort of belief a conviction is, how the former may be found happy, or how the latter may be justified. Philosophy of religion, in this understanding of the term, investigates the concepts and practices of religion and explores the limits of theology but is not itself theology or theoretics and cannot replace these. Theoretics is (or may become) the 'science of convictions'; philosophy of religion done as we have done it is not that science but rather (to borrow an old metaphor) its servant or handmaid.

We have not set out to do theoretics in this book, and we have conscientiously avoided arguments on behalf of this or that conviction set. We have also made a point of our own widely differing religious convictions. Nevertheless, we acknowledge that we share convictions that have guided our work and even made it possible. Some are so common that we undoubtedly share them with any reader: the veridical nature of some of our experience, the genetic continuity of our selves, and more. Others, though not equally common, have contributed in a specific way to our ability to work together in spite of disagreements: we are convinced that dialogue and cooperation are preferable to dispute and hostility, and, at a more general and philosophically interesting level, we subscribe to the fallibility principle, the conviction that any of our convictions might be false and that all are open to criticism, modification, and even rejection.

This is a fairly small list of fairly particular convictions, not perhaps of great interest in a world racked by conflicts between authoritarian and democrat, Arab and Jew, radical and reactionary. There are other convictions guiding our work, however, that do seem to share the character of those convictions over which people argue and fight and die. Perhaps our own rather similar life-histories have given us similar views on religious issues that are not made explicit in our work. Our arguments and disagreements and their (sometime) resolution suggest that we share common views about rationality and coherence and about the relation of our theories to our experience. Discussions with friends and colleagues persuade us that not everyone shares these views. Those who do not may expect to find our work not (merely) mistaken, inadequate, or inaccurate but unintelligible, incoherent, or incredible. Not every criticism reflects such a convictional difference, of course; and not everyone who differs with us on some conviction will necessarily disagree with all we have said.

No doubt there are still other convictions that have helped to make this work what it is. To the extent that the argument of this book is cogent, these convictions, whatever they may be, are supported and can be recommended to others. But happy or not, our convictions, like everyone else's, must stand their turn in the dock, for they too require subjection to the ongoing process of justification, with whatever adjustment that process may in turn demand of the authors of this book.

Notes

Chapter 1:
Convictions and Religion

1. "The Modes of Thought and the Logic of God," in John Hick, ed., *The Existence of God* (New York: Macmillan, 1964), 297–98.

2. Karl Marx, "Theses on Feuerbach," in Friedrich Engels, *Ludwig Feuerbach and the Outcome of Classical German Philosophy* (New York: International Publishers, 1941).

3. A valuable discussion of the concept of conviction is found in Willem F. Zuurdeeg, *An Analytical Philosophy of Religion* (Nashville: Abingdon, 1958), chap. 1.

4. Jonathan Edwards, *Concerning the End for Which God Created the World,* in Paul Ramsey, ed., *Ethical Writings: The Works of Jonathan Edwards,* vol. 8 (New Haven: Yale University Press, 1989), 533.

5. In ordinary language, what one 'believes' may be distinct from what one 'knows'; thus to call convictions a kind of belief might seem to suggest that we cannot know what we are convinced of, but this is not what we mean to say.

6. John Hick, *An Interpretation of Religion* (New Haven: Yale University Press, 1989).

7. Ibid., 235–36. "Post-axial" religions are those religions that have developed in the wake of the lives of Buddha, Confucius, Lao-Tze, Socrates, and Jesus, and that emphasize salvation or liberation or enlightenment as the human and divine goal.

8. Ibid., 124f.

9. Ibid., chaps. 19–20, see esp. 375–76.

10. "Of Miracles" is Section X of David Hume, *An Enquiry Concerning Human Understanding* (1st ed., 1777), collected in David Hume, *Enquiries Concerning the Human Understanding and Concerning the Principles of Morals,* ed. L. A. Selby-Bigge, 2d ed. (Oxford: Clarendon Press, 1961); David Hume, *Dialogues Concerning Natural Religion* (1st ed., 1779), ed. Henry D. Aiken (New York: Hafner, 1948); Immanuel Kant, *Religion within the Limits of Reason Alone*

(1st ed., 1794), trans. T. M. Greene and Hoyt H. Hudson (New York: Harper & Row, 1960).

11. We note that some who support the epistemology we are about to describe neither use nor are fond of the name "Reformed epistemology." What follows is nonetheless based on the works next to be noted, as well as on two very readable articles: Merold Westphal, "A Reader's Guide to 'Reformed Epistemology,'" and Nicholas Wolterstorff, "What 'Reformed Epistemology' Is Not," both in *Perspectives* (November 1992): 10–16, and on a useful critique by Terrence Tilley, "Reformed Epistemology in Jamesian Perspective," *Horizons* 19, no. 1 (Spring, 1992): 84–98.

12. Alvin Plantinga, "Reason and Belief in God," in Alvin Plantinga and Nicholas Wolsterstorff, eds. *Faith and Rationality: Reason and Belief in God* (Notre Dame, Ind.: University of Notre Dame Press, 1983), 73. See also Nicholas Wolterstorff, *Reason within the Bounds of Religion,* 2d ed. (Grand Rapids: Eerdmans, 1984).

13. Westphal, "A Reader's Guide," 13.

14. Alvin Plantinga, "Epistemic Probability and Evil," *Archivo da Filosofia,* ed. Marco Olivetti (Rome: Cedam, 1988), 578, cited in Tilley, "Reformed Epistemology," note 17.

15. William P. Alston, *Perceiving God: The Epistemology of Religious Experience* (Ithaca, N.Y.: Cornell University Press, 1991), chap. 4.

16. Wolterstorff, "What 'Reformed Epistemology' Is Not," 15f.

17. E.g., Tilley, "Reformed Epistemology in Jamesian Perspective."

18. Henry Fielding, *The History of Tom Jones, a Foundling* (London: Collins, 1955 [1st ed., 1749]), 107.

19. Wilfred Cantwell Smith, *The Meaning and End of Religion* (New York: Macmillan, 1963), chap. 2, "Religion' in the West," with extensive notes found on pp. 203–45.

20. Ibid., 45.

21. Frederick Ferré, "The Definition of Religion," *Journal of the American Academy of Religion* (March 1970): 3–16.

22. Frederick Ferré, *Basic Modern Philosophy of Religon* ((New York: Scribner's 1967), 69.

Chapter 2:
Recent Approaches to Religious Language

1. Ludwig Wittgenstein, *Lectures and Conversations on Aesthetics, Psychology and Religious Belief,* ed. Cyril Barrett (Berkeley and Los Angeles: University of California Press, 1967), 58. We have corrected the placement of the quotation marks, assuming it to be a typographical correction.

2. Stanley Fish, "Is There a Text in This Class?" (Cambridge, Mass.: Harvard University Press, 1980), 318.

3. William James, *The Varieties of Religious Experience* (1902), in *William James: Writings 1902–1910*, ed. Bruce Kuklick (New York: Library of America, 1987), 104.

4. The classic Logical Positivist view of religious language is found in Alfred J. Ayer, *Language, Truth and Logic* (1936; New York: Dover, 1952).

5. The difficulties of verifiability (and falsifiability, to be discussed in chap. 5) for religion were explored while it was still a live issue in a collection of short essays written from various viewpoints and gathered in Antony Flew and Alasdair MacIntyre, eds., *New Essays in Philosophical Theology* (London: SCM Press, 1955). The further fortunes of the verification criterion's role in the philosophy of religion are summarized in Diogenes Allen, *The Reasonableness of Faith: A Philosophical Essay on the Grounds for Religious Beliefs* (Washington and Cleveland: Corpus Books, 1968), chap. 2.

6. Ludwig Wittgenstein, *Tractatus Logico-philosophicus* trans. Pears and McGuiness (London: Routledge and Kegan Paul, 1974 [1st ed., 1922]). Wittgenstein, however, intended the *Tractatus* to be taken in a much more paradoxical way than the Positivists had recognized. For him the literally 'senseless' questions of philosophy and religion were already, at this his first stage, of unlimited importance, as the concluding sentences of the *Tractatus* show. See Norman Malcolm, "Wittgenstein, Ludwig Josef Johann," *The Encyclopedia of Philosophy*, ed. Paul Edwards, 8 vols. (New York: Macmillan and Free Press, 1967), 8:327–40; Ludwig Wittgenstein, *Lectures and Conversations.*

7. Ludwig Wittgenstein, *Philosophical Investigations*, trans. G. E. M. Anscombe (New York: Macmillan, 1953).

8. See note 6.

9. The following paragraphs are based on Norman Malcolm's "The Groundlessness of Belief," in R. Douglas Geivett and Brendan Sweetman, eds. *Contemporary Perspectives on Religious Epistemology* (New York: Oxford University Press, 1992).

10. Ibid., 100.

11. D[ewi] Z. Phillips, *Faith and Philosophical Enquiry* (London: Routledge and Kegan Paul, 1970), 77f.

12. Dewi Z. Phillips, *The Concept of Prayer* (London: Routledge & Kegan Paul, 1965), chaps. 1 and 2.

13. Wittgenstein, *Lectures and Conversations*, 56.

14. Phillips, *Faith and Philosophical Enquiry*, 94.

15. Ibid., 97f.

16. D. Z. Phillips, *Faith after Foundationalism* (London and New York: Routledge, 1988), part 1.

17. Phillips, *Faith after Foundationalism*, 89, 245–47. In the second case, Phillips is commenting on a similar view in another Wittgensteinian, Paul Holmer, *The Grammar of Faith* (San Francisco: Harper & Row, 1978), 131–35.

18. Saussure's teaching was powerful and influential, but he wrote little. His views can be found in the book constructed from his lectures by his followers, *Cours de linguistique générale* (Paris, 1891), trans. Wade Baskin, *Course in*

General Linguistics (New York, 1959). Our abbreviated account is drawn from standard encyclopedia articles and from the work listed in the following note.

19. The example is taken from John M. Ellis, *Against Deconstruction* (Princeton, N.J.: Princeton University Press, 1989), 46f. Ellis provides a useful overview of Saussure's system.

20. Walter Ong, "Wit and Mystery," cited in Christopher Norris, *Deconstruction: Theory and Practice,* rev. ed. (London and New York: Routledge, 1991), 13f.

21. A primary source for Deconstruction is the writings of French literary critic Jacques Derrida, notably *Of Grammatology,* trans. G. C. Spivak (Baltimore: Johns Hopkins, 1977 [French, 1967]). Among secondary sources we depend especially upon Christopher Norris, *Deconstruction: Theory and Practice,* rev. ed. (London and New York: Routledge, 1991) and even more upon Ellis, *Against Deconstruction;* further full bibliographies are found in Norris and Ellis.

22. Norris, *Deconstruction,* 18–55; Ellis, *Against Deconstruction,* 18–66.

23. Stanley Fish, *Is There a Text?*

24. The illustration is our own.

25. Fish, *Is There a Text?,* 4f.

26. Ibid., 13. We add that Fish does something a bit fishy here: if there are really only "texts," i.e., various interpretations, isn't the sentence in which he makes this claim confused? Interpretations of what? At the beginning of the sentence, he refers to "the text" that "drops out"; but the latter part of the sentence seems to say it was never there? *What* was never there?

27. Ibid., 14–16.

28. We are indebted to Nancey Murphy for this insight. Dealing with fiction, however, Fish is less concerned than we are with *reference.*

29. William James, *Some Problems of Philosophy* (posthumously published in 1911), republished in *William James: Writings 1902–1910* (New York: Library of America, 1987), 996.

30. Ibid. Emphasis added.

31. William James, *The Varieties of Religious Experience* (1902, comprising the Gifford Lectures for 1899–1901) republished in *William James,* 214–18.

32. For example, he writes, "These problems [of metaphysics] are for the most part real; that is, but few of them result from a misuse of terms in stating them" (James, *Some Problems,* 998).

33. James, *Varieties,* 202.

34. Ibid., 165n.

35. See ibid., Lectures XVIII–XX.

36. Bernard E. Meland, ed., *The Future of Empirical Theology* (Chicago: University of Chicago Press, 1969).

37. William James, *The Meaning of Truth* (1909), republished in *William James,* 826.

38. Bernard E. Meland, *Fallible Forms and Symbols: Discourses on Method in a Theology of Culture* (Philadelphia: Fortress Press, 1976), xiii, 43, 48f, 174f.

39. See ibid., chaps. 2 through 4.

40. Nancy Frankenberry, *Religion and Radical Empiricism* (Albany, N.Y.: SUNY Press, 1987), 132, quoting Meland, *Fallible Forms,* 56.

41. Frankenberry, *Religion and Radical Empiricism,* 132.

42. Ibid., 136–42.

43. These works are republished in *William James,* together with his uncompleted textbook, *Some Problems of Philosophy,* and essays from the same period.

44. Richard Rorty discusses the philosophy of language in several essays collected in part 2 of his *Objectivity, Relativism, and Truth* (New York: Cambridge University Press, 1991).

45. Richard Rorty, *Philosophy and the Mirror of Nature* (Princeton, N.J.: Princeton University Press, 1979).

46. Sallie McFague, *Metaphorical Theology: Models of God in Religious Language* (Philadelphia: Fortress, 1982).

47. See especially Ian T. Ramsey, *Religious Language* (London: SCM Press, 1957); *Models and Mystery* (London: Oxford University Press, 1964); Ramsey, ed., *Words about God: The Philosophy of Religion* (London: SCM Press, 1971). For a longer bibliography and critical discussion, see the following note.

48. A fuller, critical discussion of Ramsey is our article, "Ian Ramsey's Model of Religious Language: A Qualified Appreciation," *Jounal of the American Academy of Religion* 41, no. 3 (September 1973). The best critical survey of Ramsey's work is Terrence Tilley, "On Being Tentative in Theology," dissertation, Graduate Theological Union, Berkeley, Calif., 1976. Among other things, Tilley reports there the content of the lost Ramsey manuscript whose discovery rounds out our knowledge of his contribution to the philosophy of religion. Finally, see also pp. 35–47 and notes thereto in the first edition of the present book.

49. Following Ramsey and drawing on his own scientific competence, Ian Barbour's *Myths, Models and Paradigms: A Comparative Study in Science and Religion* (New York: Harper & Row, 1974) provides a nonideological account of symbols, myths, parables, metaphors, and models in religion. Janet Soskice, *Metaphor and Religious Language* (Oxford: Clarendon Press, 1985) offers the best account of metaphor in religion, beginning from a literary point of view.

50. See Paul Ricoeur, *The Conflict of Interpretations* (Evanston: Northwestern University Press, 1974); Anthony C. Thistleton, *New Horizons in Hermeneutics* (London: Harper Collins, 1992).

Chapter 3:
A Speech-Act Theory of Religious Language

1. J. O. Urmson and G. J. Warnock, eds., *Philosophical Papers* (Oxford: Clarendon Press, 1961), 33.

2. Stanley Cavell, *Must We Mean What We Say?* (New York: Scribner's, 1969), 19.

3. Evans's work is published as *The Logic of Self-Involvement: A Philosophical Study of Everyday Language with Special Reference to the Christian Use of Language about God as Creator* (London: SCM Press, 1963). The second part presents a 'performative' doctrine of creation that is theological in intent.

4. Austin's principal work (cut short by his early death) is available in three volumes: *Sense and Sensibilia,* reconstructed by G. J. Warnock (Oxford: Clarendon Press, 1962); *How to Do Things with Words,* the William James Lectures for 1955, ed. J. O. Urmson (Oxford: Clarendon Press, 1962); and *Philosophical Papers,* 2d ed., ed. J. O. Urmson and G. J. Warnock (Oxford: Clarendon Press, 1970). Also see "Critical Notice of J. L. Lukasiewicz' *Aristotle's Syllogistic: From the Standpoint of Modern Formal Logic,*" *Mind* 61 (1952).

Austin's best-known successor is (the early) John Searle. See his "What Is a Speech Act?" in *Philosophy in America,* ed. Max Black (Ithaca, N.Y.: Cornell University Press, 1965), and his *Speech Acts: An Essay in the Philosophy of Language* (London: Cambridge University Press, 1969). See also Mats Furberg, *Saying and Meaning, a Main Theme in J. L. Austin's Philosophy* (Oxford: Basil Blackwell, 1971), and the essays in K. T. Fann, ed., *Symposium on J. L. Austin* (London: Routledge & Kegan Paul, and New York: Humanities Press, 1969).

5. See "Performative Utterances" in *Philosophical Papers,* and *How to Do Things with Words,* 45–91.

6. *How to Do Things with Words,* 45–91; "Performative Utterances" in *Philosophical Papers.* After noting that relation to the facts is a significant test of the happiness of the 'performative' and 'constative' utterances alike, Austin remarks with his characteristic irony: "This is in itself no doubt a very trivial part of our investigations" (*How to Do Things with Words,* 45).

7. Some philosophers have argued that Austin was mistaken, that there are sure-fire tests for a narrowly defined class of performative utterances. But for what follows their cavil, even if sustained, does not matter. For the importance of performatives in Austin's thought (and in ours) was heuristic; it helped to free him from the grip of the "descriptive fallacy" and enabled him to develop the theory of speech-acts, and it is the latter that is our interest here.

8. See for example Gilbert Ryle, *The Concept of Mind* (London: Hutchinson's University Library, 1949); Anthony Kenny, *Action, Emotion and Will* (London: Routledge & Kegan Paul, 1963); Myles Brand, *The Nature of Human Action* (Glenview, Ill.: Scott, Foresman, 1970); Stuart Hampshire, *Thought and Action* (London: Chatto & Windus, 1959); Charles Taylor, *The Explanation of Behavior* (London: Routledge & Kegan Paul, 1964); and the literature cited in these.

9. This is our term; Austin and John R. Searle distinguish differently than we do the ways in which in speaking we act. Austin speaks of phonetic, phatic, and rhetic acts, and of locutions *vs.* illocutions (*How to Do Things with Words,* 91ff.); Searle speaks of utterance acts (uttering words, morphemes, sentences), propositional acts (referring and predicating), and illocutionary acts (stating, promising,

etc.) ("Austin on Locutionary and Illocutionary Acts," *Philosophical Review,* October 1968; and *Speech Acts,* 24ff.). Our distinction of phonetic acts (issuing sounds), sentential acts (uttering sentences in a language), and illocutionary acts = speech-acts (stating, promising, etc.) is for present purposes clearer and more manageable, we believe.

10. *How to Do Things with Words,* 98ff.

11. Regrettably, there is no uniformity in the usage of "speech-act." Austin usually (cf. *How to Do Things with Words,* 52, 147; *Philosophical Papers* [1961], 238) but apparently not always (cf. *How to Do Things with Words,* 146) used "speech-act" (or "speech act") of the illocution in its context — the "total speech situation." Searle instead uses "speech act" as a *generic* term for utterance acts, propositional acts, and illocutionary acts (*Speech Acts,* 22). We stick closer to the usual Austin, differ from Searle, and use "speech-act" (including, thereby, its implied subacts, the sentential act and phonetic act) because Austin's term "illocutionary act" is such a mouthful.

Paralleling the speech-act could be the "graphic-act"; each would entail a sentential act; in the former case the sentential act would be also the acts of saying words and of moving one's jaw, issuing sounds, etc.; in the latter case the sentential act would be also the acts of *writing* words, moving one's pen (or typewriter) upon the paper, etc. But since little is to be gained for present purposes by making these distinctions in each case, we shall employ "speech-act" in a sense that includes written as well as spoken language.

12. This may be seen by noting the number of works on religious language that refer to the Austinian work but continue blithely to treat "religious statements" or "religious assertions" as if they were self-evidently satisfactory linguistic categories.

13. Financial statements are useful examples to keep in mind for bringing together several of these points: (*a*) While the treasurer or accountant may prepare such a statement, the office boy, even if talented, cannot (special position required). (*b*) If the treasurer or the CPA does give us this information in proper form, it is a *statement,* not an assertion, a guess, or a telling (i.e., responsibility is fixed in a particular way upon the issuer of the statement, and the same thing is true if it is an institution that issues the statement). (*c*) Although the fact that you owe $250.37, or that the Bank of Angel Island has on deposit $135,791.35, may appropriately appear in a statement, the fact that you are a dead-beat, or that the bank is greedy, may not, even though you are, it is, and the CPA knows it (limitation of appropriateness).

14. J. L. Austin, *Philosophical Papers* (1961), 236f.

15. A similar speech-act humor characterizes a Ring Lardner line (reporting what he said to his children): " 'Shut up,' I explained carefully."

16. This section is based in part on James M. Smith and James Wm. McClendon, Jr., "Religious Language after J. L. Austin," *Religious Studies* 8 (March 1972).

17. Some might contend that the conditions we are about to lay down are too stringent. After all, isn't a mumbled request or one for an impossible task

still some sort of request? This misses our point, however, in using "happy" or "unhappy" of speech-acts. We want to call attention to the wide variety of ways in which acts, including speech-acts, can go wrong or be subject to criticism or question. Just as other acts can be clumsy, graceful, careless, or clever as well as morally wrong or legally authorized, so speech-acts can have many virtues and vices besides existing or not existing as such. It is to avoid undue concentration on traditional categories of assessment that, with Austin, we use the very broad terms "happy" and "unhappy" (or sometimes, for stylistic convenience, "felicitous" or "infelicitous") as assessments of all the faults and virtues of speech-acts.

18. Cf. a similar attempt by John R. Searle, *Speech Acts,* 66. Searle tabulates the conditions for requesting as follows:

Propositional content	Future act A of H.
Preparatory	1. H is able to do A. S believes H is able to do A.
	2. It is not obvious to both S and H that H will do A in the normal course of events of his own accord.
Sincerity	S wants H to do A.
Essential	Counts as an attempt to get H to do A.

19. Searle does call such a condition "essential."

20. Searle, *Speech Acts,* 66, incurs the latter risk by listing the essential condition of requesting as "Counts as an attempt to get H to do A." That seems to disregard the distinction between requesting and ordering, for one thing; for another it seems to disregard the (really essential) difference between linguistic and nonlinguistic ways of getting "H to do A," a difference Searle is in general deeply interested in.

21. Of course, "Hello" and "Thank you" are not in the usual technical sense 'referring expressions,' but the speech-acts that they are used to perform require certain things to be true of the world if they are to be happy.

22. On this point, cf. Searle, *Speech Acts,* 44f.; cf. also the articles by H. Paul Grice: "Meaning," *Philosophical Review* (July 1957); "Utterer's Meaning and Intentions," *Philosophical Review* (April 1969); "Utterer's Meaning, Sentence-Meaning, and Word-Meaning," *Foundations of Language* (August 1968).

23. *How to Do Things with Words,* 115f.

24. *The Confessions of St. Augustine,* trans. E. B. Pusey (New York: Washington Square Press, n.d.), 1.

25. See H. Richard Niebuhr, *The Meaning of Revelation* (New York: Macmillan, 1941), chap. 2.

26. However, Isaac Newton himself believed in miracles and was thus not a 'Newtonian' in the present sense. The plainest Newtonian in our sense is La Place, who felt no need to use the "hypothesis of God" to explain the heavens.

27. Clearly, then, these remarks are not offered as settling the question of whether it is proper *to say* that God acts in history or the question of whether

God does so; we are at best providing a kind of linguistic footnote to those related questions.

28. W. J. Harrelson, "Blessings and Cursings," in *Interpreter's Dictionary of the Bible,* ed. G. A. Buttrick (New York: Abingdon, 1962), vol. 1; our emphasis.

29. A good instance of a classic liturgy that displays these elements clearly is the Liturgy of St. James of the Eastern Church.

30. *Sabbath and Festival Prayer Book* (Rabbinical Assembly of America and the United Synagogue of America, 1946), 28.

31. *The Passover Haggadah, with English Translation, Introduction, and Commentary,* based on the commentaries of E. D. Goldschmidt, ed. Nahum H. Glatzer (New York: Schocken Books, 1953).

32. Ibid.

33. If the uptake of confession requires genuine understanding of *what* is confessed, it follows that the solitary believer is one whose speech is (necessarily) unhappy — a linguistic point of great theological interest.

34. Our guide to Buddhagosa is Ninian Smart, *Reasons and Faiths: An Investigation of Religious Discourse, Christian and Non-Christian* (London: Routledge & Kegan Paul, 1958), 95–104.

Chapter 4:
How Are Convictions Justifiable?

1. Ludwig Wittgenstein, *Philosophical Investigations,* trans. G. E. M. Anscombe (New York: Macmillan, 1953), I, 373, 116e; II, xii, 230e.

2. Norman O. Brown, *Love's Body* (New York: Random House, 1966), 82f.

3. The appropriate changes would be those that allowed for the evident differences between a speech-act and a thought or belief: speech is faulted, often, if it is not heard; it requires a certain degree of uptake for its success; it is a performance or act; it occurs at a given time and can be repeated; these features give rise to differences that could be explored in detail, but, our interests being different, we will not do so here.

4. It might be possible to examine systems of religious belief, and the apologies for such systems, in terms of these three categories.

5. We are not concerned here with legal rights.

6. It may be worth noting that a suspicion, though once justifiable and even justified, meeting every available challenge, may cease to be either. The police chief was justified, given the evidence, in suspecting Roberts, but now that Randall is caught red-handed, the suspicion of Roberts is no longer justified.

7. Willem F. Zuurdeeg, *An Analytical Philosophy of Religion* (Nashville: Abingdon, 1958), 58.

8. For example, we may not know when to count a growing youth as an adult or an immigrant as acculturated, nor when to count a play or a novel as 'great.' Yet without doubt there are full-grown adults, acculturated immigrants, and great plays, and there are as well callow youths, obvious newcomers, and

slight or insignificant novels. In case of need, we define the border: an 'adult' may then be one who has reached his or her eighteenth birthday; the great novel, one that has endured one hundred years and enjoyed a million readers. But these acts of precision are themselves but approximations, mere rules of thumb.

9. Willem F. Zuurdeeg, *An Analytical Philosophy of Religion*, 40–44.

10. Indeed, several stories in the gospels and in Christian tradition. However, let us assume that these coalesce in Aleph's mind (he may believe that many of them are variants of a single story in the gospel tradition), or that one, e.g., the healing in John 9, assumes prototypical importance for him.

11. A fact that tends to explain the resistance of many believers to critical examination of sacred texts. The critic is tampering with words that express, that are, another's convictions.

12. Wilfred Cantwell Smith, *Questions of Religious Truth* (New York: Scribner's, 1967), 89.

13. Thus R. B. Braithwaite's claim for the importance of stories is quite justified, though we believe he does not accurately identify the basis for that claim. See *An Empiricists' View of the Nature of Religious Belief* (Cambridge: Cambridge University Press, 1955).

14. See, for example, the "Christology" article in any convenient handbook or encyclopedia of Christian theology, or James Wm. McClendon, Jr., *Doctrine: Systematic Theology, Volume II* (Nashville: Abingdon, 1994), chaps. 5–6.

15. *Summa Theologica*, 1–2ae, q. 109, art. 8. We have quoted from the Library of Christian Classics edition of selections: *Nature and Grace,* trans. A. M. Fairweather (Philadelphia: Westminster, 1965), 151.

16. *The Christian Faith,* trans. H. R. Macintosh and J. Stewart (Edinburgh: T. & T. Clark, 1928), §100 (p. 425).

17. Cf. the discussion of the context of the representative force of G in our chap. 3, 66–70.

18. Van A. Harvey, *The Historian and the Believer* (New York: Macmillan, 1966), 265ff.

19. *An Analytical Philosophy of Religion*, 32–35.

20. "Is 'Transcendence' the Word We Want?" *Theological Explorations* (New York: Macmillan, 1968), 164.

21. *Tractatus Logico-Philosophicus*, ed. D. F. Pears and B. F. McGuiness (London: Routledge & Kegan Paul, 2nd impression, 1933), 44 (our translation).

22. *Theological Explorations*, 169–70.

23. Ibid., 171. We remark that the capacity to be puzzled or astonished at what most take for granted is a characteristic shared by geniuses (and lunatics) in many areas: science, poetry, and philosophy as well as religion.

24. Ibid., 172.

25. Save by specifying a code, a possibility that presupposes the very conventional structure of language that we are here invoking.

26. Cf. for example *How to Do Things with Words,* the William James Lectures for 1955, ed. J. O. Urmson (Oxford: Clarendon Press, 1962), 27 (divorce among Mohammedans, etc.).

27. Some of these convictions are, of course, at a different level from the ones that are our models in the present chapter. They do not, as far as we know, entail entirely different considerations than do the latter, however.

28. On the relation between convictions, character, and morality, see also James Wm. McClendon, Jr., *Biography as Theology* (Valley Forge, Pa.: Trinity Press International, 1990), chaps. 1 and 7, and the literature cited there.

29. We take these character traits to involve not just urges in one direction or another, but beliefs about the preferability of certain policies or goals; e.g., the ambitious person is one who believes that success of certain kinds is of great importance, while a malicious person believes that the interests of others are readily sacrificed to his or her own pleasure. If then we consider the case of the malicious person who is (therefore) conscience-stricken, we will say that such a person is not one lacking in these convictions, but rather, if "malice" and "conscience" correctly apply to him or her, one who has two (painfully contrary) convictions. Thus this is not the case we have in mind in the text.

Chapter 5:
A Perspective on Nonperspectival Reason

1. *Pensées*, trans. A. J. Krailsheimer (Harmondsworth: Penguin Books, 1966), 95.

2. *The Future of an Illusion* (Garden City, N.Y.: Doubleday, Anchor, 1957), 86.

3. Roger Trigg (in *Reason and Commitment* [Cambridge: Cambridge University Press, 1973], 145–57) argues that it makes no sense to speak as we have here of a "commitment" to reason: reason underlies all language and cannot sustain a commitment or require a justification. It is interesting that Trigg, who is in our classification an imperialist, makes the same sort of claim for reason here that relativists make for the central contents of their own perspectives. Thus our own main arguments for our view apply equally against both these. Trigg's particular mistake seems to us to be a confusion of the notion of "commitment" with that of "voluntary endorsement": but I may endorse a political candidate without being (convictionally) committed to her, and I may be committed (e.g., to reason) without choosing it. Reason may simply be presupposed by my thinking and speaking.

4. *Summa Theologica*, part I, q.2, art.3.

5. Austin Farrer, *Finite and Infinite*, 2d ed. (Westminster: Dacre Press, 1959), 262.

6. Ibid., 263.

7. Ibid., 266.

8. Ibid., 268.

9. Ibid., 268f.

10. Ibid., part 2.

11. Ibid., 168–70.

12. Ibid., 9; our emphasis.

13. Ibid., 9f.

14. Ibid., ix. After eight more years, Farrer published a restatement of his views on rational theology under the title *Faith and Speculation* (London: Adam and Charles Black, 1967). In this work, he criticized and revised his old argument at some points, especially retracting its "formalism" as opposed to the "voluntarism" he now favored in the conception of God, which was the conclusion of his argument. Yet Farrer stood by the general argument. See especially pp. 104–18. Farrer also wrote there, "We take it as axiomatic that the straight path of rational theology must be the prolongation of that basic theism which precedes all philosophising" (122).

15. We remind the reader again that we are not using "proof" as a success-word.

16. Michael Scriven, *Primary Philosophy* (New York: McGraw Hill, 1966), 11.

17. Ibid., 13.

18. Ibid., 14.

19. Ibid., 15.

20. Ibid., 87.

21. Ibid., 102.

22. Ibid., 103.

23. Ibid.

24. Regrettably, as far as the aptness of our choice of illustrations of argument is concerned, Scriven's argument leaves something to be desired here, since his discussion of the nature of God does not make it evident either that God is, in Scriven's sense, supernatural, or that the sort of God he has in mind is a sort attended by believers.

25. See the title essay in William James, *The Will to Believe and Other Essays in Popular Philosophy* (New York, 1897). See also, in the same collection, "The Sentiment of Rationality."

26. See W. K. Clifford, "The Ethics of Belief," in his *Lectures and Essays,* ed. F. Pollock, vol. 2 (London, 1879). See also Ralph Barton Perry, ed., *The Thought and Character of William James, Briefer Version* (New York: Harper & Row, 1964), 153; Richard B. Brandt, "Epistemology and Ethics, Parallel Between," in *Encyclopedia of Philosophy,* ed. Paul Edwards (New York: Macmillan and Free Press, 1967), 3:6–8; Rudolf Carnap, "Probability as a Guide in Life," *Journal of Philosophy* 44 (1947): 141–48; Roderick Chisholm, *Perceiving: A Philosophical Study* (Ithaca, N.Y.: Cornell University Press, 1958), chap. 1.

27. Dag Hammarskjöld, *Markings,* trans. Leif Sjoberg and W. H. Auden (New York: Alfred A. Knopf, 1965), 51.

28. Diogenes Allen, *The Reasonableness of Faith* (Washington and Cleveland: Corpus Books, 1968), xv–xix.

29. R. G. Collingwood, *An Essay on Metaphysics* (Oxford: Clarendon Press,

1940), 190. The Latin phrase is the familiar "something than which no greater can be conceived."

30. Ibid., 40.

31. Ibid., 198.

32. Ibid., 224–26.

33. A. C. McGill, "Recent Discussion of Anselm's Argument," in John H. Hick and Arthur C. McGill, eds., *The Many-Faced Argument* (New York: Macmillan, 1967).

34. Ibid., 39–41.

35. Ibid., 50–69.

36. Ibid., 104.

37. Ibid., 105.

38. *Proslogion* II, in ibid., 4, our emphasis.

39. McGill, "Recent Discussion of Anselm's Argument,"105f., 108.

40. Ibid., 109.

41. For this convictional definition of theology, see further our chap. 7.

42. Cf. the bibliography in Hick and McGill, *The Many-Faced Argument.*

43. Norman Malcolm, "Anselm's Ontological Arguments," *Philosophical Review* 69, no. 1 (January 1960), reprinted in Hick and McGill; Charles Hartshorne, *Man's Vision of God* (New York: Harper, 1941) and *The Logic of Perfection* (La Salle, Ill.: Open Court, 1962); J. N. Findlay, "Can God's Existence Be Disproved?" *Mind* (April 1948), reprinted in A. Flew and A. Mac-Intyre, eds., *New Essays in Philosophical Theology* (London: SCM Press, 1955).

44. White's work is cited and discussed in Claude Welch, *Protestant Thought in the Nineteenth Century,* vol. 2, 1870–1914 (New Haven: Yale University Press, 1985), 196f.

45. Vilfredo Pareto, *A Treatise on General Sociology* (New York: Dover Publications, 1963), 2:506f; emphasis added.

46. See for example Robert N. Bellah et al., *Habits of the Heart: Individualism and Commitment in American Life* (New York: Harper & Row, 1985).

47. John Milbank, *Theology and Social Theory: Beyond Secular Reason* (Oxford: Basil Blackwell, 1990), 106–9, 126–29.

48. See Claude Welch, *Protestant Thought,* vol. 2, chap. 4; Hendrik Kraemer, *The Christian Message in a Non-Christian World* (New York: International Missionary Council, 1947); Arend Theodoor van Leeuwen, *Christianity in World History,* trans. H. H. Hoskins (New York: Scribner's, 1964); Mircea Eliade, *Cosmos and History: The Myth of the Eternal Return,* trans. Willard R. Trask (New York: Harper & Bros., 1959); Mircea Eliade, *Patterns in Comparative Religion* (Cleveland: Meridian Books, World Publishing Co., 1963); Mircea Eliade and Joseph M. Kitagawa, eds., *The History of Religions: Essays in Methodology* (Chicago: University of Chicago Press, 1959); Joseph M. Kitagawa with Mircea Eliade and Charles H. Long, eds., *The History of Religions: Essays on the Problem of Understanding* (Chicago: University of Chicago Press, 1967); I. R. A. Al

Faruqi, "History of Religions: Its Nature and Significance for Christian Education and the Muslim-Christian Dialogue," with responses by Charles H. Long and H. N. Wieman, *Numen* 12, Fas., 1, 2 (1965): 35–95.

49. On scientific method in its relation to religion we are indebted in the following paragraphs to Nancey Murphy, whose original and striking contribution to this field we will cite below. Here we express our thanks for her generous gifts of time and critical attention to our account of the relation.

50. A. J. Ayer, *Language, Truth and Logic* (1936; New York: Dover, 1952), 114–20.

51. R. B. Braithwaite, *An Empiricist's View of the Nature of Religious Belief* (Cambridge: Cambridge University Press, 1955), reprinted in Ian T. Ramsey, ed., *Christian Ethics and Contemporary Philosophy* (New York: Macmillan, 1966).

52. Nancey Murphy, *Theology in the Age of Scientific Reasoning* (Ithaca, N.Y.: Cornell University Press, 1990), 53f.

53. Antony Flew and Alasdair MacIntyre, eds., *New Essays in Philosophical Theology* (London: SCM Press, 1955), 96–130. Flew's version of the parable of the gardener, borrowed from John Wisdom, is on p. 96.

54. Alastair McKinnon, *Falsification and Belief* (The Hague: Mouton, 1970).

55. Ibid., chaps. 3–4; Murphy, *Theology in the Age*, 80–82. Richard Hare makes a similar point in his contribution to the falsification discussion mentioned in the previous paragraph: Flew and MacIntyre, eds., *New Essays*, 99–103.

56. Thomas Kuhn, *The Structure of Scientific Revolutions*, (1962; 2d ed., Chicago: University of Chicago Press, 1967).

57. References to the work of these post-Kuhnian laborers in religious thought are found in Murphy, *Theology in the Age*, 84.

58. Imre Lakatos, "Falsification and the Methodology of Scientific Research Programmes," in *Criticism and the Growth of Knowledge,* ed. Imre Lakatos and Alan Musgrave (Cambridge: Cambridge University Press, 1970), 91–196; also "History of Science and Its Rational Reconstruction," *Boston Studies in the Philosophy of Science,* ed. R. C. Buck and R. S. Cohen, 8 (1971): 91–135. The latter paper is reprinted in *The Methodology of Scientific Research Programmes,* vol. 1, ed. John Worrall and Gregory Currie (Cambridge: Cambridge University Press, 1978), 8–101. As before, we will follow this work through the helpful summary in Murphy, *Theology in the Age,* 58–79. A useful, brief summary of Lakatosian philosophy of science may also be found in William C. Placher, *Unapologetic Theology: A Christian Voice in a Pluralistic Conversation* (Louisville, Ky.: Westminster/John Knox Press, 1989), chap. 3.

59. Murphy, *Theology in the Age,* 59.

60. For a general account see Walter Bauer, *Orthodoxy and Heresy in Earliest Christianity,* trans. under the editorship of Robert A. Kraft and Gerhard Krodel (Philadelphia: Fortress, 1971). A more recent and more specialized work is Jack T. Sanders, *Schismatics, Sectarians, Dissidents, Deviants: The First One Hundred Years of Jewish-Christian Relations* (Valley Forge, Pa.: Trinity Press International, 1993).

61. Rudolf Bultmann, *Theology of the New Testament,* 2 vols., trans. Grobel

Kendrick (New York: Scribner's, 1951); for a survey of more recent work, see Robert Morgan, "Theology (NT)," *Anchor Bible Dictionary,* 6 vols., ed. David Noel Freedman (New York: Doubleday, 1992), 6:473–83.

62. Murphy, *Theology in the Age,* chaps. 4–5.

63. Ibid., 130–41.

64. George Tyrrell, "Mysteries a Necessity of Life," *The Month* (November–December 1902): 175, cited in Murphy, *Theology in the Age,* 105.

65. Douglas Clyde Macintosh, *Theology as an Empirical Science* (New York: Macmillan, 1919, reprinted by Arno Press, 1980), 41.

66. See Wolfhart Pannenberg, *Jesus: God and Man,* trans. L. L. Wilkins and Duane A. Priebe, (Philadelphia: Westminster Press, 1968), 88–114; cf. Murphy, *Theology in the Age,* chaps. 2 and 6.

67. Murphy, *Theology in the Age,* 183–92.

68. Ibid., 186.

69. Ibid., 188, 136–57, 161–72.

70. A second Lakatosian project in philosophical theology, appearing at about the same time as Murphy's, is Philip Clayton, *Explanation from Physics to Theology: An Essay in Rationality and Religion* (New Haven: Yale University Press, 1989).

71. Murphy, *Theology in the Age,* 84.

72. Werner Jaeger, *The Theology of the Early Greek Philosophers* (Oxford: Oxford University Press, 1947), 1–4.

73. Wilfred Cantwell Smith, *Towards a World Theology: Faith and the Comparative History of Religion* (Philadelphia: Westminster Press, 1981).

74. Ibid., chap. 9.

Chapter 6:
The Process of Justification

1. *Tractatus Logico-Philosophicus,* trans. D. F. Pears and B. F. McGuinness (London: Routledge & Kegan Paul; New York: Humanities Press, 1961), 6.43.

2. "Aesthetic Problems of Modern Philosophy," in Max Black, ed., *Philosophy in America* (Ithaca, N.Y.: Cornell University Press, 1965), 86.

3. We would hold that known exceptions to this generalization, e.g., Hugo Grotius' apologetic poem *De Veritate religionis Christianae,* did not set the tone of the Western community's self-understanding regarding the demands of justification. Nevertheless the situation we are describing did in time change; every change has its harbingers; and most attempts to draw a line distinguishing new eras in history will meet claims that the line is not early enough.

4. Cf. chap. 5.

5. Thomas S. Kuhn, *The Structure of Scientific Revolutions,* 2d ed., enlarged,

constituting vol. 2, no. 2 of *Encyclopedia of Unified Science,* Otto Neurath, editor-in-chief (Chicago: University of Chicago Press, 1970), 53–56.

6. Ibid., 55.

7. Ibid., 53.

8. It is noteworthy that in the later 'Pauline' writings, this linguistic reserve is diminished; for example, 2 Timothy 1:12 makes 'Paul' say, "*I know* whom I have believed." And in the Gnostic writings the adept flourishes. As the apostolic revolution wanes, is the sense of the ineffable replaced by dogmatic confidence?

9. If the prophet's or apostle's appeal is to a longer run than history itself, as is suggested in John Hick's appeal to eschatalogical verification, special problems are introduced that we do not explore here. We note that it is possible that appeals to a life to come are not cogent. Our present point, however, is that the appeals are *made.* See John Hick, "Theology and Verification," *Theology Today* 17, no. 1 (April 1960), reprinted in John Hick, ed., *The Existence of God* (New York: Macmillan, 1964), and see the criticisms of Hick's theory cited there (253).

10. *Nicomachean Ethics,* 1095a, lines 14–22.

11. See the articles cross-referenced under "Truth" in Paul Edwards, ed., *The Encyclopedia of Philosophy* (New York: Macmillan and Free Press, 1967).

12. Wilfred Cantwell Smith, "Can Religions Be True or False?" in *Questions of Religious Truth* (New York: Scribner's, 1967), 78f.

13. Ibid., 77.

14. W. W. Bartley III, *The Retreat to Commitment* (New York: Random House, 1962).

15. The latter form of speech, by the way, should be used with caution. The present book maintains that the meaning of our talk lies not merely in the mind of a single hearer (or speaker), but in the act of utterance embedded in its linguistic and thus conventional context. One who fails to get the meaning of an utterance, then, does not evacuate it of meaning.

16. See Charles Stevenson, *Ethics and Language* (New Haven: Yale University Press, 1944), chap. 9.

17. An interesting brief discussion of parable, which also provides a guide to the literature in the field, is Sallie M. TeSelle's "Parable, Metaphor, and Theology," *Journal of the American Academy of Religion* 42, no. 4 (December 1974).

18. *Hamlet,* act 1, sc. 3.

19. See for example Ruth Rouse and Stephen C. Neill, eds., *A History of the Ecumenical Movement,* vol. 1, 1517–1948, 2d ed. (London: S.P.C.K., 1967), vol. 2, 1948–1968, ed. Harold Fey (London: SPCK, 1990), and for interreligious awareness, George Rupp, "Religious Pluralism in the Context of an Emerging World Culture," *Harvard Theological Review* 66, no. 2 (April 1973).

20. William Christian, *Meaning and Truth in Religion* (Princeton, N.J.: Princeton University Press, 1964), chap. 2.

21. Ibid., 18.

22. *Oppositions of Religious Doctrines: A Study in the Logic of Dialog among Religions* (New York: Herder & Herder, 1972).

23. See for example F. S. C. Northrop, *The Meeting of East and West* (New York: Macmillan, 1946); and William E. Hocking, *The Coming World Civilization* (New York: Harper & Bros., 1956), and our remarks about W. C. Smith's project in chap. 5.

24. For Paul, see Galatians 1:13–17; Acts 8, 9, 22, 26. For Gotama, see Henry C. Warren, *Buddhism in Translations* (Cambridge, Mass.: Harvard University Press, 1922), 38–87, and Kenneth Morgan, ed., *The Path of the Buddha* (New York: Ronald Press, 1956), 5–10.

25. J.-P. Sartre, quoted without further reference in J. C. Hoekendijk, *The Church Inside Out* (Philadelphia: Westminster Press, 1966), 46.

26. Cf. the paradoxical description of rebellion in Albert Camus, *The Rebel* (New York: Vintage Books, 1956), part 1.

27. This is illustrated by the concept of "passing over" in the work of John S. Dunne. See for example his *The Way of All the Earth* (New York: Macmillan, 1972).

28. See chap. 5, p. 112.

29. Cf. the discussion of the expansion of the notion of reason in chap. 5, *passim*.

30. Alasdair MacIntyre, *After Virtue: A Study in Moral Theory,* 2d ed. (Notre Dame, Ind.: University of Notre Dame Press, 1984); *Whose Justice? Which Rationality?* (Notre Dame, Ind.: University of Notre Dame Press, 1988); *Three Rival Versions of Moral Enquiry: Encyclopaedia, Genealogy, and Tradition,* Gifford Lectures (Notre Dame, Ind.: University of Notre Dame Press, 1990).

31. MacIntyre, *After Virtue,* chap. 15.

32. Do deep convictional barriers make some translation simply impossible? MacIntyre spends a chapter of *Whose Justice* ("Tradition and Translation," 370–88) in response to Donald Davidson on this theme. Davidson has staked out an antirelativist (indeed, an imperialist) claim in these terms: for him, untranslatability simply consigns the untranslatable 'speaker' to nothingness. To this, MacIntyre objects that such work in its very abstractness is "uninformed . . . by attention to empirical enquiry either about the differing uses of language in specific cultures or about the historical transformations of languages" (*Whose Justice,* 371, responding to Davidson, *Expressing Evaluations,* 20). It is such historical transformations to which appeal can be made if one seeks the middle ground between Davidsonian imperialism ("if we can't understand you, you aren't saying anything") on one side, and hopeless or mere relativism on the other. Present untranslatability, in our view, is not an insurmountable barrier to the ultimate justifiability of some conviction set. MacIntyre's standpoint, like our own, seeks the middle ground of possible future translatability, arguing, in its behalf, the actual facts of social change.

33. MacIntyre, *Three Rival Versions.*

Chapter 7:
Theology as a Science of Convictions

1. "Action and Responsibility," in Max Black, ed., *Philosophy in America* (Ithaca, N.Y.: Cornell University Press, 1965), 160.

2. "The Availability of Wittgenstein's Later Philosophy," reprinted in George Pitcher, ed., *Wittgenstein, The Philosophical Investigations* (Garden City, N.Y.: Anchor Books, 1966), 183.

3. William James, *The Varieties of Religious Experience: A Study in Human Nature,* The Gifford Lectures in Edinburgh for 1901–2 (New York: Modern Library, 1902), 422–24.

4. Ibid., 505–7.

5. Ibid., 479ff., 500f.

6. Ibid., 476ff., 494f.

7. Kai Nielsen, "The Primacy of Philosophical Theology," *Theology Today* (July 1970); our emphasis. For Nielsen's position in philosophical theology generally, see his *Contemporary Critiques of Religion* (London: Macmillan, 1971); *Scepticism* (London: Macmillan, 1973), and the succinct account in "On Speaking of God," *Theoria* (28), 1962.

8. Ibid., 162ff.

9. It is relevant to note here, as previously, that one of the present writers is by conviction more sympathetic to Nielsen than to Nielsen's religious adversaries. If we are biased, it is not against Nielsen's basic religious stance.

10. Nielsen, "The Primacy of Philosophical Theology," 166.

11. Cf. James Wm. McClendon, Jr., *Systematic Theology, Volume I, Ethics,* and *Volume II, Doctrine* (Nashville: Abingdon, 1986, 1994).

12. Michael Novak, in the introduction to *American Philosophy and the Future* (New York: Scribner's, 1968), 17.

13. Cf. Stephan Körner's characterization of metaphysics as "the exhibition of implicitly accepted categorial frameworks...their critical examination and, sometimes, also...their modification" (*Categorial Frameworks* [Oxford: Basil Blackwell, 1970], 59).

14. The Lundensians, especially Anders Nygren, Ragnar Bring, and Gustaf Aulén, as represented by Nels Ferré, *Swedish Contributions to Modern Theology* (New York: Harper Torchbook, 1967 [1st ed. 1939]), make a vigorous effort to separate the a priori justification of religion-in-general from the historical *identification* of particular religious strands; the former is the task of philosophy; the latter that of theology. "Theology is thus a special form of religious history with a special working hypothesis, according to which it accomplishes its systematic task, namely, the discovery and the systematic exposition of each religion in accordance with its organic distinctiveness. '*Nicht die begriffliche Einheit, sondern die organische Ganzheit muss das Ziel der Darstellung sein*' " (Ferré, *Swedish Contributions,* 58f.; the German quotation is from Bring, "Die neuere schwedische Theologie," in *Die Kirche in Schweden,* 74. The present enterprise parallels

Nygren and Bring in several interesting ways; we depart from both their Kantian transcendental underpinnings and their view that the theologian necessarily cannot by any means "prove the value of the disclosures of faith" (Ferré, 73) — the present essay aims to show just how such a 'proof' can be undertaken.

15. One can hardly read Anders Nygren's *Agape and Eros* or Gustaf Aulén's *Christus Victor* without feeling oneself under strong persuasion that *agape,* not *eros,* in the first case, and the 'victor' theory of atonement, in the second case, really *ought* to be determinative for Christian thought.

16. David Tracy, *The Analogical Imagination: Christian Theology and the Culture of Pluralism* (New York: Crossroad, 1981), chap. 1. See also Tracy, *Blessed Rage for Order: The New Pluralism in Theology* (New York: Seabury Press, 1975), and the review of this earlier book by Van A. Harvey, *Journal of Religion* 56, no. 4 (October 1976): 382–91.

17. Tracy, *Blessed Rage for Order,* 14.

18. Ronald F. Thiemann, *Constructing a Public Theology* (Louisville, Ky.: Westminster/John Knox, 1991); see further the bibliographical notes there and in Placher's *Unapologetic Theology* (to be cited next).

19. William C. Placher, *Unapologetic Theology: A Christian Voice in a Pluralistic Conversation* (Louisville, Ky.: Westminster/John Knox, 1989).

20. Ibid., 115.

21. Ibid., 7.

22. Kees W. Bolle, "History of Religions with a Hermeneutic toward Christian Theology?" in Joseph Kitagawa, Mircea Eliade, and Charles Long, eds., *The History of Religions: Essays on the Problem of Understanding* (Chicago: University of Chicago Press, 1967), 89–118. The quotation is from p. 102. See also Kees W. Bolle, "The History of Religions and Christian Theology," *Anglican Theological Review* (October 1971).

23. Ninian Smart, *Worldviews: Crosscultural Exploration of Human Beliefs* (New York: Scribner's, 1983).

24. Ninian Smart and Steven Konstantine, *Christian Systematic Theology in a World Context* (Minneapolis: Fortress Press, 1991).

25. Ibid., 291.

26. Wilfred Cantwell Smith, *Towards a World Theology: Faith and the Comparative History of Religions* (Philadelphia: Westminster Press, 1981).

27. Ibid., part 1.

28. Ibid., 103.

29. Ibid., chaps. 6, 8, and 9.

30. Nancey Murphy, *Theology in the Age of Scientific Reasoning* (Ithaca, N.Y.: Cornell University Press, 1990).

31. Ibid., chap. 5.

32. J. L. Austin, "A Plea for Excuses," *Philosophical Papers,* ed. J. G. Urmson and G. J. Warnock (Oxford: Clarendon Press, 1962), 175.

Index